Another Fine Mess

ALSO BY TIM MOORE

Tim Moore

Another Fine Mess
ACROSS TRUMPLAND IN A FORD MODEL T

YELLOW JERSEY PRESS

LONDON

1 3 5 7 9 10 8 6 4 2

Yellow Jersey Press, an imprint of Vintage
20 Vauxhall Bridge Road
London SW1V 2SA

Yellow Jersey Press is part of the Penguin Random House group of companies
whose addresses can be found at global.penguinrandomhouse.com.

Copyright © Tim Moore 2018

First published by Yellow Jersey Press in 2018

www.vintage-books.co.uk

A CIP catalogue record for this book is available from the British Library

ISBN 9781787290235

Typeset in 12/17 pt Fairfield LH
by Integra Software Services Pvt. Ltd, Pondicherry

Printed and bound in Great Britain by Clays Ltd, Elcograf S.p.A.

Penguin Random House is committed to a sustainable future for
our business, our readers and our planet. This book is made
from Forest Stewardship Council® certified paper.

To M8 and P8

'No blasphemy. Say piss and tits all you like, but no Jesus Christ or God Almighty. I'm serious.'

Ross Lilleker's pan-flat Derbyshire tones hung portentously in the bright blue Virginia morning. 'Oh, and don't use the C word. They're not big fans of that one over here.'

It was the first Sunday in July, and we were outside a big white house in the manicured woodlands of Charlottesville's deepest suburbia. Behind us, on a driveway delicately strewn with pine needles, stood a tall, thin, black motor car of startling antiquity. It had been a while, though much too short a while, since Ross reversed this frail relic out of the 30-foot trailer he now walked back past, en route to the huge, squat pick-up that towed it.

'Drink plenty of water, you get really dried out driving them old things.' Ross paused by the pick-up's door. Sixteen years in Texas had done nothing to blunt that Chesterfield accent. He climbed in and lowered the window. 'Right, reckon you're all good. I'll be off, then.' Then he winked with his good eye, the one that hadn't been taken out some years back by a rivet gun, fired up a brutish diesel engine and eased the colossal rig away.

I watched it disappear over a tree-topped brow, then listened as the roar faded, leaving me alone with birdsong and the distant drone of a lawnmower. That pick-up was the manliest vehicle I had ever been in, its crew-cab rear seat cluttered with greasy wrenches and boxes of rattling ironmongery, one of which I'd gamely attempted to employ as a pillow on our non-stop drive through the night. Fifteen hours earlier, Ross had picked me up outside an airport motel in Newark, New Jersey. By then he'd already driven almost 2,000 miles from Texas, having collected that tall, thin, black motor car from its previous keeper, just south of Houston. Bob Kirk was ninety-three years old, and so was the car he had owned for the last fifty-one of them. A 1924 Ford Model T Touring, now gazing warily at its new custodian through wide-set, chrome-lidded eyes. 'It looks like it's about to start talking,' my wife had said when I'd shown her a photo Ross had emailed over some weeks before. Perhaps it might start right now: 'Hey, Charlottesville! Thought I'd just let you all know how much I'm looking forward to this candy-ass Limey clownshoe trying to drive me six thousand miles across the whole damn country. Piss and tits, my friends, piss and tits.'

Our journey was to begin here by bureaucratic misadventure. Some states allow foreigners to register cars, some to insure them, but none permit both. In desperation I'd contacted Miles, who lived in the big white house behind me. The partner of my American cousin Patricia, Miles had made two critical mistakes. His first was to mention an interest in classic motoring during our first and only encounter, in London the previous summer.

His second was to live in Virginia, extremely close to the east coast, which was my intended starting point. In any event, Miles's consequent feats of trusting generosity had sent him to the brink of reckless blind faith. I'd bought the Model T (for $14,000), but in the eyes of the law and the GEICO insurance company, it was his. Learning to drive a T in confident safety was a process that by general consensus demanded a full year or a thousand miles, whichever came first. Any mishap during my protracted apprenticeship would have profound negative consequences for Miles's future insurance prospects. Even for his future liberty, in the worst-case scenarios that now luridly suggested themselves: a steaming tangle of old black metal wrapped around a bus stop, with a dozen elderly legs twitching beneath it; a tall, thin hole in a schoolhouse wall.

Anyway, Miles and Patricia were on holiday in the Bahamas. I'd been let into their house by a teenage nephew, and walked out of it with an insurance certificate and a set of licence plates: 286GQ in an angular vintage font, with 'ANTIQUE VEHICLE VA' alongside in smaller letters. With dry lips and a fluttering stomach I now bent down and screwed them on over Bob Kirk's battered tin plates. '24FORD TX' on the rear, just beneath the spare wheel bolted to the car's upright back end. On the front, behind the starting crank that drooped from the radiator like a thermometer from a patient's mouth, his poignant novelty plate: 'Too old to work, too young to die, so here we sit, just Mom and I.'

The dewy grass sparkled, more unseen mowers joined the symphony and a pair of ponytailed women in lilac vests and shorts jogged smoothly past. This Pleasant Valley Sunday was the calm before the storm, and I spun it out with a detailed appraisal of my aged charge. Old man Kirk was clearly a bit of a showman. The spindly wire wheels had been painted dark purple, girdled in flashy whitewall tyres that lent the little car an unlikely touch of the Ant Hill Mobs. Curlicued red coach lines embellished the doors and those leaping front fenders. The black paintwork had been buffed to a gaudy shine, and the outboard chrome headlamps winked in the morning sun. So too did the scripted Ford logo, making a jaunty tombstone of the radiator.

My personal effects were packed in two holdalls. I heaved one on to the rear seat, and wedged the other into the iron storage trellis that sat on one of the running-boards, its latticed sides recalling the concertina gate of an antique elevator. Then I walked slowly around the car, struggling to recall key points – any points – from the brisk tutorial Ross had delivered before he left. As a global authority on Model Ts, and the veteran of several mammoth tours in them, Ross was the best-qualified tutor I could have wished for.

But the forces of exhaustion and jabbering panic had been fighting it out in my head as he spoke, and very little had been retained. Something under there had to be oiled daily, something over here greased weekly. I pulled aloft the left-hand half of the hinged bonnet and frowned intently at the cast-iron, red-rubber innards. There wasn't a lot in there at least. The most conspicuous component, a big metal carafe bolted on top of the engine, was the horn. This let forth a tremendous *ahooga*, an evocative nostalgia-klaxon that I already knew would bring me succour in difficult times. Disconnected snatches of Ross's lecture spooled uselessly through my mind, like some lost verse from 'I Am the Walrus'. Carb's off a lawnmower, get into the hogshead, bolting on a Bendix.

There is no driver's door on a Model T, owing to the obstructive presence of a lofty floor lever, whose many functions I soon hoped to explore. On a Touring model, as this was and most were, there are also no sides. Mine was a three-door convertible without too much to convert: by way of demonstration, Ross had hauled back the iron-framed black canvas top, in the process releasing a dusty pair of clip-on sunglasses and an earring from some ancient fold in the fabric. 'Don't look like Bob had it down much. Can't blame him, at this time of year you'll be burned alive in a couple of hours.' We hauled it back aloft and I thereafter left it up.

So now, with a girding clap of the hands and a puffing out of cheeks, I unlatched the little metal flap that served as the passenger door, stepped up on the running-board and clambered across that tramp's Chesterfield of a front seat. A soon familiar chorus played out as I took my station behind the upright, split-paned windshield, dimpling my back and buttocks on Bob Kirk's minicab-style beaded seat cover. The stately creak of leather and leaf springs; the gentle slosh of petrol from the 10-gallon tank directly beneath me. Canvas brushed my scalp and the wooden steering wheel grazed the tops of my thighs. The Model T stood seven feet tall with its roof up, but half of that lay under my feet, ground clearance for the rutted rural tracks the car had been designed to tackle. The wheel was hard up to my chest, and holding it demanded splayed, bent elbows. Down on the floorboards, my shoes struggled to negotiate a thicket of pedals and levers. I sat there a while, knees to chin, back hunched, a stance I had last adopted on an infant's chair at a primary-school parents' evening. It didn't seem like the optimal driving position for a transcontinental journey.

A final stocktake of my Model T's information systems did not detain me for long. Pooh-poohing the traditional emphasis on speed and covered distance, the dashboard was home to a single, tremulous gauge that revealed if the battery was being charged or not. To its left, the ignition keyhole and headlamp switch. To its right, one of Bob Kirk's after-market additions: a jaunty little thermometer, featuring a cactus, a rattlesnake rampant and the word TEXAS, alongside a thin column of red alcohol which told me the cabin temperature was already 85 degrees Fahrenheit. Further accessories of variable period authenticity were strewn about. A single round rear-view mirror clamped to the outside upper edge of the windshield. An indicator set-up removed from an old truck, comprising a little chrome stick clamped to the steering column through a box that emitted a strident buzz in operation. A (*cough*) USB charging socket under the dash, fitted by Ross on his own initiative, into which I now inserted my telephone's power lead. Stuck to a bracket on the inside of the windscreen, this would display navigational advice and current speed, at the cost of universal derision. Ross had flipped down the final two dashboard add-ons with a flourish: 'And here's yer cupholders.' Actually, there was just one more, a silver bell-push down by my left knee. How grateful I was that by 1924, most Model Ts came fitted with an electric starter, demoting the hand crank to emergency use. I turned the little brass key, adjusted all the controls to the best of my ability, and eased a moist, unsteady index finger towards the silver button.

My journey didn't really start in Charlottesville. It had begun the previous November, with a wintry dawn fringing the curtains, when my wife and I were awoken by a commotion down in the street. Our son, who had invited a couple of friends over for a presidential-election all-nighter, was outside. We recognised him by his iron-throated baritone, an instrument that was now treating us and our neighbours to a deafening rendition of 'The Star-Spangled Banner'. Its tone of deranged sarcasm made us instantly and horribly aware that the unexpected, the unthinkable, had unfolded. 'Bollocking shit-gibbons,' I muttered, and we lay there in the half-light, hands clasped under the duvet.

Only five months had passed since that previous long, dark dawn of the soul, when 48 per cent of us woke up in Brexit Britain and stared in harrowed disbelief at our bedroom ceilings. Those 52 per cent – who were they? What had they been thinking of? And why are they right now brusquely slamming this volume back on the bookshop shelf?

At least, and at last, an upside to Brexit now presented itself: the incredulous dismay my household had endured since the referendum offered a useful inoculation against the full-blown horror of President Donald Trump. But Brexit was just our own private calamity, an idiotic shot in the foot. Electing Trump felt like shooting Earth in the face. Shit just got global. As a citizen of the free world, I dearly wished to understand why its self-styled electorate had just installed this needy, groping narcissist, this infantile bullshitter, this ridiculous, orange phony as my leader.

Brexit reminded me how close I'd grown to Europe; Trump's shocking election proved just how far I'd drifted from America. Forget that special relationship and our shared language. In terms of values, culture, lifestyle and outlook – let's call it the entire human experience – I seemed to have so much more in common with our continental cousins. Even the Finns. Even the French. Yanks were the strangers now. Most of them, anyway. Or not quite most of them, because despite Donald's ongoing bleats, he'd lost the popular vote by three million. Nearly every American I'd ever met lived near one coast or other, and I'd got on splendidly with nearly all of them. But as the election maps that scrolled up the screens next morning plainly emphasised, they hadn't voted Trump. America lay cleaved in three, two slivers of Democrat blue astride a yawning swathe of Republican red that spanned the nation's entire central bulk. The largely rural 'flyover states' had thrown a brick through the window of the coast-dwelling urban-ites, those disdainful liberals who knew them only as a greeny-brown nothingness viewed through an aeroplane window.

With a start I remembered reading a *New York Times* editor's account of his 3,000-mile motorcycle road trip across America's provincial north, a few months before the election. As most of the states he passed through traditionally leaned Republican, he didn't at first pay much attention to the Trump yard signs along the roadside. But there really were an awful lot of them – he started counting, but gave up after a hundred – and many were monu-mental labours of love: 10-foot hand-painted billboards, bed-sheet flags. A man with a 20-foot Trump banner flying from the extended ladder of an old fire-truck outside his boom-repair shop proudly revealed it had cost him $500. In Thorntown, Indiana, after 2,500 miles on the road, he finally encountered his first Hillary Clinton poster, a standard one-foot-by-two-foot campaign job stuck in a front lawn. 'And I had to drive 60 miles to pick that up,' grumbled the elderly Democrat who answered the door.

The small towns, the plains and prairies, the over-looked, over-flown US heartlands: here was where Trump won, and won bigly. If I wanted to know why – and I really, really did – this was the America I needed to visit.

Nobody, not even the Donald himself, had seen it coming; nobody, him least of all, knew what it meant. As the dumbfounding reality sank painfully in, commentators tried to take stock. The advent of Trump, by almost unanimous agreement, marked the end of an era. In 1941, *Time* magazine heralded 'The American Century', in an editorial beseeching its nation to enter the Second World War in the defence of democracy. *Time* heralded the United States as a forward-looking, outward-looking, initiative-seizing force for global good, the dynamic leader of world trade, an inter-national Samaritan that would set an example to all nations on how to behave. Those rousing words may not have always translated into matching deeds in the decades that followed, but the thought was there. It wasn't now, though. Trump was vowing to pull up America's drawbridge, and turn the nation's gaze from the future to the past. 'Most important of all,' *Time* had declaimed with a stirring flourish, 'we have that indefinable, unmistakable sign of leadership: prestige.' Well, that was that, then. The American Century had finished, twenty-five years short.

There was a more poignant, and more poetic, casualty in the headlines that tolled out around the Fox-free world.

'Is choosing Trump the end of the American Dream?'

'With Trump in the White House, the American Dream is Dead.'

I began to wonder precisely what these melodramatic obituaries were mourning. Many defined the American Dream as a simple economic progression: the expectation that you would live better than your parents had. Generational American betterment – a dependable reality for a hundred years or more – had faltered. Ninety-four per cent of Americans born in 1940 out-earned their parents; of those born in 1980, just 50 per cent were managing to. At lower income levels, the bottom tenth of earners, the decline was more profound still: from 88 per cent for the class of 1940 to 33 per cent amongst the 1980 cohort. Average household income in the US peaked back in 1999. But much as I'd love to, you could hardly pin any of that on Trump: he wasn't its cause, but its consequence.

No, the Trumpdunnit trail led back to the American Dream's core principle, the proud egalitarianism spliced deep into the land of opportunity's DNA. 'That dream of a land in which life should be better and richer and fuller for everyone,' wrote James Truslow Adams in *The Epic of America*, the 1931 treatise that spawned this emblematic coinage, 'with opportunity for each according to ability or achievement … This is the American Dream that has lured tens of millions of all nations to our shores.' At the divided, divisive, wall-building dawn of Donald you couldn't read all that without a hollow laugh, though I plumped for a demented yodel. Trump had even called it himself, at the end of the infamous speech that dismissed Mexican immigrants as drug-dealers and rapists: 'Sadly, the American Dream is dead.'

In truth, as I now learned, Adams was himself harking back to happier times. He put pen to paper in the depths of the Depression, and his words were a retrospective paean to the American Dream's preludial golden slumbers. 'As we compare America to-day with the America of 1912 it seems as though we have slipped a long way backwards,' he wrote, referencing the year that the last two mainland states joined the union, and thus providing a handy date of birth for the dream that had just died.

I read on, as Adams gamely fleshed out his shiny new catch-phrase, defining what the American Dream meant by emphasising what it didn't. 'It has not been a dream of material plenty ... nor physical comfort, and cheap amusements ... It is not a dream of motor cars.' Woah, Jimbo. I'll have to stop you there. Keep the cheap amusements if you must, but let's not be silly: take cars out of the American Dream, and you throw a bucket of iced water right in its peaceful, sleeping face. Ask anyone to envisage the Dream and they'll describe a green-lawned, blue-skied consumerist wonderland, whose every cornerstone – suburbia, shopping mall, high school, the family vacation – is connected by road. Four-wheeled desire was the bedrock of the culture that underpinned the Dream, and of the work ethic that made it come true. If you wanted a car and worked for it, you got one. In 1964, when Lyndon B. Johnson announced his War on Poverty, even the most desperate regions were full of cars. In Appalachia, 40 per cent of the poorest residents owned one, and a third of those had been bought new. Car ownership was like some unwritten constitutional right.

When the Chinese wanted to kickstart their own economic miracle in the early 1990s, they simply removed restrictions on private vehicle ownership. The 'car carrot', as I've just feebly dubbed it, sufficed to lure millions of young people from rural areas into cities. Upheaval, cramped loneliness and years of soulless toil seemed a small price to pay for your own set of wheels. In 1985, only sixty people in Beijing owned private cars. By 2000, over a million did. Even in 2008, with over three million cars on the city's streets, first-time buyers could barely contain themselves. 'I can feel it when they come into the showroom,' one Beijing dealer told the *Washington Post* that year. 'The whole family chooses the car together. I can read the eagerness in their faces. They pay attention to every detail of the car. After they take it home, they get up several times every night to see if their cars are OK.'

Today there are six million cars in Beijing, and 163 million in China as a whole. The American Dream has gone on a world tour, by car. And it has done so because universal vehicle ownership is the American Dream's most tangible expression: go-anywhere individual freedom and conspicuous consumption, in one handy package. One brief but glorious summer, my first as an ex-teenager, I lived that dream.

It was 1984, and my father had secured a three-month contract in New York. Being a one-man concern, his microfilm publishing company drafted in a team of hardened mercenaries: me, my sister, her boyfriend and my girlfriend, all veterans of Mindata Micropublications' pound-an-hour repetitive-task game. By day we sat in a dark room somewhere in upper Manhattan and depressed the shutter buttons of our Bell & Howell Filemasters several thousand times. Then we rode the subway back to our home-swap apartment in Greenwich Village, and tried to understand baseball as a platoon of questing cockroaches set out from beneath the TV cabinet. We took turns to cook, with my debut effort combining frozen onion rings and a full bottle of white Zinfandel in a casserole I have never been allowed to forget. We were being rudely awoken from our American Dream before we'd even nodded off. Then flung into a waking nightmare when some of the larger cockroaches were granted the gift of lumbering, wayward flight.

After a week of this, my father and I began scouring the classifieds, and presently caught a commuter train out to Hicksville, halfway down Long Island. We returned, after dark and in a throbbing cloud of exhaust, on the yawning bench seat of a 1970 Oldsmobile Delta 88 convertible. Mindata's new company car felt about 20 feet wide and 80 feet long, with an outermost layer of sky-blue paint largely applied by brush. It had three hubcaps and an eight-track tape player with *The Concert Sound of Henry Mancini* wedged in the slot. The passenger door was secured, after a fashion, by means of a bathroom latch bolted to its exterior. For an outlay of $350 this vehicle presented a novel twist on conspicuous consumption, though it was nothing if not conspicuous, and my word it consumed. Over the next ten weeks I think we saw about 9mpg out of it.

Our après-Filemaster routine was instantly and gloriously transformed. After dark we cruised through Chinatown and Alphabet City with the grubby white top down, Mancini's weapons-grade muzak quavering out above that throaty rumble. We would pull up outside some hip, fairylight-swagged street eatery, cut 'Moon River' off in its orchestral prime and make a showy exit, often including a bench vault straight out on to the sidewalk. An hour later we'd come out to find the car gone. 'Tow truck just came right up and took it away, man, whaddya want me to say?' We never learned. The car-pound fees cost us more than the car did.

Every weekend was a pocket road trip, barrelling up and down the eastern seaboard, in and out of New England, all the way across to Virginia. We stopped at every yard sale we passed, filling the Oldsmobile's giant, corpse-ready trunk with ironic daywear and cast-off Americana – old diner signs, a baseball mitt, the extraordinary tail lights off a 1950s Mercury, like scale models of the Sydney Opera House fashioned from chrome and red glass. The sun always shone and Henry's swelling strings always filled the warm breeze. Summertime, and the listening was easy. The driving sometimes wasn't, though. Hubcaps would routinely detach themselves and skitter gaily off into the dappled verge. The passenger door swung open on the sharper left-handers, and one day the brakes completely failed as we dived into the Lincoln Tunnel. My father somehow got us back using heavy applications of emergency brake and clenched-teeth profanity.

He was the only insured driver, which obliged me to live out my hands-on American Dream on private roads. I am still regularly reminded that when the rest of our party went off to improve themselves at Thomas Jefferson's home and many of Frank Lloyd Wright's more notable architectural creations, I was burbling around a car park the size of Hampshire with my left elbow on the top of a hot blue door. I still don't regret it. Even at walking pace there was a heady, epic quality to the experience, a sense of initiation: look at me, driving this huge car in this huge country. My formative behind-the-wheel experiences had done nothing to prepare me: this absolutely was not a Morris Minor van, and nor was it Ealing. The car was the undisputed star of that trip. When I ruminatively consult my memory's USA 1984 photo album, the Oldsmobile crops up on every page. Though, regrettably, the cover shot is that guy with the huge afro who once roller-skated past us down Fifth Avenue, wearing nothing but a yellow backpack.

One Saturday we drove out to Rhode Island and overdid the yard sales; when darkness crept upon us, my father felt too tired to drive home, and too prudent to finance three motel rooms. We bumped off the road, down a lane, and parked up in the corner of a forgotten field. But huge as the Oldsmobile was, it was not a bedroom for five adults. After an hour or two of communal fidgety huffing, my sister's boyfriend issued a frustrated imprecation, climbed noisily outside and spreadeagled himself on the bonnet. Incredibly, I soon heard him snoring.

In the frailest light of a new day, blearily unrested and blistered with insect bites, I stumbled off through the crispy weeds for a pee. I was stumbling back when a pair of headlights bounced slowly up the lane behind me. An engine died, a window buzzed down and a flashlight clicked on.

'Sir?'

I did my best to explain our situation to the very straight-faced state trooper who now stepped out of his patrol car, but it was never going to be easy. My future brother-in-law still lay out cold on the bonnet, limbs splayed to their widest extremity, with a black Lee Van Cleef hat over his face. It had been a bumper day at those suburban trestle tables, and as the trooper walked up to the Oldsmobile and peered in, I followed his flashlight beam over a sleeping riot of edgy kitsch and gaping mouths. I remember a lot of lurex and fur. Even my dad, chin on chest behind the wheel, had a tangerine-trimmed yachting cap on. Only now did I think to remove the Davy Crockett hat and over-sized John Lennon shades I had donned in a desperate small-hours bid to keep the mosquitoes at bay.

I've still got the hat, and the Mercury tail lights. And a fading Polaroid, which I chanced upon in a bedside drawer just a few days after Trump's election. It's me, in an appalling Hawaiian shirt and those wonky Lennon shades, standing on a Manhattan sidewalk with my arm around a cardboard cut-out of Ronald Reagan. We're both beaming: that's as happy as I'll ever look beside a Republican, especially one I've just paid five dollars to embrace. In 1983, a street entrepreneur could have profitably unfolded Ronnie on any sidewalk in the land. But a flat-pack Trump would be radioactive Marmite. Especially in Manhattan, his home turf, where more than 90 per cent of voters put their cross elsewhere.

And as I gazed at the Gipper and me, smiling side by side, I thought back to the summer of '84, and those halcyon top-down days on the open road, mourning my lost youth and America's lost fellowship. I thought back further, to 1912, when the American

Dream was born. A mission began to take fuzzy shape: there I was, driving through the small-town, big-country states that everyone now flew over, those suddenly alien outposts of Trumpland. The route had already laid itself out, in the form of a compelling election map I'd come across in the *Washington Post*. This split the nation into its 3,142 counties, and coloured each of them Trump red or Hillary blue, with the depth and darkness of these hues reflecting the strength of the candidate's majority. I downloaded it and printed it out, noting the crimson bruise that blotted the Appalachians and the Midwest, and the spine of rich mahogany that spread north from Texas right up to the Canadian border. Peering closer, I found it was possible to drive all the way across the nation in Trump-voting territory, with a lot of weaving and a willingness to more than double the beeline distance to a touch over 6,000 miles. That was it, then. A road trip through the American Dream, from coast to coast, and cradle to grave. In the car that had launched it, over a hundred summers before.

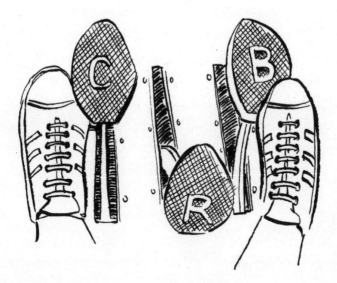

Learning to drive a Model T Ford is a fiendish, vexatious and often terrifying process, entirely at odds with the car's jolly and biddable demeanour. When you first sit behind the wheel of a T, take a while to savour the familiar feel of that circular rim before you, and its reassuringly traditional relationship with your desired direction of travel. I make this recommendation because everything else you have ever learned about driving a motor vehicle – absolutely everything – is about to be torn to shreds, stamped on and burned before your wild and weeping eyes.

Look down at your feet. There are three pedals, which appears encouragingly standard, but deceitfully so. The right-hand one, doubtless familiar to you as the accelerator, is the brake. The left-hand one is the clutch, but don't get too excited. Press it halfway down and the car is in neutral. Mashing it to the floor selects low gear; take your foot off and you put the car in high. There are no other forward gears, and no gearstick. Welcome to Henry Ford's planetary transmission: 'the automatic gearbox you drive with your feet'. By now you may not be too surprised to learn that the central pedal, the one you will have learned to love as the brake, engages reverse.

Now, with unease already puckering those inner buttocks, let us direct our attention to the big steam-engine lever that sticks high up out of the floor, and is now chafing intimately against your left thigh. Surely that's a handbrake. Why, yes – yes it is! A bit. Though it's also a kind of auxiliary clutch, which functions as a quirky parody of its foot-operated counterpart. All the way forward engages the planetary transmission in high gear. Halfway sets it in neutral, though in this position the car may proceed in low gear or reverse. Pulling it all the way back maintains neutral, applies the brakes and drives two sharpened bolts through the rim of the steering wheel and deep into your palms. I mean it might as well. Oh yeah, and that other floor lever, the one you snagged your knackers on when you climbed in? Well, that operates the Ruckstell two-speed rear axle. Look, I dunno. Says here it's an 'underdrive'.

Right – let's go for a petrifyingly chaotic drive! Slow down, sailor. You don't even know where the accelerator is yet. You won't find it either. See those two stubby iron stalks sticking out either side of the steering column, just behind the wheel? The one on the right is the gas. I'm serious: you pull it down to go faster. And the one on the left? Come on, silly, that adjusts or retards the ignition spark as appropriate. Anyone who understands how cars work will know exactly what that means. It would be great if one of them came over and told me.

'Spark up, gas down!'

My first lesson in starting a Model T was delivered by James Dean. *East of Eden*, adapted from John Steinbeck's novel, was set in the early T era and thoughtfully featured an entire scene dedicated to the exercise, during which Dean and a bevy of assembled cast-mates chant the above phrase with manic enthusiasm. As fifteen million Ts rolled off the lines during Hollywood's dawn, it was no surprise to find them popping up in umpteen period productions, though my related pre-departure viewing procured little further practical advice. In sorry truth, a Model T only ever seemed to be wheeled on to the silver screen for derisive comic effect. In *It Happened One Night*, a young Clark Gable borrows a Model T – a 1924 Touring exactly like mine – for an urgent romantic mission, only to find this hopeless old jalopy steadily overtaken by every other car on the road. Sad trombones all round. That scene in *East of Eden* was built around the rib-tickling palaver required to get a Model T running: after pushing the spark lever up and pulling the accelerator lever down, there remain no fewer than seven further stages for Jimmy and friends to enact and bellow aloud. Even Steinbeck, a writer who typically dealt with grandparents starving to death in lay-bys and the mercy killings of gentle giants with learning difficulties, couldn't resist having a giggle at the Model T's expense. There was something about the T – its ubiquity, its sloth, the curious marriage of spartan virtues and maddening operational complexity – that made the car an irresistible figure of fun. Inevitably, the Model T found itself a staple prop in the slapstick works of Fatty Arbuckle, Buster Keaton and, most regularly, Laurel and Hardy. I watched a lot of those before I left. If nothing else, they offered a handy primer on what facial expression to adopt should my T find itself compressed between two streetcars, bisected in a sawmill or driven into a bottomless, slurry-filled pothole.

But as helpful as the Chant of Jimmy Dean most surely was – I would intone it silently before my first few hundred starting rituals – it needed padding out. I was preparing for a drive that would occupy several months, in a car I'd been warned might take a year to master. So a few weeks before leaving home, I'd plugged myself into the UK's Model T network, whose throbbing nodes of helpful activity swiftly put me in contact with Ross Lilleker, and coordinated two test drives.

The first took me around a damp Buckinghamshire farmyard in the company of Neil Tuckett, a straight-talking old T hand with curly grey hair, red cheeks and a boiler suit. The second, through the sunset-dappled lanes of deepest Kent, was undertaken with Deke Martin and his wife Rachel, who met me in full period costume: flapper hat and floral dress for her, waistcoat and *Peaky Blinders* cap for him. Aside from their common generosity, Deke and Neil were very different people, with very different cars. Neil's Model T, or the one he selected for me from his extensive fleet, was an early model with big brass coach-lamps and wooden cartwheels: two parts Chitty, two parts Bang. Deke's was one of the last Ts, a wire-wheeled, more compact dark-red 1926 Touring model.

Together these drives had totalled perhaps four miles. But despite their brevity and umpteen contrasts, the two experiences had left many consistent impressions. The clattering explosion of start-up, all hisses, clanks and lateral shudders. The painful threshes and howls as the planetary transmission bit into its fabric bands and I groaned off the mark, at once replaced by the sensation of wobbly runaway speed. Neck-snapping kangaroo hops, then the death lurch of a stall. And the inescapable, creeping dread that something was just about to go mechanically awry, mainly because in both cases it had. Neil spent his time in the passenger seat continually rapping his oily knuckles against a wooden box bolted to the firewall, an activity that sometimes roused its resident ignition coils to full attention, but twice left us coasting to a silent halt. Deke kept his ear cocked doubtfully throughout my micro stint at the wheel, and when I bumped to a stop in his orchard he leapt out, yanked up the bonnet and began muttering about band slip. That seemed like a lot of issues to face in four miles, particularly when considered on the start line of a journey 1,500 times longer.

And so, three weeks on and an ocean away, I said a silent prayer, jabbed that silver button and shattered Virginia's Sunday calm with roaring, spluttery judders. Some experimental twiddling with the gas and spark levers amplified this crackpot-inventor's cacophony into a thunderous biplane flypast, then, via a startling volley of shotgun backfires, muted it to an irregular tugboat burble. I heaved the brake lever forward and planted my left foot heavily on to the clutch, filling the air with protesting moans as the T trundled down Miles's drive. How could this ancient machine possibly tolerate such a wild and injurious procedure? And how would I ever tame it? I swung the wheel right and weaved off into the morning on the wrong side of the road.

As a tale of desperation, upheaval and spectacular triumph over tragic adversity, the story of Henry Ford is the story of fledgling America. Huddled-mass refugee voyage – tick. Serial bereavement – tick. Back-breaking toil, surfeit of children, gung-ho foolhardiness in dogged pursuit of opportunity – tick, tick, tick. Ford's humble ancestry and hard-won glory might qualify him as the most representative American in history. In fact, I've just decided it does.

Henry's Irish father, William, emigrated from Cork at the age of twenty-one, in the year that came to be known as 'Black '47', the grim nadir of the potato famine that killed a million and drove almost twice as many out of the country. William's mother would perish on the voyage, leaving him and his father responsible for six younger siblings. They settled in Dearborn, near Detroit, built a log cabin, and found employment as navvies on the extension of the Michigan Central Railroad. Eighty acres of local woodland were in due course bought from an old Irish acquaintance, then arduously cleared and cultivated. In 1861, three years after purchasing half the family farm from his father, William married Mary Litogot, adopted daughter of another Irish neighbour. Mary was the daughter of Belgian immigrants who had both died in Dearborn before she turned three; her mother in childbirth, and her father while leading a team of oxen across the inadequately frozen Rouge River.

Henry was William and Mary's eldest, born in 1863, three weeks after the Civil War tide turned against the Confederacy at Gettysburg. By then, the farming Fords were beginning to prosper. Its proximity to the Great Lakes and Canada's vast natural resources had already established Detroit as a transport hub and industrial power-in-waiting, a city whose burgeoning population – 80,000 in 1870, almost half of them foreign born – represented an ever hungrier market for the Ford family's wheat, meat and orchard fruit. The farm doubled in size, more children arrived, and William – by now a justice of the peace and church deacon – extended the family home into a ten-roomed bungalow, imposing by the standards of the time.

Young Henry, in common with every farm-child of the age, worked long hours in barn and field before and after school. Sunday began with an eight-mile walk to church and back. As fond as he would always be of the rural lifestyle, this routine fostered a profound resentment for manual and pedestrian chores, and a fixation with their mechanical fulfilment. His determined curiosity in this arena soon earned him a reputation as a reckless tinkerer, with an especially wayward fascination for the harnessing of power. One summer afternoon he dammed and diverted a creek to propel a small water wheel, inadvertently flooding a neighbour's potato field. To explore the potential of steam he filled a clay pot with water, bound the lid tightly shut and surreptitiously placed it in the family's dining-room fireplace. The resultant explosion smashed a mirror, a window and left a lifelong scar on his fore-head. A later and more ambitious study involved a 10-gallon drum, a home-made tin turbine and a parallel catastrophe which burned down the schoolyard fence and bequeathed Henry another blemish, on his left cheek, that he would be wryly explaining for the rest of his days. He took apart his neighbours' pocket watches, using his indulgent mother's corset stays and knitting needles for tools, and sometimes successfully reassembled them. He almost lost a finger examining his father's hay cutter. And all the while, he honed a deep loathing for agricultural inefficiency in all its forms. He nursed a particular aversion for the horse: sickly, expensive, unreliable, and each one a living reminder of the humiliation he'd once suffered when a colt dragged him all the way home on his arse, a boot stuck in the stirrups.

'Horses and mules eat their fool heads off six months out of the year,' the young Henry ranted in a notebook, his way of explaining that a quarter of all the farmland in the US was given over to feeding the nation's twenty-five million horses. 'And you can't fix a dead horse with a monkey wrench,' he added bluntly. (Many years later, after selling a million Model Ts, Henry got out his ever-ready notebook and scrawled: 'The horse is DONE!')

But that homely, hapless, horse-hating heaven was turned upside down in 1876. Twelve days after delivering a stillborn baby that would have been her seventh child, Mary died. 'I never had any particular affection for the farm itself,' Henry would recall. 'It was the mother on the farm I loved.' But a month later, the thirteen-year-old Henry experienced an epiphany that provided a durable distraction from his grief, and would in due course change the world. Riding alongside his father in the family cart, Henry detected a clattering, huffing commotion from up the lane and jumped out to investigate. The source of this tumult was a Nichols and Shepard steam-powered traction engine, the first horseless vehicle he had ever beheld. (At the time over 75,000 steam engines were plying their trade across America's Corn Belt, threshing and reaping.) Henry looked up at the machine in awe, then bombarded the operator with technical enquiries. 'This encounter showed me I was by instinct an engineer,' he rather blandly recollected three decades later. But as he stood there amongst the din and sooty vapour, his teenage mind was blown by the overwhelming possibilities of a self-contained, self-propelled conveyance. Henry Ford was, thenceforth, a young man obsessed. For the rest of his life he kept a photograph of a traction engine on prominent display, 'somewhere I could see it every day'.

At this point we had better apply a finger to the fast-forward button, and hold it there, watching blurry sepia figures dart to and fro before our eyes with entertaining haste. Zoom, there goes the sixteen-year-old Henry, scooting away to Detroit to work in a streetcar factory. Then at a dry dock. Then as an apprentice machinist. Three years pass and he's speeding back home, operating and fixing traction engines for neighbouring farmers. Look, he's getting married to Clara Bryant, and they're living on a farm his dad gave them. What's he up to? Doesn't look like farming. Nope, he's using a steam engine to log wood. For two years. And now – whee! – he's off again, whisking Clara to Detroit where he's bagged an engineering job at the Edison Illuminating Company. Pop! Their only child, Edsel, is born at the new family home in November 1893. Bang! A month later, on Christmas Eve, our man rigs up a little petrol engine in his kitchen sink, with Clara dripping the fuel in while Henry – seriously, mate? – holds a wire from the ceiling light socket to the spark plug. Three years on, and Henry is still clocking in at Edison, but whizzing in and out of his woodshed late into the night. He's only gone and built a car! But – what are you like, Hezza? – it's too big to get out through the shed door, so there he is demolishing half the front wall at 4 a.m. to take his petrol-powered Quadricycle for its debut run through the Detroit dawn. Hmm, looks a bit rubbish, like a big pram steered by a narrow-boat tiller. Still, it soon gets attention and look, there he is scuttling about in a smart new coat and a big moustache, getting well in with Thomas Edison, the mayor of Detroit and plenty of bigwig moneymen and industrialists. It's 1899 and Henry has left the electric company to head up the new Detroit Automobile Company. But his backers have no interest beyond a quick buck, and if we slow the action we can see them losing patience with Henry's vision of a perfectly engineered car pitched at a mass market that doesn't yet exist. Within two years the firm folds. Henry is pushing forty and has to date built twenty-three cars. Let's hit pause, just as he's shaving his 'tache off.

At the hectic dawn of the automobile age, Ford found himself up against 2,500 rival US start-ups, with Detroit home to more backstreet car makers than any other city. Had the cards fallen differently, we might all now be driving about in Kerosene Surreys, or American Beauties, or Juveniles, Gaylords and Cuckmobiles. Like some pioneering but less punchable Richard Branson, Henry decided that a grand gesture was needed to set himself and his cars apart from the crowd, a daredevil publicity stunt. And so, summoning the youthful bravado that had scarred him for life and laid waste to half of Dearborn, in the autumn of 1901 he entered the first motor race Michigan had ever hosted.

Ford was by then entering middle age, and the only vehicle he'd driven with any regularity was that wobbly 20mph Quadricycle. His sole competitor for the $1,000 prize would be Alexander Winton, millionaire owner of the largest petrol-engined car manufacturer in the US, and the nation's most famous racing driver. It was a dramatic statement of Henry Ford's relentless, unbounded ambition, and from Clara's viewpoint a pigheadedly irresponsible one.

The event, held at Detroit's Grosse Pointe race track on 10 October, incited great excitement in the nascent Motor City. Shops closed for the day. Courts were adjourned. Eight thousand spectators travelled to the track, in packed streetcars that ran from the city centre every thirty seconds. Yet when the two rivals puttered up to the start line, the crowd were dismayed by an embarrassing mismatch. Winton's mighty 70hp Bullet dwarfed Ford's Sweepstakes, a frail-looking, stripped-down machine with a 26hp engine that Henry had built with his young associate Ed Huff. Huff, a self-taught electrical engineer who had worked with Ford since the age of sixteen, had fitted Sweepstakes with a revolutionary fuel-injection system incorporating porcelain insulators – in effect the first modern spark plug – fashioned to order from denture ceramic by a local dentist. However, he was now making a rather more conspicuous contribution: in order to facilitate on-the-move adjustments to his ignition set-up, Huff would spend the entire race clinging to the car's running-board. The plucky and dextrous adhesion he displayed that afternoon earned him a lifelong nickname: Spider.

When the flag fell, nobody was surprised to see Bullet roar away to an impressive lead. Unburdened by relevant experience, Ford struggled to control his car at 60mph through the corners, requiring Huff to supplement his alfresco tinkering with dramatic redistributions of body weight. But the lighter car began to close the gap after five laps, and when Bullet overheated on lap 8, sputtering and misfiring, Sweepstakes sped past. As the precarious combo took the flag, the crowd erupted into something approaching mass hysteria. 'The people went wild,' wrote a relieved but alarmed Clara to her brother. 'One man threw his hat up and when it came down he stamped on it. Another man had to hit his wife on the head to keep her from going off the handle.'

To the victor, the spoils. Alexander Winton, the first man to put a steering wheel on a car, builder of the first V8 engine and the first presidential motor carriage, is no more than a footnote in motoring history. But Henry's memorable triumph, in his first and last motor race, made his name and that of the cars that would bear it. Speed sold cars to the rich few; the hare-and-tortoise reliability that had won the day for Sweepstakes was a far greater draw to the mid-market masses. (Though just for the hell of it, at the age of forty-one Henry upset Clara one last time by setting a world land speed record of 91.37mph on the frozen waters of Detroit's Lake St Clair.) 'It is not uninteresting,' noted a rather dry press advertisement, 'that the builder and driver of this car is also the designer and builder of the regular Ford Runabout.' The public would keep the faith for seven years, one further failed company and nine models of gently ratcheting appeal, before Henry Ford and his team – Spider Huff prominent amongst them – launched their self-styled Universal Car, the world-changing Model T.

My determination to complete a full coast-to-coast journey meant I first had to drive 160 miles back to the Atlantic shore, heading south-east against the American road trip's magnetic westward lure. I can't say this detour troubled me when there was so much else on my metaphorical plate, much of it already spilling into my metaphorical lap. Indeed, I'd already blithely bolted on another detour, factoring in a side trip to Detroit – a city which had roundly rejected Trump, but one that in the circumstances seemed to demand a pilgrimage.

After a nerve-settling preamble on empty side roads, during which I reoriented the car rightwards in compliance with native traffic regulations, I turned on to a thoroughfare which quite quickly swelled into Charlottesville's many-laned bypass. I grasped the wheel as tight as my slickened palms allowed and tucked into the slow lane, nodding rigidly to acknowledge the supportive waves and toots of passing motorists. Green light, green light, green light. Neil Tuckett's headline mantra spooled through my head: *If you can stop a T, you can drive a T.* Green light, green light, red li— PISS AND FREAKING TITS. High up on an over-head gantry with a giant sun for company, the first stop signal took me by spleen-shrivelling surprise. With the front wheels almost up to the white junction line I stamped both feet on the pedals, any pedals, and flipped the hand levers aloft. If it hadn't been a Sunday, these would have been my final actions on earth. The T squirrelled about the tarmac, the motor popped and died and I came to rest, at a rakish angle, about two feet past the six-lane intersection's deserted geometrical centre.

Humming reedily, I punched the starter. *Ker-dug-a-dug-a-dug-a-dug-a-dug-a-dug-a-wheeeck.* Then silence. I tried again, and again. The motor just wouldn't catch. Again. Again. Again, and by now the battery was audibly tiring. At this point an extremely large blue object entered my right-side peripheral vision at great speed, while an extremely loud air horn tore through every hole in my head.

'Hail pew?'

My eyes were clamped shut, braced for terminal impact or death by embarrassment. I opened them and saw a very round and very red face, underpinned by a moist smile accessorised with a small number of beige teeth. I realised these words were an offer of assistance when two meaty hands grasped the frame of the wind-shield and began pushing the car backwards to safety. As we inched out of the junction and on to the verge-side gravel a many-wheeled blue truck, hissing and rumbling, weaved slowly past in front of us.

I thanked my saviour, who appeared to have deserted his vending duties at a fruit-stacked roadside trestle table some way behind us. 'Your car is a old car,' he said, with great deliberation, and I sensed his utility might have peaked. I clanked open a bonnet flap and was met by an almost visible wave of heat. The Model T motor's prodigious talent for thermal radiation would always amaze me. It was as if Henry had made a terrible miscalculation and perfected the external combustion engine.

Having burned deep welts in the tips of three fingers and failed to stare the T better, I remembered how I had regularly coaxed my old Morris Minor van back to life in these exact circumstances. Thus inspired, I bent down, removed my right shoe and whacked its sole firmly and repeatedly against anything that looked like part of the ignition system. Then I leapt back in and hit the starter. *Ker-dug-a-dug-a-dug-a-whockwhockwhock-wheeeeeeck.* 'That were no good,' noted my assistant, drawing the back of a large hand slowly across his nostrils. The rattlesnake thermometer was already past 100, and broiled befuddlement was pushing my stupidity levels into the red zone. I phoned Ross.

In the hour that followed I rearranged my Model T's contents, and quite large parts of the car itself, into a creative roadside installation across the hot gravel. The toolbox that Bob Kirk had bolted on to the passenger running-board donated its well-used wrenches and screwdrivers to the base layer. Atop these, and between the two plastic crates that had accommodated them in the rear-seat footwell, lay the spare parts and touring essentials donated by Ross or thrown in by Bob. A military cartridge case with its heavy top flap agape, exposing a jostle of small bottles, jars and cardboard boxes of archaic appearance. A heap of little chewing-tobacco tins with legends such as 'COTTER KEYS' and 'STARTER PARTS' scrawled on their lids in shaky marker pen. A 2-gallon plastic drum full of petrol, a smaller one full of water, and three quarts of oil. A sheaf of cable ties, a roll of duct tape and sundry aerosol solvents. A box of gaskets and a foot pump I'd found under the rear-seat cushion. The rear-seat cushion. The bonnet, which had completely detached itself when I raised the opposing side flap, now stood on its hinges in the dust. And draped over this, like one of Salvador Dali's floppy clocks, the heavy black folds of an inner tube.

I performed this grand transplant, before the placid, curious gaze of my rescuer, in futile search of an electrical test probe that Ross had left somewhere in the car, and which he advised I would need to inaugurate the diagnostic process. I had begun my hunt, after that first brief call, with quite a detailed mental image of the device in question: it would be a calculator-sized affair with a needled meter window and two poky contact sticks. This was such a compelling personal vision that I felt no need to ask Ross to confirm its accuracy. Now, sweatily assessing my pop-up junkyard, I reappraised a tool sticking out from the bottom of the heap, one of the earliest items extracted, and called him back. 'This probe thing. I don't suppose it looks like a screwdriver with a big cable coming out the end?'

This episode's useful legacy was in finally convincing Ross that all my declarations of mechanical hopelessness had no roots in false modesty. I really was attempting to keep a needy, fragile relic on the road for 6,000 miles from a position of the profoundest imbecility. The very first time I talked to Ross on the phone, he'd sought to fix my whereabouts on the foothills of basic mechanical competence by asking if I had ever removed a cylinder head. 'Well, you're going to have some fun,' he'd said after I told him I hadn't. 'On every Model T trip I've done there are people and cars that don't make it.'

Now I held the phone to my reddening ear expecting, and deserving, to hear a long period of silence, followed by an exasperated imprecation and a terminal click. Instead, Ross very patiently talked me through the electro-analytics, sympathetically recalibrating his tone to that of an emergency-services operator asking a toddler to assess a comatose parent's vital signs. And then to surgically resuscitate them, because having pinpointed the fault

I now had to remedy it – with Ross on speaker phone – by taking the distributor to pieces, then retarding and advancing the ignition timing through a memorable combo of intricate, thousandth-inch twiddles and lusty, cast-iron heaves on the crank handle. These activities greatly excited my companion, who sidled closer, lowered his large round head into the engine bay, and began to gurgle.

'What the hell's that?' called out Ross as I jabbed at the screen with filthy fingers, vainly attempting to locate and deactivate the speaker function.

'It's a … I've got a chap here who, um … Does this sound any better?' By way of distraction I snaked a hand into the car and punched the starter button, initiating a reedy, electro-mechanical cough.

'Too retarded!' yelled Ross. 'Just way, way too retarded.'

Ker-dug-a-BRRRRRRAGGHHH!

After two roadside hours the car abruptly burst into fast and furious life. Neither I nor Ross had any idea what we'd just done to persuade it. As would invariably prove the case, the T seemed to cooperate of its own accord, on its own terms and in its own time, a fickle stubbornness that had no place in the world of inanimate machinery. Alongside me, five brown teeth broke into a smile and a big red hand was held aloft. I returned it with a wave of my own, then noticed it was holding a small plastic disk that I recognised as the distributor's internal dust cover. And so, following a further fiddlesome under-bonnet hiatus, I meandered noisily away over the plump green hills of central Virginia.

One hundred and sixty miles doesn't sound like much of a drive. Especially not in America, where in many states that's a daily commute, or a shopping run, or a ride to the movies and back. But for a novice at the wheel of a Model T, let me assure you that

160 miles in one stint is a life-changing odyssey. At its conclusion I sank fully clothed into the motel nylon, limbs akimbo, ears still ringing with roars and clunks. Then I tilted my empty head towards the net curtains, and tried to refill it. I saw myself puttering through King William County, a colonial realm of steepled, witch-trial churches and sun-washed village greens. I heard all the cheery shouts and toots and waves, which had even poured forth from overtakers I'd led for slothful miles through the winding, low hills. *Ahoooga!* I felt the heat of Ford's furnace rise up through the floorboards and the soles of my shoes, smelled the first, breezy tang of salt and seaweed. I recalled those laps of a busy petrol-station forecourt in ever decreasing circles, feet and hands working overtime, trying to master a controlled halt before a pump-edge kerb did a more brutal job for me. Yanking the front seat up, unscrewing the tank cap thus revealed, plumbing its contents with a marked wooden ruler. Hosing in 8 gallons of regular as the questioners assembled. What year is that, sir? How fast does it go? No seat belts? I guess there ain't much point when you're sitting on the gas tank. Where you from? How long you had this? You taking it to that antique rally in Richmond? Watching those keen and open expressions evolve into something very different when I answered the last three: I'm from London, England; I've owned this car for seven hours and I'm driving it to the Pacific.

Through the net curtains, the T fixed me with that guileless, wide-eyed stare. You've got some front, I thought, sitting there looking all sweet and old and innocent. And now I recalled the demonic growl of low gear; the angry, bucking stalls, and above all the blanching terror that sprang from those free-spirited front wheels. The slightest imperfection in or on the road surface – a dimple, a ridge, a pebble, a twig – dispatched us across the tarmac in a bracingly random manner; on cambered corners, I had to steer in the bend's opposite direction to stop the T wandering over to greet oncoming traffic. Less lethal but more humiliating were my struggles to engage reverse. This operation, remember, was afforded its own pedal, but pressing it to the floorboards achieved nothing unless I simultaneously rammed the throttle to its skull-shuddering extremity. Even then, rearward progress was feebly reluctant, creating an overall audio-visual performance that attracted the wrong sort of attention.

The motel manager – a middle-aged Indian, from India – had insisted that I back my precious antique up to the front door of my room. How sad to behold his regret and alarm at the appalling manoeuvre this spawned. At least he didn't argue when I then flung my bags in through the door and announced that I'd walk to his recommended eatery, a Subway, even though it was a mile and a half away down the dual carriageway outside. Ninety minutes later I shuffled back up the hard shoulder, with breakfast slapping against my knees in a plastic bag: five tepid, leftover inches of a foot-long sub of the day.

I only remembered why I'd come here when I woke up. This was the nearest motel to the quietest-looking Trump-voting stretch of Atlantic I could find, and it was in Ordinary. As the emblematic starting point for a journey through small-town, everyday, run-of-the-mill America this had seemed irresistible. And I must say, looking back, that as a template of typicality, Ordinary, Virginia, did a stand-up job. It was a seamless zone rather than a town, a settlement with no identifiable centre, just a wide-meshed grid of silent residential streets bisected by four lanes of through traffic. No pedestrians; indeed few visible signs of life beyond the cars that sped past every few seconds.

The Subway I'd walked to lay amid the stripped-down strip mall that lined the George Washington Memorial Highway, a struggling retail parade with a lot of vacant, weed-invaded space between the thrift stores and Hunter's Heaven Guns & Archery. An enormous Stars and Stripes, a good 20 feet across, flapped gently atop a road-side pole. A dead racoon swelled in the verge below. A sign outside one of the pre-fab churches read: 'PRAYER – AMERICA'S ONLY HOPE.' I'd counted half a dozen TRUMP–PENCE bumper stickers on my weary Subway stumble, plus a home-made placard in the yard of a side-road bungalow that said, 'FOR SALE – AMERICA' in very large letters, with 'CONTACT CLINTON FOUNDATION' in smaller ones beneath. Handy reminders that Ordinary, and so many thousands of slightly run-down little towns like it, had just played a role in something extraordinary. Without question the most incredible political event in post-war democracy. Trump picked up two-thirds of the votes here; the Democrats returned their worst result in forty-four years.

I was out on the motel forecourt at 7 a.m., the sun already blazing down from a cloudless sky, the T's bonnet already propped open. In one hand: a quart bottle of SAE30 engine oil. In the other: my phone, with the Google homepage open, and 'Where is the oil filler on a Model T Ford?' entered in the search box. Nobody had ever insulted my intelligence by showing me, and I'd therefore been too ashamed to ask. I now flipped the appointed cap and poured, checking the dipstick at regular intervals. To my alarm it swallowed the whole bottle before reaching the requisite notch, a rate of consumption that couldn't be entirely explained by the slick little puddles the car had leaked on to the forecourt overnight. At least I knew where the water went: straight under the graceful silver-winged cap, with its incorporated 'motometer' temperature gauge, that crowned the radiator. But despite my empurpling efforts, it wouldn't budge. I pulled and twisted and tugged and swore. Then, trying not to picture his reaction as he read it, I sent an enquiring text message to Ross. 'It just unscrews,' he replied. Though not until an hour later, by which time I had brutalised that lovely thing loose with a plumber's wrench. I had also done something even worse, and much less successful, with a cartridge of thick, red lubricant. A tiny amount of this had made its way into the empty chamber of Ross's grease gun. The rest had been forcefully expelled into places that the poor motel manager is probably still discovering.

I'd plotted my official start long in advance on Google Street View, and I had plotted well. Fleming Road, just a quick and panicky pootle from Ordinary, was a peaceful, pine-bordered lane that ran right into the Atlantic, or at least the salty wedge of Chesapeake Bay that I hoped would count. I crunched over the last fir cones and killed the engine with the front wheels on a sliver of pale sand. Two ramshackle jetties prodded into the shallow, still water; across the bay, smoke rose from a distant pair of industrial chimneys. I hopped out. My word it was warm. A large bird of prey circled high in the windless blue sky. The Stars and Stripes hung limply from its pole in the picket-fenced yard of a beach-front bungalow. I drained the little water bottle in my hand, then walked over the sand, bent down and rather laboriously filled it with tepid brine. To endow my journey with a romantic sense of purpose, I planned to crown it by tipping a few fluid ounces of Atlantic into the Pacific.

I gazed around and sighed. Photoshop the chimneys out and this was a scene to linger in. Instead, I savagely despoiled it with a belching, roaring twelve-point turn and a spirited klaxon reveille. Ahooga! Ahooga! *Ahoooooooooooga!*

The car that rolled out from the Ford Motor Company's Piquette plant in Detroit on 27 September 1908 didn't look like a world-beater. Those gangly, disembodied fenders, fat-spoked cartwheels and stubby, four-square proportions were all throwbacks to the age of the horse carriage. So too was the body construction: sheet metal bent over a hardwood skeleton. The Rolls-Royce Silver Ghost, released the year before, was inestimably more represent-ative of the era's automotive market – a sleek rich-man's plaything that ran like silk on the smooth city roads of Europe.

But Ford had pinned his hopes on America's booming middle class, in particular the farmers who'd struck it rich feeding the nation's burgeoning population: from 1900 to 1910, the price index for farm produce shot up by an unparalleled 52 per cent. No other manufacturer seemed to know or care that most Americans lived in small towns or on the nation's six million farms. As a farm-reared boy, Henry knew the demographic's priorities: ruggedness, simplicity, practicality. American roads then ranked amongst the worst in the world, so the Model T's wheels were spaced to slot into the cart-horse ruts that ran down most of them, and its chassis, set high above the ground, was designed to flex and pivot over extravagant imperfections. Short and light, it could pull itself out of the loosest sand and the thickest mud. Pertinently, the T's 200-mile range was 50 miles longer than the entire national network of paved roads. The Model T would boldly go where no car had ever gone. And it would do it for just $825, a lot less than any competitor, and – more crucially for his intended sector – around $150 cheaper than a team of horses.

Henry was supremely confident in his Universal Car: on a 1,300-mile test drive around the Great Lakes, he'd suffered nothing worse than a puncture. But because nobody had previously attempted to sell a lot of cars to a lot of people – only 2 per cent of rural families owned one – he had no idea how his utilitarian offering would go down with the public until the first newspaper adverts went out on 2 October, a Friday. 'No car under $2,000 offers more,' wheedled the copy, 'and no car over $2,000 offers more except the trimmings.' For Henry Ford, now forty-five years old, this was the last roll of the dice.

He didn't have long to wait. 'Saturday's mail', recalled the *Ford Times* many years later, 'brought nearly one thousand enquiries. Monday's response swamped our mail clerks and by Tuesday night, the office was well nigh inundated.' No car had ever managed more than 7,000 sales. The Model T doubled that before it had even gone into full production. One dealer in Pennsylvania gushed: 'It is without doubt the greatest creation in automobiles ever placed before a people.'

In May 1909, the overwhelmed company had to stop taking orders for two months. Within a year Ford had outgrown its Piquette factory, and moved to a purpose-built facility up the road at Highland Park. 'It was the right car at the right time at the right price,' said Philip Van Doren Stern, who wrote the story on which *It's a Wonderful Life* was based, and should thus be regarded as an authority on small-town miracles. That price kept getting righter. In 1911, the firm sold 35,000 Model Ts, and Henry dropped the RRP to $680. Two years later, he shifted 170,000 at $525 a pop – a few bucks below the nation's average annual wage.

In the early years of the twentieth century, the life of an American farm family was, from most human perspectives, a thanklessly shit one: up at 4 a.m. in an unheated room, with nothing but supper and sleep to look forward to when another hard day was done. So while Ford's provincial customers may have convinced themselves they were buying a Model T to carry sacks of grain around the farm or pick up a bale of barbed wire from town, in truth they'd been seduced by its breathless, horizon-busting possibilities: nipping out for a country picnic or over the hills to visit the in-laws, top down on the open road for a day at the state fair, the fun of driving for driving's sake. Heady thrills for farmers who typically never ventured more than 10 miles from their homes, fulfilling desires they barely knew they had. Speed and freedom, owning the future, undoing the fearsome isolation of rural life. Hanging out with people you actually liked, not just happened to live near.

Norval Hawkins, Ford's pioneering sales manager, understood all this. 'You do not sell goods,' he presciently noted, 'but ideas about goods.' His campaigns targeted emotions, depicting proud, lone Model Ts above slogans like 'Boss of the Road' and the frankly startling 'Obey that impulse!' There were early dabblings with automotive sex appeal: one ad featured a young chap and two girls in the back seat of a Model T, captioned, 'Look at this picture and decide for yourselves.' Henry Ford had a more prosaic grasp of marketing, but still felt he knew his customers better than they knew themselves. 'If I had asked these people what they wanted, they would have said: a faster horse.'

The planetary transmission, a serious deterrent for those of us with previous gear-shifting experience to unlearn, could be swiftly mastered by rustics who had never driven before. And the Model T had been designed to appeal to their redneck fixing skills: a car that every farmer could repair by the road with baling wire and a hammer. As an indicator of Henry's success with his rural demographic, by 1910, the vehicle ownership rate in Iowa was six times higher than New York City's. And almost every car in the state was a Model T. In that year, the US Department of Agriculture composed a paean to the Model T's liberation of rural America, concluding: 'Never before have any such proportions of the nationals of any land known the lifting spirit that free exercise of power and independence can bring.'

By 1912, Ford employed more salesmen than any other US company. The firm had 3,500 dealers across the US, each required to stock every one of the Model T's 5,000 component parts. An unprecedented promotional mania set in as Ford sellers outdid each other with demonstrations of the car's remarkable capabilities. Dealers drove Ts up the steps of the YMCA in Columbus, Nebraska, down a staircase at Alamo Square in San Francisco, up two flights and into the hall of a Kentucky courthouse. They drove them through the streets laden to the gunwales: fifty boys in one, three hogsheads of tobacco in another, an entire graduate class, the St Louis Browns baseball team. A dealer in Houston ran his car at 10mph for six days and nights without once stopping the motor. Another who had lost both his arms put on a show in which he crank-started a T with his feet.

T owners were no less keen to explore the capabilities. Farmers employed their cars as a portable power source for shelling corn, sawing logs and pumping water. They were driven up to the farmhouse porch and used to churn butter and wash clothes. Preachers stuck a shed and a clapboard steeple on the back and had themselves a mobile chapel. After-market accessory manufacturers offered a multitude of gadgets: heaters, 'anti-rattle' vibration muters, cigar-shaped speedster bodies.

The Model T phenomenon went into overdrive in 1913, after Ford and his team introduced the moving assembly line at Highland Park. Henry was not so much an inventor as a superlative innovator, an enhancer and refiner of existing products and methods, and the process was an aggregation of borrowed techniques. His principal inspiration: the slaughterhouses of Chicago, where meat workers hacked methodically at carcasses that passed before them on a moving, overhead 'disassembly line'. Ford simply reversed this system, confident that the repetition of straightforward manual tasks at a conveyor belt would offer a giant leap in efficiency over standard manufacturing practice, in which teams of skilled workers assembled components at static stations.

But just as he had with the launch of the Model T, Henry was taking a bold leap into the dark. He expanded Highland Park into the largest factory on earth, where 14,000 assembly-line operatives worked at conveyors and overhead cranes that hauled bits of car in unbroken 300-yard lines, at a steady 6 feet per minute. No one had ever seen anything like it. 'Wonderful, wonderful!' cried President Taft, after a tour of the new facility. 'I am amazed by the magnitude of the establishment, and can still hear the hum of its machinery now!' 'The Ford plant is a miracle,' wrote one of the many breathless journalists who visited Highland Park. 'Hundreds of parts, made in vast quantities at incredible speed, flow toward one point. The final assembly is the most miraculous thing of all.'

Well, Henry was right again. The time taken to manufacture a Model T plummeted from thirteen hours to ninety-three minutes, and a finished car was soon rolling off the Highland Park lines every eleven seconds. In 1916, Ford sold 500,000 Ts, and cut the price to $345. 'Like the New Testament story of the loaves and fishes,' writes Ford's biographer Steven Watts, 'Ford seemed to be creating material sustenance for thousands of people by a superhuman process. His fellow citizens responded with a kind of worship.' Only now did Henry coin the Model T's most fabled maxim. Before 1915, cars had left the factory green, blue, red and grey, but black was cheaper and more durable, and with a near monopoly in the market he felt emboldened to impose it as a no-choice option. Ford stopped advertising the car in 1917, and didn't start again for almost seven years. There was simply no point. By this time not even the manufacturer referred to it as the Model T. It was just 'the Ford car', the only show on the road.

The ubiquitous T, a national treasure before its tenth birthday, quickly embedded itself into popular culture. Nicknames were inevitably bestowed, and two stuck. 'Flivver', a colloquial term for any cheap and cheerful machine, was in widespread use by 1910. Nobody seems entirely sure how 'Tin Lizzie' originated, though the *New Dictionary of American Slang* offers a derivation that strikes an uncomfortable note today: 'Sturdy, dependable and black, like the traditional, ideal Southern servant, called Elizabeth.' There were dozens of Ford joke books and thousands of humorous postcards, poking gentle fun at the little car's rattling bumpiness or admiring its doughty pluck. Henry's own favourite, related to the *Denver Express* when he visited the city in 1915, told of the old man who asked to be buried with his Ford, 'because the darned thing has pulled me out of every hole I ever got into'.

Music halls rang with comic doggerel: 'My Bonnie leaned over the gas tank, The depth of its contents to see, I lighted a match to assist her, Oh bring back my Bonnie to me.' America's earliest in-car fumbles were celebrated in a popular ditty, 'On the Old Back Seat of the Henry Ford'. Up the other end of the cultural spectrum, the avant-garde composer Frederick Shepherd Converse wrote a fourteen-minute fantasia entitled *Flivver Ten Million*, scored for real car horns and featuring squeaks, rattles and a tremendous collision, which was well reviewed and performed by several leading orchestras. It was all good publicity. Ford didn't even mind when the likes of Laurel and Hardy kept brutalising his beloved machines on screen, as the joke depended on those flattened, halved and submerged Ts proceeding doggedly onwards.

Henry's Universal Car went global during the Great War, when 125,000 Model Ts served the Allied cause, impressively outperforming their heavier European rivals in muddy, shell-pocked combat zones. Assembly plants were duly opened in France, Denmark, Argentina, Spain, Uruguay, Italy, Belgium, South Africa, Mexico, Germany, Malaya and India. Some 300,000 Model Ts were built at Ford's factory in Manchester, and over 750,000 at Ford Canada, the British Empire's largest manufacturing concern. In 1921, when Ford shifted a million Ts at $325 each, almost two-thirds of the cars in America were Model T Fords. So were half the cars on earth. Black and black and black all over.

Peak T was reached in 1924, when Ford built and sold two million Model Ts at a unit price of $260. It was all downhill from there. But what an extremely big hill it had been. By the time production ended on 26 May 1927, more than fifteen million Ford Model Ts had been manufactured in nineteen years. The VW Beetle took almost twice as long to match the feat, and no other car has come close.

*

'You have more speed at your command than you can safely use on average roads, or even on the best roads save under exceptional conditions, and a great deal more than you ought to attempt to use until you become thoroughly familiar with your machine, and the manipulation of brakes and levers has become practically automatic.' So reads a section in the 1909 Model T owner's manual, headed 'Go It Easy' and aimed at the novice driver. It's an intriguing insight into the constraints of the early motoring age, when a car with a top speed of 39mph could be considered a liability in the wrong hands.

I had two of those hands and a pair of matching feet, all of them a very long way from automatic manipulation. But I was also driving on roads that were better than the very best on offer in 1909. By 1920, a billion dollars were being spent every year on new and improved roads, and speeds nosed steadily upwards. Heading back north-west through Virginia I cruised down broad, empty tarmac, past mailboxes with five-digit house numbers on them, past plagues of yellow school buses parked up for the summer, past founding-father settlements: Gloucester, Essex, Port Royal. Confidence laid its comforting hand upon my shoulder, then began to tug surreptitiously at the throttle lever. The GPS flashed up 39mph. The T settled into a thrumming, sweet-spot rhythm. I unhunched just a little, relaxing as much as those wooden beads allowed, and let the warm, green world spool towards me through that split windscreen, the winged motometer bobbing steadily up and down on my prow like a figurehead. This was better. This was much better.

And so, for a few hot and heady days, I fell into something like a routine. I'd be up early to beat the heat, bung in a bottle of oil, then chug and rumble north-east in the general direction of Detroit, via the reddest blots on my map. I broached the prosperous outposts of pick-up country, trim clapboard farmhouses with a boutique vineyard out front, golf courses set amongst the sun-kissed maize. The road began to pitch and roll through hills stacked with hickory, oaks and sugar maples. It was an idyll compromised only by the over-ripe death pasted across the rural tarmac, delivering waves of the very headiest putrefaction through my open cabin: raccoons, deer, foxes, squirrels, fat-rat opossums, the question mark of a flat black snake. And those poor little Mohawk-tufted skunks, wrinkling my nose from a mile away.

I'd refill gas tank and stomach at petrol stations, shooting the breeze with the aimless sheriffs who always seemed to congregate there. Quite often an amiable old-timer would shuffle up and lean into the T's cabin. 'Learned to drive in one of these,' said one, with a wheezy chuckle. 'That there's the brake pedal, that's reverse, and that's the one that puts you straight through the side of the barn.' Some drastic maintenance issue would typically manifest itself during these early pit stops. I'd check the tyre pressures and find them all 70 per cent below Ross's recommendations, or discover that half my wheel nuts had rattled themselves loose, or hear a faint chink when I slammed the door, then get out and spot a large mystery bolt on the concrete below. This was the shakedown: after decades of fitful pensioner pottering, my blameless old car was being rattled apart by the rigours of long-haul use.

And I joined battle with my first serious traffic, enmeshed in many jockeying lanes when I passed close to larger towns. Reluctant to hazard a glance over my shoulder through the letterbox back window, my awareness of rearward activity was restricted to the shuddering, juddering driver's-side mirror. It was like Tom's view of the world after Jerry belts him in the face with a frying pan. Was that one truck steaming up behind me, or six? Out on the open road it hardly mattered: in a Model T, whatever's behind you will shortly be in front. But in traffic the uncertainty was deeply unsettling, especially with unseen undertakers shooting up my blindside. I'd veer gingerly across into the slow lane, braced for impact, then find it filled with a stationary motorhome, or evolve into a compulsory right-turn filter, or simply disappear. The stress was compounded by the parade of red lights that clutter American ring roads: it would be more than a thousand miles before I encountered the reviled symbol of nannying European traffic socialism that is the roundabout.

One early motorist neatly described the activation of a Model T's braking system as 'a ritual, not a function'. Mine was an ill-starred marriage of uselessness and wayward instability, which when applied *in extremis* would have the car fishtailing helplessly about the carriageway, rear wheels locked, with only the tiniest diminishment of speed. 'Good brakes encourage bad driving,' said Herbert Austin, the British Henry Ford, a man who very unfairly died of pneumonia.

When a light ahead changed from green to amber, I had to make a snap decision: floor the brakes and risk careening into the middle of the intersection, sideways, or yank the throttle wide open and shoot through the red with a volley of warning ahooogas. And all this whilst endeavouring to respond in kind to the supportive waves, and answer all those bellowed and ever more familiar through-the-window questions ('Sweet ride – what year?'), and force a smile for the camera-phones. How very closely overtakers would weave in the quest for the optimum snap. But however alarming, I could hardly condemn their insouciance. Of all the thoughts that might suggest themselves on passing an extremely old motor car – Ah, that's cute; What a terrible racket; Praise be for the twenty-first century – there is one that never would: I bet the guy driving that has absolutely no idea what he's doing, and might at any moment swing blindly over and kill us all.

Into another gas station to take aboard fluids and nutrition; a few hot hours later, into another to offload them. As I came to discover, a lot of small-town life revolves around the local petrol stop. Rural Americans drive a lot, and generally in a pick-up truck with the fuel economy of an icebreaker, so they need to refill a lot. And not just with unleaded. Even the tiniest gas station is almost walled in by batteries of towering glass-doored fridges, all geometrically stacked with rows of shiny, garish soda cans. I was transfixed. With their clinical interior lighting and wisps of cryo-genic mist, these installations had a reverential, futuristic air, a climate-controlled preservation facility for life-giving treasures.

Rare was the customer who left without condensation-beaded refreshment. In the larger gas stations, they'd also have fast-food-style soda dispensers with nested cups alongside, ranging in capacity from top hat to water butt. On my third morning, I saw a well-built sheriff emerge from a gas station nursing a beaker the size of an office bin. As I walked inside to pay, I took a sidelong glance into his patrol car and saw him carefully wedging it in an extended funnel-shaped adaptor stuck in the console cupholder.

Now that we've passed Peak Cig, America's addiction to soda pop stands alone as the greatest first-world public-health scandal of our age. Let's take a look at the sticky-faced facts. In the past three decades, as America's consumption of sugary beverages has doubled – to 45 gallons per head annually – its diabetes rates have trebled. The incidence of obesity has more than doubled for adults, and quadrupled for children aged six to eleven. J. D. Vance, the Appalachia-reared author of *Hillbilly Elegy*, was nine months old when his mother started putting Pepsi in his bottle. More than a third of Americans are now classified as obese – that's twice the British ratio, and we're the fat man of Europe.

CHAPTER 4

In the 1970s, the largest 'fountain drink' sold at McDonald's was 20 fluid ounces. It's now 40 fluid ounces, more than a litre. In 1995, the Wendy's fast-food chain introduced the 42-ounce 'Great Biggie', billed as 'a river of icy cold enjoyment'. A standard 12-ounce can of soda contains the equivalent of nine teaspoons of sugar. Down a Great Biggie and you have just ingested thirty-one teaspoons. Yet this fizzy, sweet river is dwarfed by a syrup tsunami that defies physiological logic: at 50 fluid ounces, the 7/11 Double Big Gulp is 156 per cent larger than the stomach capacity of an average human. Young men aged twelve to twenty-nine now consume an average 160 gallons of carbonated soft drinks a year – nearly two quarts, or well over two litres, every single day. That's an extraordinary level of dedication, almost a part-time job.

I'd first confronted the helpless, hardwired extent of this addiction at a Civil War re-enactment in the Louisiana woods ten years before, during the research phase of a book I wrote about living history. The civilian refugees I camped with ranked amongst the most fanatically authentic re-enactors I met anywhere. They had built their ox wagon from scratch, even forging the nails in a backyard, charcoal-fired iron foundry. They made their own buttons out of animal bone, wove clothes on a hand loom, spooned grits from onion-tainted wooden bowls and said 'good enough' instead of 'OK'. They knew more about English history than I did, whimpered a lot less about spiders, and didn't disgrace themselves when somebody said they lived in Knob Lick. Then one night, a blacksmith beckoned me to the back of the mess tent with a shifty wink, and lifted the lid of a big wooden pail. Inside it sat three enormous bottles of Mountain Dew.

'Don't tell anyone I showed you this,' he whispered.

'Good enough,' I lied.

For the avoidance of doubt, I point out none of this from a position of moral or nutritional superiority. The only reason I didn't

– spoiler alert! – drink myself into a diabetic coma on this trip is a historic personal correlation between the consumption of liquid sugar and the development of agonising kidney stones. But along with those 99¢ gallon drums of water perched precariously in my lap all day, I still drank plenty of total rubbish. As I grew more at ease behind that ancient wheel, and those mind-focusing splurts of adrenalin ebbed away, I had to rely on a hefty afternoon dose of sugar-free taurine to maintain alertness. Energy drinks really are the silliest, crappiest grocery products known to man, with those puerile, death-metal names – Relentless, Monster Rehab, No Fear – and logos like a footballer's tattoo. As a bonus, they're also way more dangerous than straight soda, and in an excitingly immediate manner: energy drinks have been linked to dozens of fatal heart attacks in recent years.

Neither did I resent having to sustain myself on the fearsomely processed fare that fills every gas station. Not once did I gaze wanly along the shelves and shelves of plastic-sealed snacks and think: Oh *no*, Fire Cracker Giant Red Hot Pickled Sausage for elevenses AGAIN. The truth is I love all that crap. I love staining my puckered lips with extreme and unearthly snack sensations, the scarlet-red Flamin' Hot Pork Rinds, the peanuts encrusted with honey chipotle, those unspeakable dill pickles that come in a clear pouch of psychedelic flavoured vinegar, like take-home souvenirs from the intimate gangrene clinic. I drew the line at beef jerky, but only because it was so bloody expensive. Seven bucks a pack? Why, that's a week's supply of the foot-long finger of mechanically recovered, deep-smoked meat that is the Slim Jim – the snack you can eat behind the wheel of a speeding antique vehicle and STILL maintain partial control!

But I could afford to eat all this delicious garbage, and to savour doing so, because I was on holiday, sort of, and in the fullness of time would be returning to a Nordic-run, snack-intolerant household with enforced access to fresh food. What on earth must this diet do to you in the long term? And in such button-popping profusion? The Model T was a slim and nimble car for a hungry, go-getting nation. When Americans had a body-image problem back then, it was unappealing scrawniness. After Angelo Siciliano changed his name to Charles Atlas in 1922, he pitched his bodybuilding regime at '97-pound weaklings', and went as far as patenting the phrase, 'Hey Skinny, Your Ribs Are Showing!' Right up to the early 1960s, US newspapers were full of ads for feminine weight-gain supplements, depicting mildly curvaceous women in swimsuits with speech bubbles saying things like 'I have plenty of dates since I put on 10lbs!' and 'It's hard to believe they once called me skinny!'

Well, whatever those hungry go-getters were after back then, they'd long since gone and got it, and stuffed it down their throats. Americans spend six times more on processed savoury snacks than the per-capita global average. A standard serving of McDonald's fries is now three times larger than it was in the 1950s. Let us consider the current president's standard – and very regular – McDonald's order, as revealed by his former campaign manager: two Big Macs, two Filets-O-Fish and a chocolate milk-shake. Weighing in at 2,500 calories, that single meal is rather more than the recommended daily intake for a man of his age. As the embodiment of the American Dream's bloated, decadent endgame, Trump leads from the front. Of the twenty-five fattest states in the US, only two didn't vote for him.

Henry Ford, however, despised obesity, evidence of indulgent laziness and guarantor of 'a sluggish brain'. 'If people cut down on their rations,' he opined, 'they wouldn't need doctors.' How very upset he'd have been to learn that many twenty-first-century Model T owners turned their steering wheels back to front to allow a couple of extra inches of gut clearance, or fitted a hinged 'Fat Man' wheel that could be folded back down over their bellies once they had taken their station. While searching for a suitable T, I'd read two or three classified ads penned by regretful owners who explained they were now 'too big' to drive one.

My word, what a protracted outburst! Let us return, with a jarring jump-cut, to a day in the life of our antique motorist, as he putters gamely towards the Appalachians. After 150 or so miles of heat, noise and carbonated taurine, his day is drawing to a close, and he pulls into some forlorn motel, a relic of that 'King of the Road' no-pool-no-pets era. There'll be a Gideon bible and a chunky old phone on the bedside table, and a yellow glow from the underpowered lamp will pick out walls scarred by long-gone decades of high jinks and hot tempers. Perhaps there's a Mexican restaurant nearby. If there isn't, he will make a regrettable mistake with some leftover stubs of Subway, adding many new layers to the room's ingrained odour of male-pattern transience. Then he'll click on the telly.

A White House staffer once described working there as 'trying to take a sip of water from a fire hose that never shuts off'. That was me trying to take stock of Trumpland in those early days, lost in the jarring disconnect between the benign, bucolic world outside my hinged windscreen and the cacophonous panic that ruled inside it. No time to ponder the state of the nation with more pressing and immediate mysteries to resolve, like how the fuck to reverse and why the passenger door kept flying open. The TV news was my hope for a calm, insightful overview of developments, but it only ramped up the manic bewilderment, a shouty confusion of backstabbing, frontstabbing, fear and loathing as Trump's presidency careered madly on. Harrowed correspondents would stare blankly down the lens and say: 'Jim, in thirty years of political reporting I have never witnessed anything like this.' Then the next day they'd have to say it again.

And the adverts; oh my, the adverts. We're always being told that television news is on the way out, and in America that's because its viewers are old, fat, sickly and therefore dying in droves. (Not just a heartless insult but a startling demographic fact: the life expectancy of white male Americans has been in slow but steady decline since 2009, and in some West Virginian counties now stands at sixty-four, the same as Namibia's.) Almost every single commercial I saw on the big three news stations – CNN, MSNBC, Fox News – related to serious ill-health, obesity treatment or aged frailty. I'd jab the motel remote and there'd be Marie Osmond in a belted pink dress, patting her stomach and trilling, 'Bye-bye, stubborn belly fat!' Or a swimsuited old dear beaming away in a plastic sarcophagus: 'A walk-in tub – with a heated seat!' 'Find the catheter that's right for you with our free sample pack – there are so many catheters to choose from! Pre-lubricated catheter! Anti-bacterial catheter! Steel-barbed catheter! High-voltage catheter!'

My motel TV began to seem like a porthole into the American Dream's decadent, sickly endgame, a vision of consumerism eating itself. When I switched over to *The Simpsons*, pitched at a younger audience, the commercials almost exclusively urged viewers to gorge themselves silly. 'Eat like you mean it at Hardee's!' 'Here at Carl's Junior we're all about doubling down on breakfast!' 'Trip-le thick, trip-le thick, brown-sugar-bacon: at Arby's WE HAVE THE MEATS.' 'All Red Robin burgers are just $6.99 – of course with our famous bottomless fries!'

And then back on the news networks, the old were trying to tackle the bloated, immobile consequences of their indulgent youth, and turning on each other if they failed. 'Hernia Mesh complications? Infection, wound-reopening, chronic pain? You may be entitled to compensation.' America's famously litigious healthcare culture has really gone into overdrive. Even CNN's closed-caption subtitles were brought to me by the Mesothelioma Awareness Legal Helpline. Most compellingly, the downside disclaimers at the end of all those prescription drug adverts now lasted far longer than the upside sales pitch, and were no longer blurted in that incoherent after-garble of yore (*may-cause-headaches-and-crutch-rot-don't-blame-us-if-spleen-explodes*).

The net effect of all these extraneous costs – the billions spent on advertising and legal settlements – is that the average American now pays 50 per cent more for their healthcare than anyone else on earth. You'd never think it given the fuss about Obamacare and so on, but the US has for years been spending about the same on public healthcare, per capita, as countries like the UK, Japan,

France and Germany. It's just that they've also been spending the same amount again – twice as much as the Swiss, their nearest rivals – on private care.

It's scandalous, but also rather sad. Those watered-down, mealy-mouthed pharmaceutical adverts with their endless toll of disclaimers seemed so jarringly out of place in this country, a gung-ho, hard-sell nation now beset by faltering uncertainties. All that self-confident vigour exhausted, whittled down to bloated, lethargic sickbed blame and bickering. I remembered the scrawny loser in those Charles Atlas strip-cartoon ads, getting sand kicked in his face before turning the tables two frames later. Now there'd be asterisks all over the page. *Results not typical. *Prolonged muscular exercise may cause pain and boredom. *Stretchy spring device may twang into nose. *Consult your lawyer if bullying persists.

On Independence Day the road began to rise and weave and the Appalachians took hazy shape before me: the actual Blue Ridge Mountains of Virginia, in my actual Laurel and Hardy car. The holiday brought a few other antiques out on to the road to exchange ahoogas with, and draped balconies with patriotic bunting. Someone had slung a big placard up on their porch: 'HAPPY BIRTHDAY AMERICA. HOPE YOU MAKE IT ANOTHER YEAR.' Trumpophobe, doomsday prepper or both? That was a door I wanted to stop and knock on. But stopping, without ample notice and preparation, was a four-limb dance I had yet to master.

'Ain't no July Four for farmers,' called the pimpled, straw-haired youth when I juddered and squealed to a complicated halt beside his tractor at a lonely four-way stop sign. 'Get some eggs go see the chips wool fireworks if I git done playin' the john naughty.'

Appalachia was clearly going to present new challenges. Steep inclines would rank amongst them. The T had trundled redoubtably over its first blue ridge, a leafy, winding bona fide mountain momma that delivered me into West Virginia. (There are only so many times you can bellow the chorus to 'Country Roads', but it does seem to be an awful lot of times.) On the second pass, though, the engine began to falter, and my speed dropped to an erratic shuffle. If the car died on a steep gradient, so might I: Ross had warned me a Model T's handbrake wouldn't hold on a big hill. To this end he'd supplied a pair of plastic chocks, which now lay ready on the passenger seat beside me. Should the motor fail and the T begin to roll backwards, I was expected to snatch the chocks up, vault out, then in one fluid movement wedge them under the nearest two wheels. And to do all this before accumulated speed rendered it impossible, guaranteeing runaway destruction of the T, or me, or both.

It was a scenario that concentrated my mind so completely that I failed to notice passing the bearded old guy in the army cap. A creak and a tilt and there he was beside me: up on the passenger running-board with one bony hand on the roof and the other braced to the frame of the windshield. 'Mand if I catcher rad?' he drawled, settling into a practised hunch and gazing casually straight up the hill. How very weird, but how very wonderful: a living link to the age of running-boards, when cars went so slowly you could jump aboard one as it passed. Furthermore, a handy quid pro quo now suggested itself. 'That's absolutely fine,' I called out above the T's jerky splutters, 'but if the motor stops, could you do me a favour and jam these things under the wheels?' He peered into the cabin and squinted doubtfully at the chocks, and the elbow I was jabbing in their direction. Then, without a word, he hopped off.

When the engine did give up the ghost, it chose a thought-fully gentle incline just outside Harrisonburg: I coasted on to the shoulder, pulled up the bonnet and called Ross. Or tried to. As would increasingly be the case, I had no phone signal. After half an hour of hopeful prodding, a huge and macho pick-up pulled in, and from it emerged a matching gentleman. Bruce C. Wood II – 'Bruce the Deuce' – had country-star hair, a checked shirt and a big dog riding shotgun. It didn't take him long to fix the T – my distributor's points had cracked in half, and he installed a spare set from one of Bob Kirk's tobacco tins – but in that time I learned quite a lot about Bruce. I learned that he was a mili-tary contractor in the field of aero electronics, who would shortly be off to pilot spy drones around Afghanistan in the search for improvised explosive devices. I also learned that he had a boat, lived alone, never locked his front door and always carried a gun: 'Sure do, got one in my truck right now.' He briskly flipped the distributor cover back on and bid me hit the starter. The car roared into life. Good old Bruce. Good old permanently armed, Taliban-bustin' Bruce the Deuce.

I was nosing deep into small-town Trumpland, and its inhabitants seemed very much nicer than my lazy imagination had feared. A Hells Angel in a Nazi helmet had given me the thumbs-up. Everyone I'd met had been friendly and helpful. They knew how to fix stuff, and did so with a smile. But my word they were conservative. The Adidas trainers I'd bought for this trip were chosen on the grounds of girth alone: my first farmyard test drive had proved that operating the T's tightly clustered pedals demanded extremely narrow shoes, and those were the slimmest I could find. But because they were also a bit red, my feet were routinely gawped at in utter astonishment. 'Neat ride you got there, what year w— Hot *damn*, that is one HELL of a pair of sneakers. Marlene, feller out here's got him some shoes and they are R-E-D red!' To create an equivalent footwear commotion on a British street, you'd need to go out in a pair of gold fishing waders. And nothing else.

That stolid traditionalism extended to a genteel, almost Victorian primness in personal matters. Consider the excretion of human fluid – you know you want to. I encountered a phobic reluctance to admit this ever happened. It began with those euphemisms, that door in the gas-station corner prissily dedicated to bath or rest. Within, the urinals would invariably be divided by neck-to-knee privacy barriers, lest your fellow resters snatch even the tiniest peek of pecker. And the globally indulged tradition of the roadside splash-and-dash behind a tree – a permanent temptation thanks to my gallon-a-day water habit, and one to which I occasionally succumbed – was frowned upon so sternly that I never once saw a rival practitioner.

Yet curiously, small-towners seemed much more relaxed about the solid small-room occupation – you know, the, um, the Full Bath, the Big Rest. Of all the strange and worrisome things I saw stickered to the rear of a pick-up – a crowded field from 'IF YOU CAN READ THIS, YOU'RE IN RANGE' to 'I ♣ BABY SEALS' – the worst, and by a margin, was 'HONK IF YOU HAVE TO POOP'. I spotted three of those. After the third I did some online retail research. 'Make driving fun with this "honk if you have to poop" magnet! Put it on the back of your car and see how many people around you need to use the bathroom! *Use outside the USA at your own risk.*' Why would one ever wish to ask this of their fellow motorists? Why would they ever wish to answer? What an incredibly odd state of affairs.

But then Americans could be incredibly odd, even the ones you really didn't expect to be. Take Henry Ford and Donald Trump. Two very different characters in most ways: Ford was an honest, frugal grown-up who lived an unostentatious life bereft of scandal, and once said, 'I would rather be right than be president.' But less different in others. The towering arrogance. The distrust of mainstream media. Both dismissive of experts and intellectuals, both sometimes alarmingly ignorant and inarticulate (interviewers complained that Ford routinely offered 'dubious quotations' and 'lacked the facility to explain his ideas', and he once told a court-room that the American Revolution had been fought in 1812). And both quite surprisingly eccentric.

Donald Trump smirks and gurns but never, ever laughs, not even when he's launching his own-brand steaks or vodka. The twelve daily cans of Diet Coke. The hair. This is a self-styled germophobe who won't touch elevator buttons, but will shake hands with visiting statesmen for whole minutes, in ludicrous parody of an alpha-male executive. For his part, Henry Ford burst into song every morning to 'start the day right', and liked to dine on 'roadside greens': clumps of random weeds plucked from the verge and stuffed between two slices of bread. He nurtured a fixation with the nursery rhyme 'Mary Had a Little Lamb', employing a team of researchers to investigate its possible origins, and in due course publishing his theories in a forty-page treatise (he later bought the early-nineteenth-century Massachusetts schoolhouse that Mary Sawyer was purportedly once followed into by a baby sheep). It seems wholly unfair to toss Ford's lifelong pacifism into this madcap mix, but the American press certainly did. When war broke out in 1914, he was ridiculed for pledging to burn down his factories rather than see them repurposed for munitions manufacture, and for suggesting that 'MURDERER' should be embroidered on every service uniform. After Henry blew $500,000 on a 1915 'Peace Ship' mission in a naive bid to keep the US out of the war, journalists dubbed it the 'Good Ship Nutty' and poured scorn all over 'Ford's folly'.

Still, however cheery and practical small-town Americans might be, and however traditional yet rather peculiar, they can also be extremely thin on the ground. Nobody was about when the car died in a silent Appalachian valley a few miles beyond the little town of Franklin, and for an hour nobody passed. Then, as I sat in that lonely lay-by, bonnet up and clueless, something abruptly possessed me. Without quite knowing what I was doing or why, I unscrewed the ancient ignition switch from the dash, prised the cover off and scraped ninety-six years' worth of sooty crud off its brass contacts. Ker-*BRRAAAGH*! Beneath that glorious roar of triumph I heard John-Boy narrating his monologue at the end of a *Waltons* episode. 'The truth is: things rarely go just the way we want them to, and when they don't, there's no shame in getting a hand from someone a little wiser. Because one day, maybe even later that same day, that someone might be you, motherfucker.'

I turned back and stayed at Franklin, in a $42 motel with a polystyrene ceiling and a bed propped up on bricks. 'You got a real purty old car, sir,' said the young waitress at the motel's conjoined diner, watching me wipe Texas Pete hot sauce from the plate with my final wodge of fajita. The reflexive bonhomie of America's service industry is so often delivered with dead-eyed phoniness, a product of their tipping culture, but out in the small towns the warmth was always genuine. 'Now, how 'bout some ass cream?'

'Hmm?'

'We got vanilla or strawberry.'

'Oh, right. I really couldn't.'

She greeted my refusal as if I'd ordered a 10-gallon sundae. 'Awesome! A coffee?'

'No thanks.'

'Alrighty!'

I looked out through the window, where my T sat alone under a broken neon VACANCY sign. The Model T singlehandedly spawned the age of the motor vacation, America's default holiday for the balance of the twentieth century. Families who had never ventured past the nearest lake or mountain would pile into their Ts and spend summer on the road, exploring the boundless majesty of their nation and tapping into the migratory heritage that had delivered their immigrant forebears to its shores. The American Dream went on tour: by 1919, ten million motorists were stopping to sleep in new 'auto courts', and the word 'motel' was coined the year after my T was born, in 1925. A typical family road trip lasted a month, and cost around $100 all in. But younger and bolder motorists set off on much more ambitious tours, and the cheap and doughty Flivver was their conveyance of choice: after it went out of production, you could pick one up for peanuts.

The modest library of related literature I had brought along described several such adventures. In July 1934, Darlene Bjorkman, a twenty-two-year-old schoolmistress from Bradford, Illinois, crammed five friends into a silver-painted 1926 Model T her dad bought for ten bucks, and set off on the first of seven summer tours that would take them through forty-four states, covering a remarkable 80,000 miles in the process. Less epic but more personally resonant was the story of Dib Fewer and Tod Snedeker, two nineteen-year-old San Franciscans who completed a three-month road trip to New York and back in 1931. Their T was a black 1921 coupé that Dib had been given free by a neighbour who'd written it off at a busy junction, breaking his arm in the process.

As a coast-to-coast drive in a black T, this adventure struck a chord. The cast of characters probably helped. I mean: Dib Fewer! And that neighbour? Pinky Robinson. Their car got in on the act too. One of Dib's old school chums ran an identical black coupé, and their friends had dubbed the cars in honour of a set of twins who appeared in a popular newspaper strip cartoon: 'Mike and Ike – They Look Alike.' Dib's T bagged the former appellation, and before he and Tod set off, he painted the name across its nickel-plated radiator grille, in bold, black capitals. MIKE. I'd bought a couple of books with me to dinner, and flicked through one until I came to the relevant photo. It would always raise a smile. Dib and Tod – jeans, open shirts, slicked-back hair, Errol Flynn moustaches – are the debonair embodiment of America's coming generation. But the frail, stiff-backed car they're standing astride, though barely a teenager, seems a cart-wheeled, matronly relic of an already distant age. And that name on its grille did me every time, so blunt, so bland, so defiantly, gloriously antiheroic. It did me again now. I liked Mike. Then I looked back out the window at my own fragile black old-timer. 'Evening, Mike,' I said, without thinking.

'If you're wanting to drive that vee-hickle north I would go around the mountain, sir. It's raining like all heck up there and you got some 10 per cent grades.' Small-town America is infested with sheriffs, who seem to have little else to do beyond dispensing helpful and courteous advice to foreign antique motorists. 'You take care now.'

The rain had built all morning, and I'd spent a wet and sweaty hour out on the motel forecourt wrapping up my car – Mike! – in Bob Kirk's weather curtains: four sheets of greasy, semi-transparent plastic attached by turnbuckles and leather straps around the open sides. It was like a leaky engine room in there, hot, moist and noisy, the T's throb amplified to clattering thunder. Rain dripped steadily from the dashboard and flew into my eyes through the half-inch gap betwixt roof and windscreen. Fumes that were normally dispersed through the open sides began to fill the cabin. I gave up on the stubby hand-powered windshield wiper after a single smeary sweep, and pressed my face right up to the spattered glass, trying to make sense of the unfolding impressionist roadscape.

The sheriff had walked up as I was disembarking at a gas station, an awkward and humiliating grovel through the tiny under-curtain door hatch. It was like crawling out of a catflap. Re-entry was worse still: I squirmed in on all fours, raised my bowed head and introduced the iron throttle stalk firmly into my right eye. I was beginning to understand why old Bob had got rid after fifty-one years: driving a T just wasn't an old man's game. Especially over long, wet distances, when I wasn't driving a T at all, more attempting to control a deafening, runaway gazebo. Part of me began to regret this whole undertaking. That part was my brain.

As advised, I went around that mountain, though there would be plenty more to follow. The detour took Mike and me through a funeral procession of struggling valley settlements, their main streets cluttered with derelict retail hulks and bookended by moribund industrial concerns. The principal source of wealth and employment in this part of West Virginia appeared to be industrial-grade poultry farms and processing plants, whose squawking, stinking trucks slooshed past me at regular intervals. By the state's class-leading standards of poverty and decline, towns like Moorefield and Petersburg weren't in fact doing too badly: their populations had dipped rather than collapsed, and only a fifth of the citizens lived below the poverty line. But in the residential outskirts, I noticed what would become a durable trend. The people with money, who pottered about in trim clapboard homes with neat yards, who drove past in shiny Buicks looking well-kempt and placid, were always old. When I saw someone scowling under a saggy porch, or slamming the door of a lichen-streaked pick-up with mismatched wheels, they were men of my age or a bit younger. Those silvery gentlefolk enjoying a prosperous retirement were their parents. The drive-by demographics were stark, and by general socio-economic agreement conclusive. I was watching the end of the American Dream.

Ford's Highland Park assembly line might have seemed a wonder of the world to the notables and journalists who toured the factory, but for the workers it was a deafening, monotonous hell. Few could hack it for long. By the end of 1913, labour turnover at the plant hit 380 per cent, and Henry was having to employ a thousand people just to expand his workforce by 100. On 5 January 1914 he revealed his dramatic solution: the company's daily wage, hitherto $2.34

for a nine-hour shift, would henceforth be $5 for an eight-hour one. The announcement sent shockwaves around the nation. Every newspaper in the land led with Ford's $5 day, with quotes that read like standing ovations: 'A new epoch in the world's industrial history!' 'A magnificent act of generosity!' One commentator heralded Ford as 'one of God's noblemen'; socialists and unionists hailed the $5 day as 'the solution of the labour wars in the country'. Down the other end of the economic spectrum, of course, disquiet merged into blind panic. 'He's crazy, isn't he?' asked the publisher of the *New York Times* when he heard the news. 'Don't you think he's gone crazy?' The *Wall Street Journal* called the $5 day 'a blunder, if not a crime'. 'Good for him if he can afford it,' said J. J. Cole, a rival car maker. 'Others can't.' But as it transpired, they could.

The remarkable Model T made Henry Ford famous, but his $5 day left a more profound legacy. Fordism – the mass-production of consumer goods by operatives paid well enough to buy them – was a paradigm shift in the relationship between boss and worker, nurturing an expectation of blue-collar prosperity that swiftly became the American norm. Highland Park workers woke up and found that they'd effectively become middle class overnight. They could suddenly afford to buy the cars they were building. And electric irons, and refrigerators, and phonographs, and radios. By accident or design, Henry Ford had made what should have been a self-evident connection: mass production didn't make sense without mass consumption. 'You can't get rich by making folk poor,' he said later. 'They can't buy your goods, and there you are.' Millions more people were suddenly in the market for a Model T, so he needed to make millions more of them. Where Ford led, others soon followed. Industrial wages shot up everywhere, and the eight-hour day – which just happened to allow Highland Park to operate three shifts around the clock – became standard. Within a year Ford raised its daily pay to $6, to stay ahead of the game. With consumer goods flying out of factories and off store shelves, workers held all the cards: in due course they unionised, securing paid vacations, healthcare benefits and generous pensions. Fordism democratised prosperity and launched mass-market consumerism, and in doing so set a template for the American Dream and a materialist way of life that spread right across the first world. Ford never called himself an inventor. But he invented the twentieth century.

The suddenly lucrative appeal of factory work drew migrants to Detroit and its regional industrial rivals from right across the impoverished Appalachians. Turned out you didn't need an education to make good money after all, as long as you were prepared to up sticks. Towns like the ones I'd been driving through were slowly leeched for fifty years. All the hungry go-getters went north to the factories, and local businesses closed down. So when the Rust Belt started corroding in the 1980s, there was no unskilled work anywhere: no manufacturing jobs to migrate for, and very few left in town. But regrettably that disdain for education lingered, and lingers still, an enduring frustration for the post-industrial employers who periodically attempt to set up shop in Appalachian towns, and struggle to attract applicants with basic skills or any appetite for training. Ford created a whole new class of wealthy workers, but when the good times stopped rolling they were left desperately ill-prepared.

The desire to out-earn your parents, a driving aspiration throughout American history, evolved into complacent certainty once Henry Ford unleashed the $5 day and blue-collar wages went nuts. But in the last thirty years, it had all unravelled. Most of the jobs vanished and the ones that remained were poorly rewarded: high-school-educated American men now earn 40 per cent less in real terms than they did in 1970. The forward momentum that sustained the American Dream stalled, then slid, and a whole generation became downwardly mobile. Guys in their forties and fifties are battling through on low wages and welfare as their dads live it up on fat company pensions.

Some of that battling looked pretty relative, it has to be said. Half the listless porch-scowlers had a rusty satellite dish on their roof, and ride-on mowers were parked by most stoops: the right to sit on your arse while cutting your grass is written into the rural constitution. It wasn't quite *The Grapes of Wrath*, but nonetheless, an awful lot of middle-aged mojos had been visibly mislaid. These were the first Americans who watched Mike drive by with sullen indifference. Things had gone to shit and it all seemed so unfair. Surveys consistently show that the white working class is the country's most pessimistic demographic: almost two-thirds of them believe the country has changed for the worse since the 1950s. J. D. Vance, who as a self-declared hillbilly is allowed to say these things, suggests Appalachian men find it increasingly easy to blame everyone but themselves: Obama closed down the coal mines, China stole all our good jobs, Hispanics stole all our bad ones. He quotes surveys that show people living a lie, insisting that they work far longer hours than they actually do, that they borrow less and go to church more. And lo, it came to pass that bitterness, apathy, despair and a towering sense of disillusionment with the status quo did coagulate into the forces that begat the Donald. Bullet-point summary: Trump was all Henry's fault.

'That a 'twenty-four?'

It was the first time anyone had guessed right. 'Those later wheels must fool a lot of people. I've got a 'twenty-four and a 'twenty-five, found them both at the back of an uncle's barn and did a full restoration.' I was at a mountain-top gas station, and had just met my first Model T guy. He seemed young by the community's standards, resting a sweet little daughter of about three on his hip as he stood by my car and scrolled through his phone's collection of T photos. 'This is my uncle with the 'twenty-five, just after I finished it. He didn't even know who I was by then, but man, when he saw that car he was just tickled to tears.' I tried to maintain polite interest but it wasn't easy: I'd parked too far from the pump, and was straining to jam the nozzle into Mike's under-seat tank orifice with the stout and stubborn hose pulled taut.

'How are your brakes? You got thirty-three bends and a thousand-foot drop coming up just— Honey! Oh my God, honey, did he get you in the face?'

I had, and the forecourt was filled with the ghastly, high-pitched screams that proved it. A premature squeeze of the trigger had sent a brief but violent jet of petroleum spirit across my car's interior and straight between a pair of wide young eyes. I stood helpless and horrified, trigger dangling from my hand, as the father bore his wailing daughter rapidly away into the gas-station store. How did they deal with these things here? This was already the longest I'd spent at a gas station without the local law-enforcers dropping in, so justice would surely be imminent. I pictured a sheriff in mirrored aviator shades pinning me regretfully to the concrete, one firm hand under my chin and the other tensing around the petrol-pump trigger. 'I'm real sorry 'bout this, sir, but you gonna have to learn yourself a West Virginia lesson.'

I stood for a long five minutes out there. When at length the father emerged, daughter in arms with a huge wodge of wet tissues over her face, I gabbled a stream of craven apologies. He accepted them with a sort of post-traumatic bemusement, still struggling to comprehend how a fellow T guy, by association an authorised proper man, could be so criminally cack-handed. Or perhaps he felt no need for anger, knowing that the forthcoming descent would prove punishment enough. It nearly meted out a capital sentence.

I ground down those swooping curves in low gear and sheeting rain, an impatient armada of headlights massed in my mirror, and suffered a heart-stopping loss of traction at a steeply pitched T-junction in the valley's fundament. In the battle for control, the steering wheel almost came off in my hands. After that, and for many weeks hence, I had to tighten the big nut in the middle with my fingers every half hour or so. Then the skies darkened, the hills receded and I was looking at my next state across a big, brown river.

St Mary's was West Virginia's last outpost, another worn-out town with a lot of empty buildings looking glumly at each other across the rain-filled potholes. I stopped there to fill up, and was about to feed coins into the gas station's air machine when a guy in overalls with a splendid twin-pronged grey goatee trotted up across the forecourt: 'Put those quarters back in your pocket, my friend, I've got a compressor in my shop right around the corner.'

His name was KD; his rendition of mine added an extra syllable that would stretch ever longer the further west I travelled. 'Well, Teeum,' he said, ramming an air hose on to my front left tyre shortly afterwards, 'I guess things have been pretty tough for St Mary's since the refinery closed.' KD was a school bus driver who had a sideline building custom hot rods, many of which lay in garish, flame-painted bits around us. 'My bus route gets shorter every year, just ain't enough kids these days.' He let a brief and practised sigh through his grizzled face-forks. I'd already briefed him on my mission and the alarums endured to date, and with some relief he now returned to the topic. 'But anyway, Teeum, what you're trying to do in this old beauty is just *awesome*. I'm real pleased to be a little part of it. Car guys will always help car guys.'

A car guy? Me? The promotion went straight to my head, pushing out all memory of that petrol-blinded toddler and the shameful ignorance betrayed in those Google searches. As KD stooped down to each tyre in turn, I leaned an elbow on Mike's bonnet and began to hold forth. 'Ironically, KD, the distributor that's been giving me all that trouble was an after-market replacement for the Model T's famously unreliable coil box,' I heard myself drone. 'Though it's perhaps fitting that it came off a VW Beetle, which of course superseded the Model T as the world's most numerous production car.' But KD now had his face pressed very intently to a rear wheel and wasn't listening.

'Know your left brake had fell off?'

I bent over and shared his discovery: half of my slowing-down apparatus had dropped from its support bracket and was dangling limp and useless, several inches below the wheel hub. God only knows how long it had been like that. My morning checks, such as they were, had been cancelled that day due to inclement weather.

'Shit,' I said. This sounded a little bald, so I said something else. 'Well: good brakes encourage bad driving!'

It didn't take long for KD to reattach the relevant bracket and bolt on a lock washer, though he did so in a silence steeped in dismay. The dynamics of our relationship shifted further to my disadvantage when I reversed out of his shop and stalled on the wet gravel outside. Then Mike wouldn't start: not even a wheezy cough, just stony silence. KD slid underneath on a little wheeled trolley, then slid out, stood up and wiped raindrops off his glasses.

'Battery cable was loose. Try the headlights.'

I flicked the switch and a flashbulb popped.

'You just blew out the left one.'

KD rolled back under the car, belaboured things beneath my feet, and re-emerged. 'Starter motor's bust,' he concluded levelly. 'We'll have to crank it.' I wasn't Teeum any more.

I jumped out, grasped wet metal and heaved in vain, trying to forget the horrible injuries that were a routine consequence of this process (if a T backfired while being cranked, the typical result was a back-to-front thumb, though Ross had once contrived to snap his forearm in two). KD tried; three passers-by tried. None enjoyed that Excalibur moment. 'Push start,' said KD, in something approaching a bark. Four pairs of hands were instantly applied to Mike's backside; incredibly, I managed to do the right things with all those levers and pedals and he jerked abruptly to life. Less incredibly, I rumbled to the end of the road, realised at the very last second that I was about to turn into a one-way street, veered wildly back on to the gas station forecourt and bucked to a dead, stalled halt with my left fender half an inch from a shiny parked Cadillac.

Ten minutes and another push of shame later I was behind the wheel at the other end of the forecourt, with the throttle set at a thunderous idle. 'The Pacific Ocean, right?' yelled KD, with misgiving and the frankest incredulity writ large across his sodden visage. I couldn't muster more than a pale nod, features settling into the gormless befuddlement that would become a default mask in adversity: my Stan Laurel face. How had so much gone wrong in one go? I could barely stop this car, and now I couldn't start it. In bucketing rain I barrelled over a girder bridge and into Ohio. The one silver lining to this whole, raging shitstorm: I had a full tank of gas. And I'd need it, because although help was at hand, that hand was 111 non-stop miles away.

The rain was fearsome, relentless, insane, machine-gunning the roof and sweeping across the asphalt in squally waves. I could barely make out the road through the raindrops crazily sperming across the glass. The dashboard drips swelled into unbroken streams that quickly drenched my knees and feet. A steady waterfall cascaded from the ignition switch. So much water was now flying into my eyes through the top of the screen that I put my sunglasses on. It seemed utter madness to drive on, in a spindly-tyred museum piece with one headlight and no wipers, but I was too scared to pull over and risk stalling. Instead, I slowed to a sloshing crawl, watching headlights cluster and dance in the mirror, until at length they were replaced by a billion-watt flash of red and blue and a hair-raising *BWOOOOOP* blared out.

I pulled over, a sodden, red-shoed foreigner with no legal claim to the one-eyed antique he was wobbling about in. Mike was now two states away from his registered home and the only insurance and title documentation I could offer were a couple of blurry scans on my phone.

Someone later told me that state troopers were the meanest of all law enforcers, humourless, unbiddable and pernickety. But the female trooper who now presented herself at my parted kerb-side curtain seemed no more than mildly petulant, and didn't even request my driving licence. I had a strong feeling her main focus was on minimising personal exposure to precipitation, and the thunder-gutted idle I'd set the engine at.

'Could you shut that off?'

I very loudly explained why I couldn't.

'OK, well, you got a line of eighteen cars behind you. I've been tailing you since Coopersville. You gotta speed up, or you gotta pull over.'

'Absolutely,' I lied. 'Ma'am.'

She nodded sceptically, then leaned in.

'And you might think about taking those sunglasses off.'

Well, I made it. The rain relented, and after 111 stall-free, non-stop, bladder-busting miles I roared up a grand driveway on the rural outskirts of Granville, Ohio, and wearily killed the engine. The many buildings grouped around me, and the landscaped grounds in which they were marooned, belonged to a man who had made contact a couple of days before through the Model T

Ford Club of America. I'd joined the MTFCA many months before setting off: they were the world's largest T owners' club, so large that I wasn't even its only Tim Moore. When my membership came through I posted up my ambitious intent on their internet forum, spawning responses that had progressed in stages from derision to enthusiastic support. Now club member Paul Griesse had opened up a whole new front of amenability, by offering to put me up for the night. But things had moved on a little since he'd emailed that invitation, and I would be taking the most extravagant advantage of his good nature. One night became three, and in the intervening days Paul would drive me 150 miles to source a replacement starter, spend hours and hours masterminding its installation, feed me like a big fat king and share head-swimming sundown doses of fine bourbon. Paul and his wife Linda dispensed their hospitality with relaxed conviviality, putting me so literally at home that I was given my own house: a multi-bathroomed affair built over one of their many garages. What very excellent people.

Paul was extremely big on Fords. At the age of seventy-four he'd recently whittled down his collection of fifty classics to half a dozen Ford favourites, including two Model Ts and a Model A he'd owned for more than forty years. His passion ran right back through the company's bloodline to its founding father. One afternoon, leaving my half-fixed T hydraulically aloft in his garage, Paul led me into a little side office that was a bona fide shrine to Old Man Ford. There were photographic portraits of Henry everywhere, young Henry at the tiller of his Quadricycle, old Henry steering the fifteen millionth T off the production line. The shelves groaned with Henry-centric literature. Paul, like so many of the old T guys I came to depend upon, was a helpless Fordaholic: when he talked about the Model T production line or Henry's $5 day, he shook his head gently, still in awe of what the great man had achieved.

In 1917, an especially pithy newspaper columnist compiled a 'Brief History of the US' that ran: 'Columbus, Washington, Lincoln, Roosevelt, Ford!' Henry's fame had by then blossomed into full-blown hero worship. The $5 day was already the $6 day, and he'd just handed his workers the first slice of a shared-profit bonus that would split $48 million amongst them in the next four years. No less incredibly, he'd made good on a promise to post a $50 cheque to everyone who bought a Model T in 1914 if Ford sold more than 300,000 cars that year, a pledge that cost his company more than $15 million. He was the richest man in the land, accumulating wealth at $20 million a year, but he was also one of their own: a farm boy made good, who never forgot his roots and those Midwestern values. 'America is not about Chicago and New York,' he declared, 'it is out there among the old village sites, the small towns and the farms. God made the country; man made the town.' Henry had quite the eye for an everyman catchphrase. 'When a man's hands are calloused and women's hands are worn, you can be sure honesty is there.' 'It is a disgrace to die wealthy.' 'Obstacles are those frightful things you see when you take your eyes off your goal.' 'I'm just a teenage dirtbag, baby.'

Henry was the farmer's friend and the small-town sweetheart. When the *American Magazine* ran the soar-away cover line 'Henry Ford Talks About His Mother', they shifted 1.9 million copies. ('Pray God may prosper you for what you said about your mother,' wrote a female admirer. 'When I read about the old-fashioned embroidered slippers, I could not keep back the tears.') For fifteen years, he received more than a thousand letters every single day. 'Until you gave us low-cost transportation,' wrote a farmer from Berea, Ohio, 'nobody I know had been 5 miles from home. God bless you, Henry Ford.' People told him they'd squeezed a pony in their T and driven it to the vet. They wrote of Model Ts that mowed lawns, sheared sheep and even cracked nuts. 'My T does everything but rock the baby to sleep and make love to the hired girl,' boasted one rural correspondent. But plenty of people just posted him reams of idle chatter, as if writing to a close friend or relative. 'We planted our potatoes today, but the rest of the garden isn't up yet.' 'We have eighty-five chicks three weeks old.' 'Could you stop in and help us churn butter?' An Oregon family wrote inviting Henry and his wife to dinner, and asking if they preferred their chicken fried or boiled. 'It seems we have known you all our lives.'

A hundred years on, this was still how my old car guys felt about Henry. Though few of them shared his rather spartan sense of moderation – Henry didn't drink, and despised all forms of indulgence – they revered the culture in which it was rooted. Because, in almost every case, it was their culture too. Like him, they were down-to-earth Middle Americans of humble origins, who had prospered through determined hard work and the application of bold ideas.

These days in Granville were my introduction to the orderly realm of traditional, capable masculinity that was every Model T owner's garage, or 'shop' as I would learn to call it. Neat banks of tool chests and parts cabinets, shelves of sealing unguents and lubricants, labels facing out, and a T or two with a drip tray under its incontinent business end. There'd generally be a pet, in this instance a rotund tabby cat with his head in a plastic trough full of dry food, and evidence of light-hearted conservatism: Paul had a sticker on a tool chest that read, 'I support PETA: People Eating Tasty Animals'. And within this realm, I assumed what would become my typical station of hovering uncertainty, offering to point a flashlight or unscrew something large and obvious. At least on a Model T there were plenty of such things: however reliable by the standards of its age, a T was still expected to break down a lot, and to be fixed by farmers when it did. My reprint of the original workshop manual began thus: '1. Disassembling Your Vehicle.' Undo six bolts and you could remove the whole body. It tickled me that almost every repair on my car would begin with the same two orders: 'OK, Teeum, take the hood off and pull up the floorboards.'

For three hot afternoons, Paul and I took turns filthying our fingers under the T. As we worked I heard his story. His father was one of nine Nebraskan brothers who'd all became Lutheran pastors – a family fate Paul was so keen to avoid that at nineteen he bought a $100 air ticket to Hawaii. Six years later, he flew back to the mainland with a wife, three kids and his first million. It's fair to say I left Granville knowing more about the manufacture of industrial dehumidifiers than I ever expected to. Paul moved to Ohio, expanded his firm into a global concern – India proved an especially lucrative market – and got into old cars. It was the definitive American lifestyle of yore: working hard and playing hard. 'I worked nine hours in the office, came home, put on my overalls, and worked four or five hours on the cars.' Even in retirement and plagued with a dicky hip, Paul remained a man of practical action. When I spotted a hornets' nest above the shop's door, he went straight outside and smote it clean from the eaves with a big stick.

In the evenings, after a stiff drink on the terrace of Paul's poolhouse, we'd head into central Granville for dinner. It was a most becoming little town, built around a venerable, picture-perfect college campus and a tastefully gentrified old main street, its broad sidewalks full of smart people dining under stripy awnings. The balmy air and Paul's easy hand on the bourbon compounded the favourable impression. There was a general mood of relaxed prosperity that seemed at odds with my experience to date, and presently I found out why. I had strayed off-piste: Granville was a dot of Democrat blue in Ohio's red sea, home to college academics and wealthy young professionals who commuted into nearby Columbus, the state capital. Urban America overwhelmingly voted Democrat – the most populous city to plump for Trump was Mesa, Arizona, a place whose existence had previously evaded me, and which ranks as the thirty-seventh largest settlement in the US. Yet Paul was a card-carrying Republican: at the back of an outbuilding I'd spotted a parade-ready plywood pachyderm, the party's symbol, looming behind a shiny red 1950s Ford convertible. There was an elephant in the garage, and Paul let it out as we strolled through Granville, licking after-dinner ice creams bought from a parlour on the corner of East Broadway, and taking the odd hip-soothing rest on a sidewalk bench.

'Obviously Trump is a jackass, but, you know – we're Republicans.' Paul shrugged helplessly: his preference, one he had bolstered with campaign donations, had been the inestimably less appalling Ohio governor, John Kasich. I could only sympathise. This must be how it feels when the football club you've supported all your life appoints a manager you find it very difficult to warm to, on the grounds that he's an absolutely colossal anus. And who then wins the league, but does it by playing with seventeen Russians up front.

'So, Tim, you think we've had our day as number one?'

The question seemed an obvious follow-on, and the catch in Paul's voice suggested he already knew my answer. Putting Donald Trump in the White House was hardly the act of a confident, optimistic nation, comfortable in its own skin. I hadn't been alone in seeing his election as an end-of-era event, a superpower on the wane raging against the dying of its light. When had that light shone brightest? Since setting off I'd been routinely struck by the anachronistic trappings of daily life, the fixtures and fittings that dated America's high-water mark to somewhere around 1962. The weedy 110-volt power supply that struggled to boil my bedroom kettles. The crappy, wobbly two-pin plugs. The cumbersome top-load washers in the motel laundry, like props from a monochrome sitcom. The speed-stick deodorant that I'd bought by default in a West Virginian pharmacy, a real blast from the personal-care past which harvested short and curlies while pasting my pits in mentholated lard.

However poorly all these accoutrements had aged, half a century back they were the trailblazing future. Domestic appliances and hot showers for all! America was a proving ground for the modern way of first-world living. It proudly invented all these home comforts, then popularised and standardised them, while the rest of the benighted, unwashed, steam-powered world looked on in awe. For more than half a century, they led and we followed. They were number one by a million miles. I remember when my American cousin Patricia, Miles's partner, first visited us in London in 1976, and left her toiletries laid out in the family bathroom. I was agog. A bottle of strawberry hair conditioner held particular fascination. I'd never even heard of hair conditioner – I'm pretty sure it didn't exist in Britain back then, except perhaps as some harshly medicated slurry that stank like Vicks VapoRub and made your scalp shriek. This stuff was a creamy pale rose and (sorry, Patricia) smelled good enough to drink. It was also graced with a runic robot tattoo – the first barcode I had ever seen. Patricia had bottled the future and brought it over.

But that was about as far as they got. Europe and the Far East stealthily reeled them in, and because Americans never leave their country – Patricia was the exception that proved this rule – they didn't notice. When my wife and I first watched *Friends* back in the mid-1990s, we were amazed to see Chandler dispense high-end Manhattanite sarcasm into a house-phone the size of a wine box, the sort of hulking embarrassment even my parents had long since chucked out. And because Americans are so cocksure and headstrong, even when they belatedly did notice, they took forever to react. The fossil-fuelled, eight-track American Way was the original and best.

I thought about all this, and felt chocolate ice cream dribble down my hand as I did so. Then I licked my sticky wrist and said: 'If you want my opinion, Paul, I'm afraid I do.'

'Well, I sure hope you're wrong.'

It was difficult to hear such an upbeat, irrepressible character sound so crestfallen. I wanted to comfort him. I wanted to explain that my country had been there and done that, had made its own sombre journey from globe-bestriding superpower to outmoded also-ran. That morning I'd enjoyed a diner breakfast with Paul and half a dozen of his oldest friends – doctors, lawyers, apple farmers, all fellow pillars of the community, and most of them car guys. On learning my nationality, a chap who owned a vintage Triumph rattled off a series of one-liners poking fun at Lucas Industries, the now defunct manufacturer of British automotive electrical components. 'Know what we call Lucas? The Prince of Darkness! Ever wondered why you guys drink warm beer? Because Lucas makes your refrigerators! I had a Lucas pacemaker fitted last week, and it hasn't given me any tr-tr-tr-aaaagh!'

I chortled politely. Yes, Britain had once been great and ruled the waves and all that, then we rested on our laurels, let everything decline and wound up as a laughing stock. But afterwards, though it took a while, we learned our lesson. We accepted our limitations and a lowlier place on the world stage. We conceded that designing and building stuff like cars and car parts on the cheap was daft, and that it was therefore prudent to stop bothering until we bagged some proper – which is to say foreign – investment. We swallowed our pride and admitted that imperial measurements, as per the absurd compound fractions stamped into every wrench in my Model T's toolbox ('Teeum, you done give me a 5/8 but I need a 9/16') could not compete with the cogent simplicity of metrics. Most of all, we learned to laugh at ourselves. I'd heard most of those Lucas jokes before, because we cracked them first.

Scooping out silver to supplement the breakfast waitress's tip, I'd been struck by another pig-headed native anachronism. The highest denomination coin in mass circulation was still the quarter, with a face value of less than 20p. My pockets always jangled heavily: I had to harvest quarters, ready to stuff them by the fistful into a forecourt air compressor, or a motel washer or tumble dryer. Every few years the US Treasury attempts to relaunch the dollar coin, reminding Americans of the vast savings the nation could make with a switch from dollar bills (the current estimate is $4.4 billion over thirty years, the typical life of a coin). And every time it fails. Of the 1.4 billion dollar coins ever minted, over half have been returned, unloved and unwanted, to federal reserve banks. I didn't encounter a single one of the circulating remainders. Consumers just can't be doing with them. They want a great sweaty wodge of good old American greenbacks.

The federal authorities could of course force the issue by removing dollar bills from circulation, as the Canadian author-ities did all the way back in 1989 (a year after the Bank of England killed off the pound note). But they won't, because they're too scared of the backlash. As I would discover, the most reviled adjective in Middle America is that other F-word: federal. The American small-town public is so conservative, so obstinately proud of its parochial old ways, so deeply hostile to federal meddling, that the authorities haven't even dared to change the size of its coins in over a hundred years. As a result, pennies, nickels and dimes all now cost more to produce than their face value. Minting a one-cent coin sets the Treasury back 1.7 cents. What a remarkable state of affairs. The Bank of England introduced plastic banknotes while I was away. If the US Treasury tried to pull that, Donald Trump could probably declare himself emperor and be done with it.

I took a lot more than a fixed Ford away from Granville. I finally learned how to reverse (as Paul patiently demonstrated, a simple matter of heaving that big lever into the halfway position before stomping the requisite pedal). I finessed my theory that America's increasingly tempestuous socio-politics might somehow be a reflection of their increasingly tempestuous weather: on the way to pick up my replacement starter, a pocket apocalypse bent trees in half and took the power out in a gas station we pulled into to take cover, and a couple of days later, taking the T for a test drive around Paul's yawning grounds, we found our path blocked by storm-felled boughs. And I added a bitter-sweet stanza to my inner elegy to the American Dream. Paul was one of the last off Henry Ford's other production line, the one that churned out hard-grafting, ballsy manufacturing entrepreneurs. A lost age when Americans still made money on Main Street, not just on Wall Street. Proper businessmen who employed lots of people and produced actual stuff. Still proud, still practical and prosperous, but now gently on the wane, with dicky hips and hearing aids. As I swung the T round the drive and waved Paul and Linda a heartfelt

'FARMING – OHIO'S LARGEST INDUSTRY!'

It's easy to forget how very agricultural America still is, which is perhaps why they put up huge roadside billboards to remind you. I'd never really thought of Ohio as farming country – this was the state that all those Kentuckians in *Hillbilly Elegy* headed north to in search of a prosperous factory-based future. But in fact almost every state in the US is farming country. There are still 2.2 million farms in America, covering an area a lot larger than India. Compare that with the UK, where more people now make and sell sandwiches than work in agriculture.

On a hot and humid morning, rural Ohio obediently exuded its fertility. It was like rattling through an open-air greenhouse: the storm-watered cornfields shone luminously and the sun blazed down from on high, slowly grilling my left forearm alive. It struck me that the only way I'd ever develop an even tan would be to turn around and drive back after hitting the west coast. These were some of the loneliest roads I'd been down. A buzzard pecked at a crimson smear on the asphalt. I passed a couple of rickety wooden outbuildings with 'CHEW MAIL POUCH TOBACCO' painted elegiacally across them in huge, fading letters, shabby-chic survivors of a promotional drive that once embellished 20,000 barns across twenty-two states. And for once I wasn't the most lethargic road-user, nor the messiest. This was Amish country, and for pleasing swathes of the day the predominant vehicle was a shiny black horse-drawn buggy, with a bench seat full of beards and bonnets, leaving a trail of steamy nuggets in its wake.

There are 320,000 Amish in the US, and though these wood-fired comfort-shunners are most famously associated with Pennsylvania, Ohio is home to just as many. A third live exclusively in the distant arable past, the ones I saw ambling out of hip-roofed white barns with scythes over their shoulders, or hanging out *Little Women* dresses on a veranda laundry line. But there was plenty of evidence of a rather more nuanced integration with the present: a roadside advert for fibre-glass buggy wheels, and countdown billboards to Amish-run commercial concerns ('GRANDPA'S CHEESEBARN, 11 MILES AHEAD'; 'NURSERY FURNITURE – TURN LEFT, TWO MILES'). 'They're Americans too, so of course they like making money,' Paul had said when we chanced upon an Amish family selling ambitiously priced zucchini at Granville's upscale farmers' market.

He'd filled me in on some of the anomalies and grey areas of Amish life, generally dictated by the whims of their local bishop. One community had been split in two by a dispute over the number of permissible pleats in a woman's bonnet. Another was allowed to own cars, as long as they were black. I saw a horse pulling a diesel-powered baler across a field, and a lot of solar panels. As a rule, it's apparently OK to go down a lot of banned techno-logical avenues as long as you go down them off-grid, or using borrowed equipment. Stopping for gas, I saw men in straw hats and face-girdling moustache-less beards queuing up by the forecourt's payphone. The Amish are past masters at zoning out the twenty-first century, but I'd already noticed a couple of buggy drivers eyeing Mike with keen curiosity, and now the last beard in the line – a middle-aged chap with pebble specs and a plastic gallon of milk in each hand – came over and engaged me in conversation.

'So you must get a little wet in there, I suppose.'

The Amish speak a dialect known as Pennsylvanian German at home, and though this fellow's manner was shy, his words were delivered in a toneless Schwarzenegger blare.

'No seat belts, no radio, nothing like that?'

He appraised Mike's cabin over the top of his glasses and I suddenly understood: my shiny black T was the missing link between his shiny black buggy and the modern world. You know what, he seemed to be thinking, I reckon the bishop could get on board with this. As he furrowed his brow and nodded, curious and approving, I glanced over at the buggy-hitched horses tied up to a railing by the car wash, and began to feel like some early-adopting farmer at the wheel of the first motor car in the county. This was a scene from Henry Ford's earliest promotional campaign: say goodbye to hopeless old Dobbin. On cue, a bushy tail was raised and a harvest of road apples slapped on to the concrete. Alongside its superior efficiency and cheaper running costs, the T was also sold as a greener alternative to the animals that hosed and splattered the streets of New York alone with 60,000 gallons of urine and a thousand tons of manure every single day, and whose dead bodies were generally left to putrefy in the gutter to facilitate dismemberment and removal. For a heady moment, Mike was the bright, new future, not the clunking, filthy past. Though for a symbolic insight into America's backward-looking present, its retrogressive fondness for the old ways, consider this: in the last fifteen years, the Amish population has doubled.

And then, quite suddenly, I was into the Rust Belt, bumping over weed-pierced train crossings, creaking down streets lined with boarded-up small businesses and shuffling drunks, readjusting to a world with Democrats, black people and tall buildings that weren't churches or grain elevators. Squadrons of Great Lake seagulls squawked about in the blue sky. An old man at a gas station offered me $20,000 for my car, wheeling away with a strained laugh when I held out my hand to shake on it. (No offence, Mike – making a quick buck is just the American way.) Toledo was a run-down mess when Dib Fewer and Tod Snedeker drove Mike Mark 1 through the city in 1931, shocked to find its riverbanks and parks thick with unemployed shamblers. To judge from the roofless, burned-out, full-fat dereliction I drove through, the place had clearly never recovered. I was taking a wayward swerve from Trumpland, on a pilgrimage to the Rust Belt's scabbiest buckle. After ninety-three years, my T was coming home.

Detroit was a car city before Henry Ford doubled down on Motown, and it seems a minor miracle that he just happened to grow up nearby: in some parallel universe, Henry is born in Kansas, never makes a single car and the twentieth century takes an awful lot longer to get going. In the 1900s Detroit was home to many carriage builders and bicycle manufacturers, which together offered the core skills that attracted many fledgling automotive concerns: by the time the Model T was launched, forty car makers and more than 200 vehicle component manufacturers were already based there.

But the T's success and the phenomenon that was Highland Park elevated Detroit into a global industrial powerhouse. Huge new factories sprang up across the city, manufacturing rival motor vehicles, spark plugs, tyres and machine tools. Work-hungry migrants poured in from the white Appalachians and the black south, from Canada, from eastern and southern Europe. Ford outgrew the 120-acre Highland Park site, and in 1926 opened a substantially more enormous plant at River Rouge, a few miles west in Dearborn, Henry's hometown. This 1,000-acre facility incorporated the world's largest foundry, and employed a flabbergasting total of 103,000 people. Two million visitors a year were soon turning up to pay homage. By the late 1920s, Detroit had established itself as one of the wealthiest cities on the planet. It was still growing thirty years later, by then the fifth largest metropolis in the US with almost two million residents. Michigan Central Station was the tallest on earth, and Chrysler's Detroit headquarters ranked as the second biggest office in the world, after the Pentagon.

But as you may be aware, the story of Detroit then took a rather dramatic turn for the worse. I did my best to review the evidence as I steered Mike through its outskirts, but when you're driving a Model T up an urban dual carriageway you need both eyes on the road. Especially when that road is very wet and strewn with potholes. It didn't help that my ears were picking up an ominous under-bonnet backbeat to the clatter of heavy rain on canvas, a muffled, percussive tonk-tonk-tonk, like someone trying to punch their way out of an oil drum.

The rain-fuzzed silhouette of a windowless factory, yawning roadside voids, a misty glimpse of Canada, there across the Detroit River. Tonk-tonk-TUNK-TUNK-TUNK. A derelict bus terminal. Ow: a spine-cracking kerb-side crater. More open space. TUNK-TUNKITY-TINKETY-TONK. Empty pavements. A tree growing out through a roof. The unsettling realisation that the traffic was steadily thinning as the downtown skyline approached.

'We shall solve the city problem by leaving the city,' Henry Ford once predicted, and Motown, a metropolis built on cars, was the first redrawn to suit them. From the 1940s, suburbs began to leach far out into the Michigan countryside, linked to the mid-town offices and factories by interconnected freeways. These were laid right through the original residential zones, destroying some and cutting others off, hemmed in by eight-lane barriers of concrete and speeding metal. But those new suburban dreamlands had been built with a particular kind of Detroiter in mind: the white kind. Detroit's black residents, who in 1950 made up just 20 per cent of the city's population, discovered that the federal government would only subsidise mortgage loans for white people to move to the suburbs. For good measure, suburban municipalities drew up policies to stop black people moving in – typically a points system that took account of religion, ethnicity, accent and

'Americanisation'. 'They can't get in here,' the mayor of Dearborn, Orville Hubbard, boasted to a reporter. 'Every time we hear of a Negro moving, we respond quicker than you do to a fire.'

Detroit had been a pretty good place to be black up until then. Henry Ford was remarkably even-handed by the standards of the time, and his insistence that black workers were paid the same as their white counterparts helped establish the city as the birthplace of the black middle class. But now Detroit's black population found itself imprisoned by giant highways in a deteriorating inner city, neglected by slum landlords and the authorities. In 1966, fewer than 5 per cent of Detroit's inner-city homes were deemed to be in 'sound condition'. It was such an unappealing environment that even the factories decamped to the suburbs, leaving central Detroit jobless as well as run-down.

The 1967 Detroit riot ranks amongst the most shocking in American history. Of the forty-three people killed that July, thirty were shot dead by police and national guardsmen. More than 2,500 premises were looted or burned; there were 7,200 arrests. White flight, the ugly tag for Detroit's urban-suburban segregation, accelerated dramatically thereafter. Within six years, half a million white residents had left for the suburbs, and the city that had been 80 per cent white in 1950 was soon 80 per cent black. The overall population fell and kept falling: America's fifth largest city would soon drop out of the top twenty. Unemployment ballooned, urban decay redoubled, and the cash-strapped Detroit authorities floundered.

By the Eighties, there were more guns than people in Detroit, and the city's murder rate was the highest in the country, three times that of New York's. In 1986, a child was shot every day on average. There weren't just crack houses but crack towers, derelict downtown office blocks repurposed by drug gangs. Arsonists torched entire streets of abandoned buildings. On a single night in 1984, 800 houses were razed to the ground. Yet there are still 70,000 derelict structures in Detroit, and some 40 square miles of empty land, an area larger than metropolitan Paris. In 2013, $18 billion in debt, the city of Detroit filed for bankruptcy. Once again, if you boil it all down and have a weakness for completely unfair sweeping judgements, there's only one person to point the finger at. Cars made Detroit, then destroyed it. And who made the cars? Sorry, Henry.

TUNK-TUNK-DONKDONKDONKDONK-*pttthhhhhh*. The rain had stopped when I put Mike out of his misery, killing the engine on the drive of a well-tended 1920s executive home. Every lawn on the street was a golf green, and a flag flew from every porch. This was a very different Detroit to the one I'd left just a couple of minutes before, turning off East Jefferson Avenue into the leafy confines of Grosse Pointe. Presently a vast pick-up rumbled to a stop, and a well-built man in a crisp pink shirt climbed down, strode over and shook me mightily by the hand.

My cousin Marshall, Patricia's brother, is probably the most American American I know. When I first met him, as a teenager, he was a champion wrestler, and more than thirty years on he still has the neck to prove it. After many years in the Army, serving as a military intelligence officer in some of the sandier foreign theatres, Marshall took a white-collar job in Ford's emerging-markets division. I'd phoned him a few mornings before, and he'd very kindly offered to host me at the house he shared with his wife Libby and their two young daughters. Now I explained Mike's malaise to Marshall, adding that I'd already made contact with a kind local soul from the MTFCA – a chap called Peter who lived in Dearborn and had offered a mechanical assessment.

'Sounds like you may be here a while,' said Marshall. I smiled awkwardly. 'Come on, I'll give you the tour.'

A while later we were cruising through the dappled avenues. Marshall's company pick-up seemed the right ride – the Ford F150 is America's top-selling vehicle and a mobile MAGA metaphor. 'The Ford F series doesn't just raise the bar,' growled the TV-ad voiceovers, 'it IS the bar.' What a classic slice of Trump-era rhetoric – it had a no-nonsense, tough-guy ring to it, but meant absolutely nothing. And though the F150 might have been the Model T's successor as America's four-wheeled favourite, it was the clod-hopping antithesis of Henry's light and nimble Universal Car. However, the Marshallmobile proved admirably suited to 'the tour'. Grosse Pointe was all manicured lawns and lakeside country clubs. Then we crossed an intersection, and suddenly found ourselves in Stalingrad.

'It's a lot better here than it was a few years ago,' said Marshall, thundering through crater-grade potholes, 'which I guess is kinda scary.'

I stared out of the window, dumbstruck by a spectacle that had largely eluded me from behind Mike's spattered, juddering windshield. East Jefferson Avenue, the main thoroughfare into downtown Detroit, was strewn with charred hulks, rusted shutters and boarded windows. Some of the vacant gas stations and warehouses had been reclaimed by scratchy-looking gyms and car washes, but most had been demolished, leaving huge voids of mossy, fractured concrete. Everyone in Grosse Pointe was white; now the few people out and about were all black. Marshall pointed to a derelict movie theatre with shrubs sprouting from its roof. 'Just going to do a roll here,' he muttered as we slid through a red light. 'Buddy of mine stopped there a couple years back and had a bullet go straight through two windows.' I nodded blankly and sunk down in my seat a little. Never have I experienced such a jarring, brutal shift in an urban setting, and I say that as someone who crawled through a hole in the Berlin Wall in 1990.

We turned north off Jefferson into a residential side street, and the mood took another shift. The first few houses looked fairly trim and prosperous, of similar style and vintage to Marshall's. A couple even had pleasure boats in their driveways. 'You could pick one of these homes up for $30,000 here in the East Side,' he murmured. 'Same house in Grosse Pointe would cost a half-million.' I understood this disparity when the housing stock grew scrappier, and thinner, then presently vanished entirely, replaced by wispy grassland crowned here and there with mature trees.

'This was the Italian neighbourhood back in the Fifties and Sixties.' Marshall's voice was now muted to an Attenborough whisper. 'One of my best friends grew up here.'

I gazed at the yawning savannah around, thinking: Who was he, then – Mowgli? Without all the forlorn fire hydrants and Marshall's commentary I could never have believed that this was once a densely populated residential area.

'When I say things have improved, what I really mean is that the city has got a lot better at pulling down empty buildings. Every house in this area was derelict or burned-out when we relocated here twenty years ago. Even in the better districts, when people moved out they just threw the keys on the lawn. You couldn't give houses away.'

We drove on through freshly planted commercial forests, hardwood saplings laid out in neat grids across ex-residential meadows. Marshall told me that wild turkeys and pheasants are now a common sight in the more rural swathes of East Side Detroit, roaming those fledgling forests and the 1,400 vegetable gardens and orchards that have been planted over recent years. On some streets a single remaining home stood marooned amidst the encroaching overgrowth, like a lonely farmhouse. In many areas only the churches survived, by virtue of their non-combustible stone construction (American housebuilders retain a stubborn, pioneer attachment to wood: the walls and roofs of the typical home are considered consumable features with a twenty-year lifespan). But most of these churches lay derelict, and the only one we passed that remained open for ecclesiastical business had a sign outside promising free hot meals every Tuesday. Grass leached ever further into the road, along with broken furniture, tyres and dumped cars. Even the less desperate-looking streets, those with a decent quorum of glazed homes and vehicles, lay eerily silent. The only people enjoying the summer breeze were a few old black guys, each sitting alone on a battered porch, watching what was left of the world go by.

It went on and on, and we said less and less. Every few blocks Marshall would quietly call my attention to some point of interest. The gas station Libby once pulled into, only for the cashier to run outside and scream at her to drive on. The terrace of derelict shops that marked the starting point of the 1967 riot. Henry Ford's first grand home, on Edison Street, where a fair number of rival mansions now stood torched and roofless. The much grander home that his great-grandson Alfred had transformed, to the Ford family's mortification, into a Hare Krishna temple. 'Lotta peacocks get out of there,' said Marshall as we drove past the scabby wrought-iron gates. 'One took up in our street for a few years – we called him Fred.'

Just round the corner we passed by a gracefully low-slung modernist structure with 'Stark School of Technology' above its shuttered entrance, behind a sign that read: 'FOR SALE/LEASE CONTACT DETROIT PUBLIC SCHOOLS'. In case you need a reminder of Detroit's decline, seventy-nine abandoned schools are now for sale across the city, on account of an ever-dwindling intake: as late as 2003 there were 170,000 kids in the Detroit public school system, compared to 50,000 today. And in case you need another: the Stark School of Technology was built on the site of the Grosse Pointe race track, where in 1901 Henry Ford had made his name.

It was awful and tragic, but my word it was grimly compelling. Detroiters have grown forgivably weary of 'ruin porn' tourists, though I sensed that Marshall was secretly enjoying himself just a little too. 'See, I know what dead bodies smell like,' he breathed dramatically as we drove through a ramshackle waterfront park, 'and the first time I got out of the car in this place, I smelled 'em.'

At length, with shadows spreading over the grassy sidewalks, we headed back towards East Jefferson. A few blocks before that extraordinary intersection, the unseen wall between black and white, wealth and poverty, life and death, Marshall jabbed a finger down a lonely lane. 'Couple years back, five kids from my neighbourhood were sat down there one night, smoking pot in a car. You can't do that shit in Grosse Pointe without getting caught. Anyway, some guy drives by and just lets off thirty rounds with an AK, one of the girls is killed and three are shot up pretty bad. They never caught him.' He put his foot down and we sped over East Jefferson and into Grosse Pointe. 'I've told my daughters that I never, ever want to see them cross that street.' Less than a mile later we pulled up at his house.

In the morning I followed Marshall's F150 to Dearborn, through a thousand traffic lights and as many potholes. The awful shudders and bangs cost me a little chrome hubcap and perhaps 5 per cent of my liver function, but did at least drown out the worst of Mike's ever-deepening engine knock. After an hour we pulled into our first stop, in a convoy of like-minded, like-gendered pilgrims: The Henry Ford, America's largest indoor-outdoor museum complex, is Disneyland for old men.

Henry might not have been flash, but he wasn't exactly humble. The Model T phenomenon blurred the line between arrogance and plain realism: when Ford described himself as 'the author of the industrial age', he was simply stating a fair-minded fact. As the T era's dust settled in the late 1920s, Henry began to take stock of his revolutionary achievements. In a few short decades, America had exploded into a manufacturing superpower, and changed the world for ever. And it had done so largely thanks to him and a clutch of kindred spirits, men like Thomas Edison, Harvey Firestone, the Wright brothers and Henry J. Heinz: Middle Americans of everyday origin, without a college degree between them. These were the underpinnings of Ford's most fabled quote: 'History is more or less bunk. It is tradition. The only history that is worth a tinker's dam is the history we make today.' Why trouble yourself with the dusty past, in other words, when my friends and I are forging all these shiny chunks of present? In this spirit, we can at least try to forgive him for devoting much of his later life to enshrining a slavish personality cult at a museum he named after himself.

Built on a vast site three miles from his childhood home, The Henry Ford first opened to the public in 1933. Its cavernous exhibition halls were dutifully stocked with machines from Henry's private collection: player pianos, steam engines, grease pumps and a fleet of significant motor vehicles. But the site's spiritual home lay in the landscaped acreage outside. Greenfield Village, whose verdant outskirts Marshall and I now strolled across, was a homespun shrine to the legends, most of them then living, who had built this bold new America. The parochial buildings sunning themselves around us were transplanted by Henry from their original sites: that was the actual bike shop where the Wright brothers first conceived their flying machine, and over there stood H. J. Heinz's actual childhood home. And there: the garden office of Luther Burbank, the amateur biologist who created the Russet Burbank, the Model T of spuds that remains the world's most widely cultivated potato. Workshops and laboratories associated with his best mates Edison and Firestone were given especial prominence; I was intrigued to see the three legendary figures photographed together on what were apparently regular camping trips. You might be interested to learn that Thomas Edison invented the beer bong on the first of these outings, although you shouldn't be as I just made that up.

But most attention was focused on Henry, by Henry, and with a breezy lack of restraint. At Greenfield Village's inauguration, the old man strode portentously into the very schoolhouse in which he had daydreamed his first machines, sat down at a desk placed in the same location as his had been, and carved his initials into it, as his eight-year-old self had done. This building was overlooked by an exact replica of the school Henry subsequently attended, and by his favourite teacher's house. Refitting Ford's childhood home to the last detail was a particular labour of self-love. These days the Greenfield staff are all dressed in period costume, and a kindly old dear in a pinafore buttonholed me as I bent down to inspect the panelling around the dining-room stove, hoping to spot shrapnel damage caused by those youthful dabblings with steam power. 'Mr Ford sent teams of people all across the country looking for that precise type of stove,' she trilled. 'Everything had to be just right. We're told they took eighteen months to find it.' A similar quest was launched after Henry kicked up a shard of patterned pottery in the farmhouse yard. Eight staff were employed on this nationwide ephemera hunt, sometimes exchanging a hundred letters in pursuit of a single item. Ford's own history was never bunk.

And of course there were Model Ts wherever you looked. It was quite emotional to set eyes on the actual fifteen millionth T, the one I'd seen grey-haired Henry driving out of the factory. And quite surprising to find out that when you weren't looking at it in black and white, it was dark green. More compelling still were the fleet of Ts that puttered up and down the Greenfield avenues, each with a man in a derby hat and a waistcoat behind the wheel, and a couple of fleshy visitors in the back. The smooth assurance of their progress, relative as it was, seemed an affront to my travails. At least until I asked a guy in a straw boater about the maintenance regime, and he rolled his eyes. 'Three full-time mechanics working on thirteen cars. Can you believe that?' I told him I could. It struck me, a thousand miles and five breakdowns too late, that if a vehicle struggles to complete a fairground joyride, you probably shouldn't try to drive it across an immense continent.

The museum proper paid lavish tribute to the motor vehicle's starring role in the twentieth century. I went aboard the actual Alabama bus in which Rosa Parks refused to give up her seat to a white man in 1955, thereby catalysing the civil-rights movement. I gawped at the very Lincoln that JFK was shot in, and the fixed roof someone had subsequently bolted on to it ('Better late than never,' I whispered to Marshall). I spent twenty minutes on an arcade-style Model T driving simulator, waiting in vain for my mastery to be rewarded with wild acclaim.

Henry's Universal Car was precisely thus rewarded, by a sprawling, multi-media celebration introduced with a hall-of-fame-style plaque:

The Model T Ford transformed the world, reordering the nature of cities and countryside, work and leisure by demonstrating the broad appeal of automobility. Henry Ford adopted and extended assembly-line techniques to reduce the car's price by nearly 60 per cent while improving its quality. The Model T became a universal symbol of the capacity of modern engineering to transform luxuries into mass commodities.

I read these heady words and understood why I was surrounded by old people. That final sentence paid tribute to Henry and his Greenfield Village posse, and recaptured the boundless, revolutionary excitements of their age. What a time to be alive! Life-changing domestic upgrades that were beyond the average American's wildest dreams at the start of the T era had become commonplace at its conclusion. By 1930, 70 per cent of US homes were electrified; more than half had a radio; 40 per cent had a telephone; 45 per cent a car. There were a million domestic refrigerators. For fifty years, the big-ticket innovations just kept coming, all breathlessly hailed. I was especially taken by a poster advertising a demonstration of Edison's phonograph at Friedrich's Music Hall in Grand Rapids, Minnesota, in 1878: 'It Will Talk, Sing, Laugh, Crow, Whistle and REPEAT CORNET SOLOS.'

Being both quite young and extremely capable, Peter Nikolajevs offered some hope for America's future. And, much more importantly, for mine: on the short drive to his trim little suburban house in Dearborn, the T's engine knock amplified horribly, a Gatling gun firing empty tin cans. Peter was the latest white knight I had summoned through the MTFCA, a diagnostic-equipment programmer at Ford with a cheery wife, two small kids and a lovely red Model T, shoehorned into a compact garage amongst much brightly coloured juvenilia. We shook hands, rearranged things and heaved the T inside. 'Take the hood off and pull up the floorboards,' ordered Peter, and so it began again.

In the following hours I held a torch while Peter removed the cylinder head from above, and the oil pan from below. While he worked, Peter told me that he'd fallen for Ts at the age of eight, when he encountered one on display at a local fair. 'If you can start it, you can have it,' the owner had smirked as young Peter fruitlessly heaved the crank handle. But the die was cast, and with a very Edisonian sense of resolve – 'Everything comes to him who hustles while he waits,' history's most prolific inventor once said – Peter spent the following five years doing odd jobs and collecting can deposits, saving up $2,500 and buying his first T.

'Well, it's nice at least to have a simple answer.'

Night had long since fallen when Peter emerged from beneath the car with a piston connecting rod in his oily hands. Even I could see what was wrong: the layer of shiny, soft metal that covered its contact surface had been almost completely chipped off. I had intended to furnish you with a full history of the tin-based alloy known as Babbitt, but given the endless grief its uselessness would cause me, I'm afraid I can't face it. Take that, long-dead Isaac Babbitt of Taunton, Massachusetts.

Peter measured the rod with great care, while I dredged out the chunks, slivers and snow-dome flakes of Babbitt that had dispersed themselves around the oil pan and elsewhere. A replacement rod was ordered; it would take two days to arrive. Then, having filthied one family's sink, I took an Uber back to Grosse Pointe and decorated another's shower with tin-based fairy dust.

I went full Ford in the next forty-eight hours. The family still dominates Detroit: beyond all the corporate headquarters and the River Rouge plant, where 6,000 workers now build F150s, their name is writ large across the umpteen schools and medical centres they've endowed over the years, and the city's NFL stadium, whose incumbent team, the Detroit Lions, they own. First up was Henry's pile, Fair Lane, a squat, stolid manor house he built in a quiet corner of Dearborn, on the banks of the Rouge River, in 1915. My Uber driver took me there through the centre of Dearborn, which in fitting tribute to Orville Hubbard, its fanatically racist former mayor, is now home to the largest Muslim community in the US. The most obvious city-wide legacy is the shawarma, a keenly priced and dependably delicious kebaby wrap thing that has established itself as the favoured lunch option across Detroit. I had several. Somewhere in the town stands a billboard which states, in Arabic, 'Donald Trump can't read this, but it scares him anyway.'

My driver – an Iraqi, as it happens – dropped me off by an empty visitors' car park. Under cadaverous skies, Fair Lane looked dreary and grim with its dumpy grey towers and mean windows, more like a squashed Colditz than the home of the world's richest man. As simple souls, Henry and Clara would gladly have stayed on at their modest downtown mansion, but the public hysteria unleashed by the $5 day made that untenable: for a weary year, the Fords had to run a doorstep gauntlet of fans and journalists. Fair Lane, dour and forbidding, hardly looked like a labour of love. I can't imagine what persuaded Henry to site his home on the banks of the river his granddad had frozen to death in.

Anyway, the younger Fords waited five whole years after Clara's demise before donating the place to the University of Michigan, and I wasn't upset to find the house closed. Henry's true passion expressed itself in a mighty riverside outbuilding: how convenient to have Thomas Edison on hand to design your own hydroelectric plant, and how typical that it put out enough juice to power the entire city of Dearborn.

What a contrast with his son Edsel's suave, high-tech home, built about as far away from his dad's place as he could get: 24 miles east on the shores of Lake St Clair, or just a short hop from Marshall's house in the passenger seat of his German au pair's Jeep. Designed to suggest a homely cluster of Cotswold cottages, the innards of Ford House combined aesthetic sensitivity, period innovation and gigantic wealth in a manner that caused our tour group to glide through the rooms on a rolling coo of approval.

A formative trip to Europe endowed the young Edsel with a taste for furniture that was much older than anything his homeland had to offer, design that was much newer, and art that was much better. He came back with a lot of Chesterfield sideboards and Elizabethan panelling, and the entire main staircase from Lyveden House in Northamptonshire, apparently in settlement of a gambling debt. On the walls were copies of the Renoirs and Van Goghs that today sit in the Detroit Institute of Arts, some worth over $100 million a pop. There was a fabulous art deco study, all circular wood and uplighters. And so many innovative comforts and luxuries: a refrigerated fresh-flower room, a centralised vacuum system and an extraordinary network of hidden hoses connected to an organ concealed in a cupboard, allowing the imprisoned musician's output to be piped around the home. How curious that all this extravagance was paid for by the utilitarian Model T.

And in that contrast, we find the root of Henry's famously difficult relationship with his only child. When the young Edsel cut off a fingertip in the family's home workshop, his father was infuriated by his clumsiness. After giving Edsel a seat on the board, he took every opportunity to undermine him: discovering his son was responsible for a new office block taking shape in the corner of Highland Park, Henry ordered construction to be halted at once, and let the half-built hulk stand for years as a lesson. He made Edsel president of the company, gave him his own marque to play with (Lincoln) and a vast salary, then resented him for not having worked for any of it. Edsel, in turn, seems to have delighted in winding up his stern and abstemious father. He smoked, and liked a drink. (Once, when Edsel was abroad, Henry sent a team of heavies round to smash up his liquor cabinet.) He commuted to work in a speedboat fitted with a 600hp aeroplane engine, and bought the first MG imported to the US. In 1935 he was voted the best dressed man in America, beating Fred Astaire. He commissioned Diego Rivera, a Mexican communist, to paint twenty-seven epic murals of workers at the River Rouge plant. He won a staircase at cards.

The battle between father and son was the battle between form and function, horny-handed hard work and pencil-chewing contemplation, old and new. A plaque in junior's honour highlighted the void: 'Edsel Bryant Ford – automobile stylist, patron of the arts, benefactor of polar exploration, philanthropist, gentleman.' He was the highfalutin liberal elitist to Henry's plain-spoken Midwestern everyman. No one ever saw Henry with a book, and his favourite song was a folk tune entitled 'Who Threw the Overalls in Mrs Murphy's Chowder?' After Henry bought the schoolhouse that he decided Mary and her little lamb had attended, he had a plaque installed hailing 'Sarah Josepha Hale, whose genius completed the poem in its present form'. When a group of art dealers tried to interest the world's wealthiest man in some old masters, he thumbed through their illustrated brochures with great delight, then was nonplussed when they tried to close a sale: 'But why would I buy an original when I can look at it in these catalogues you've given me?'

Henry was a Model T made flesh; Edsel's defining venture was the first Lincoln Continental, a streamlined, modernist coupé, shaped like a teardrop and powered by a V12 engine. The Continental was gorgeous – it's one of only eight cars deemed 'automotive works of art' by New York's Museum of Modern Art – but it was also the exact sort of high-end, small-volume ponce-mobile that Henry despised. At $3,000, the first Continental cost ten times as much as the last T, and sold a lot less than ten times fewer: in the first full year of production, 1940, just 400 were shifted.

Edsel died of stomach cancer three years later, at the age of forty-nine; Henry would outlast him by four years. The old man had the bitter last laugh beyond the grave: launched in 1958, the Ford Edsel was received so disastrously that the mid-range saloon remains a byword for commercial failure. Only 118,000 Edsels were sold, leaving the firm with a $350 million loss on the project. Some blamed the marketing; some the car's poor reliability. But there's a much simpler lesson to be learned: if you want a car to sell, don't model its front end on a front bottom.

And, one sullen, dank afternoon, I went back to where it all began.

The Piquette plant's continued existence is almost as astounding as its history. Viewed from the puddled street, that careworn, three-floor brick facade looked more like some artfully dilapidated craft brewery than the birthplace of the automotive age. Piquette Avenue made a far more convincing deathplace: the little building where the first Model Ts were made is a lonely survivor amongst the ruins of post-industrial Detroit, a wasteland of graffiti-flanked hulks and lumpy undergrowth that stretched as far as the eye could see. Its sole active rivals were a pair of old warehouses opposite, one repurposed as the Abundant Faith Cathedral, the other as the Soul Saving Church. Parked between them, its kerbside wheels deep in brown water, sat a scabby Honda with a PSALM37 licence plate.

America isn't exactly embarrassed with historic sites of global import, so I was rather taken aback to discover that the Piquette plant had lain forlorn and forgotten until 2000, when a group of Model T enthusiasts acquired the building. It was only recognised by the heritage authorities in 2002. The ground floor is let to an industrial laundry, and the museum on the upper storeys was created by the amateur volunteers who still run it. They could clearly do with some funding. When another of those micro storms turned day to night and shattered the heavens, rain blew in around the old sash windows and speckled the factory planks.

Between 1903 and 1908, Ford produced seven models of scattergun appeal, from the snobby $2,500 Model K phaeton to the cheap and cheerful $500 two-seater Model N. The Model N notched 7,000 sales: a record figure for the era, and one that sealed Henry's determination to target the mass market, as well as banking the funds for some serious related research and development. Late in 1906, he walled off a 15-foot-square corner of Piquette's narrow top floor, and put in a single door with a big padlock. Only seven chosen men – fourteen-year-old Edsel amongst them – would be given the key. The dominant fixtures within were an old rocking chair that had belonged to Henry's mother and a blackboard. He was planning to do something that had never been done, and to do it from scratch in a year – a schedule that necessitated free thinkers who weren't afraid to defy accepted wisdom. College degrees, which he felt restricted the imagination, were unwelcome. Trust and loyalty, though, were essential, and though Henry was not an easy man to work for, these qualities would in due course be stupendously rewarded.

I found Ford's hallowed 'secret room' in the early stages of a reconstruction project, which together with the clattering horizontal rain made it tricky to tap into the vibe. So too did the curator who followed me around, though I could hardly blame him. I was one of four visitors, and by far the most troublesome: I just couldn't stop touching stuff. It was so difficult to treat all these Model Ts with due reverence when I'd been more or less living in one, strewing it with crisps and cans and farting deep into its ancient upholstery.

'Sir, we do ask visitors not to . . .'

'Sorry!'

Every time I thought I'd reined myself in I'd have a relapse, and a good prod. Hmm – I wonder if this exploded Model T engine and gearbox has that same funny bi—

'Sir, we do ask . . .'

'Sorry!'

Wow, a 1924 Touring just like mi—

'Sir . . .'

'Sorry!'

'Now, let's see: "1927 Ford Model T Tudor Sedan, owner: Peter Nikolajevs." Hey – that's Pe—'

'*Sir . . .*'

'Sorry!'

Anyway, the young improvisers Ford picked to bring his dream to life, behind that padlocked door up in the Piquette eaves, were all well known to him. The museum saluted them in a series of information boards, but I'm going for jazz-combo introductions (with apologies to Henry, who hated jazz with a depthless passion). On flow charts: Peter Martin, a Canadian who had been in full-time industrial employment since the age of twelve, and was the fifth person Henry ever gave a job to. He'd been pencilled in as production manager. On spreadsheets: James Couzens, son of a Canadian soapmaker, who spent seven years checking railroad freight cars, then blagged a clerical job with a coal dealer who happened to be one of Ford's major investors. Couzens was Henry's business manager, and would have an impressively broad remit spanning sales, advertising, purchasing, shipping and accounts. On the lathe: Charles Sorensen, a Dane who joined Ford in 1905 as a twenty-four-year-old pattern maker, and wowed Henry with his talent for translating half-formed engineering ideas into actual metal parts. On blueprints: József Galamb, a hotshot Hungarian mechanical engineer who had been in the US for less than two years when Ford hired him at the end of 1905, and still spoke very patchy English. And on the fuse box: our old friend Spider Huff, a Ford employee since the age of sixteen, and a mercurial volt wizard. Hit it, boys!

You could say that Henry Ford was blessed with an unusually good eye for talent – and you should, because it's true. Yet it still seems remarkable, if not astonishing, that his small, young team not only rose to the challenge of designing a truly universal car, but then mustered the communal wherewithal to mastermind its production, marketing and distribution on a scale beyond imagination. That they did so is a testament to the all-round, commonplace brilliance that was miraculously generated in turn-of-the-century Middle America, as celebrated at Greenfield Village. It's also worth noting that not one of Henry's team, with the possible exception of the enigmatic Spider, was born in the United States.

Henry's vision for the Model T was constructed around material lightness. A light car could cope better with country mud, and by needing a smaller engine would also be cheaper to produce. After examining some surprisingly unbent components from a wrecked French racing car he developed a fascination with vanadium steel, which was three times stronger than other steel alloys and could thus be used far more sparingly. But no one in the US had even dabbled with vanadium, whose production process demanded temperatures way higher than any domestic foundry had achieved. When his team suggested hiring a metallurgical engineer to tackle this dilemma, Henry unleashed his trademark scorn for graduate specialists. 'Make an expert of Wandersee!' he shouted, to every-one's alarm: John Wandersee was a dogsbody mechanic who had started his career with Ford sweeping the factory floor. But Henry knew. He always did. Wandersee dutifully tracked down a small foundry in Ohio, accrued the necessary skills and within months was supervising production of high-grade vanadium.

József Galamb at last had the raw material he needed, and drew up a design to Henry's brief: a featherweight, functional family car, cheap to produce, buy, run and repair. The Model T was no looker – from an aesthetic perspective, it shared an awful lot with the ungainly predecessors lined up around me in the Piquette shadows. Most of its running gear – including that sodding planetary transmission – was lifted straight from previous Ford models. The Model T's only significant innovations were its use of vanadium; a removable cylinder head, which would vastly simplify engine repairs; and Spider Huff's flywheel magneto, an ambitious arrangement of magnets and copper coils which – uniquely for a low-priced car – allowed the T to operate without a battery of any sort, a huge attraction in rural areas at a time when batteries were horrendously unreliable. But as a cheap car that worked, it was an irresistible package.

As the orders piled up, Sorensen and Martin began to dabble with moving assembly lines, putting a chassis on skis and dragging it by rope past various Piquette workstations. But the firm had simply outgrown the little plant, and before the year was out Henry started looking for a new home. He'd assembled and sold 14,000 Model Ts in little more than a year, and had $9 million in the bank. By the start of 1910, at a site four miles north in Highland Park, he also had the largest manufacturing facility in the world. Two days later, I drove a little black car there to meet its maker.

East Side Detroit, so alarming in a semi-armoured pick-up with a meaty veteran at the wheel, seemed curiously benign when alone in an open-sided antique. Mike was such a disarming presence, so friendly and frail, that I increasingly struggled to imagine anyone wishing ill upon him or his occupants. And the car no longer advertised its approach with a painful steel-band drum roll. The previous afternoon, Peter and I had successfully installed the new piston rod in his sweltering garage: a task of unexpected precision, which required us to peel off papery brass shims in the quest for a microscopically perfect fit. I'd offered him my fulsome thanks, then puttered back to Grosse Pointe for a last night at Marshall's. Sick as he'd been, Mike would never look more felicitously at home than he had outside that period executive residence, parked beneath a graceful brick arch that led to Marshall's garage – so graceful that no modern car could squeeze through it. Now, after further farewells and expressions of deep gratitude, I was weaving around potholes through the dusty dereliction.

I might not have been scared, but it was all still terribly affecting – doubly so from behind the wobbly wheel of the car that put this city on the map, and built so many of the smart new homes that had once annexed the East Side. Grubby tarpaulins flapped on punctured roofs and porches. Bleak home-made billboards sprouted above the tall grass: 'AFTER YOU DIE, YOU WILL MEET GOD'; 'I CASH CHECKS'; 'SELLING THIS HOME DIRT CHEAP. PHONE NICK.' I ticked up the full house of those endgame retailers of last resort: thrift stores, liquor stores, Bible book stores. Saddest, as ever, were the once proud and mighty public structures, all those schools and libraries, now daubed and glassless hulks lost in deep vegetation.

Absolutely everyone was black. At 83 per cent, Detroit has the highest black population of any US city. Yet so entrenched is the segregation that in my five-day tour of car museums and humid suburban garages – the world of old white guys – I hadn't really engaged with a single black person. Take the transport network. I kept wanting to get on buses, and kept being discouraged, often with dramatic urgency. 'I was a police officer for a long time and I wouldn't take it,' said the security guard at Edsel's gatehouse when I asked which bus went into town. 'Just no, I'm serious.' Others were no less alarmist, and none of them had the slightest idea how much a bus ticket might cost, or if I could buy one off the driver. So when the T was out of action, I travelled every-where by Uber, or German au pair. It took me a while to realise it was a race thing: I never saw one white face in a passing bus. I'm pretty sure that wasn't what Rosa Parks made her stand for. This isn't an implication of racial hatred, more a sad reflection of lives that never overlap, and the mutual wariness thus engendered. Still, as a Londoner, born and bred in one of the world's most successfully multi-ethnic cities, I found it all rather shocking.

Downtown Detroit, until a few years back a photogenic ruin, has of late been slickly regenerated through the billion-dollar input of a local boy made good, Dan Gilbert of Quicken Loans (from manufacturing to mortgages – a hundred-year spin on Detroit's millionaire merry-go-round). Its wonderful Aztec-tiled art deco skyscrapers have been reglazed, reroofed and reoccupied. There's a swish new tram line. Marshall and Libby took me into the centre one evening, admitting that before the makeover they never went downtown after dark. 'We weren't scared – there was just nothing open, no people, nothing to do.' When they fancied a night out, they hit the Ambassador Bridge and crossed over to Canada. So vast was the glut of unwanted and derelict real estate back then that the city authorities started building a huge prison right in the middle of town, though the burdens of corruption and inefficiency meant they never finished it.

These days the students and hipsters are downtown in force, bringing their vape pens and cupcake factories, their bike paths and farmers' markets. Yet in Detroit's bigger picture, the desolate landscape I was now bumping slowly across, downtown is no more than a shiny detail. However glitzy and appealing, it is dwarfed and engulfed by post-suburban wastelands that will never be repopulated. The one million residents who have moved away since the 1950s – two-thirds of the city's population – are never coming back. As I drove through another urban forest it struck me that what Detroit really needs is a boil wash and a big round of urban Tetris: shrink it down, then fill in the gaps.

At length I hit Woodward Avenue, turned right, and there it was: a battered four-storey old office with a flagless pole on the roof and ivy spreading up its front. Behind it stood a six-floor stack of more industrial aspect, with huge, filthy windows framed in rust-streaked concrete and wonky fire escapes laddering its flanks. Beyond, occupying several toes of Highland Park's former footprint, lay the 'Model T Plaza': two shoe shops, a dollar store and a

McDonald's, all engulfed by acres of empty parking. There was a certain rough justice in seeing the Universal Car's home annexed by the lowest form of mall shopping, that defining legacy of America's automobile age. I bumped on to a forecourt of broken, moss-veined concrete, then pushed all the levers up and croaked to a halt. Well, there we were. Welcome home, Michael.

A faded historical marker stood outside the office, slightly tilted in the daisy-dotted grass. 'HOME OF MODEL T' read its headline.

Here at his Highland Park Plant, Henry Ford in 1913 began the mass production of automobiles on a moving assembly line. By 1915 Ford built a million Model Ts. In 1925, over 9,000 were assembled in a single day. Mass production soon spread from here to all phases of American industry and set the pattern of abundance for 20th Century living.

Emotions fizzed down my spine and back up. How, *how* was a machine that first rumbled to life outside this ruin still at it? Whither the '14,000, raving, tearing maniacs' who once worked here, as described by a visiting journalist in a shell-shocked account of Highland Park's hyper-productive cacophony? It was too much to imagine. The Model T's gawky, amateur demeanour seemed perfectly consistent with the Piquette plant, where artisan mechanics bolted together a couple of dozen a day. The vision of hundreds being spewed out of this place every single hour – almost a million a year for seventeen years – just didn't make sense. Inside Highland Park, a mighty automatic drill press machined a whole Model T cylinder block in one go, boring forty-five simultaneous holes from four directions. But outside, most of the raw materials were still creaking up on horse-carts.

Woodward Avenue was the world's first concrete highway, the first road ever divided by a painted line, the first cleared by a snowplough. In its raucous heyday, Woodward hosted America's earliest street-drag races (the rod in 'hot rod' is a compaction of roadster, the two-seat Model T that was the platform of choice for pioneering speed tweakers). But its six lanes were now four too many for the threadbare traffic droning fitfully past. Highland Park, a separate municipality surrounded by Detroit on all sides, has shed 80 per cent of its population since the 1950s. A few years ago, to keep its creditors at the electric company happy, the city pulled down all its street lights. In 2001, the entire Highland Park police department was fired. The city no longer has an ambulance. Its fire department, which operates out of an old warehouse and pays its crews $10 an hour, deals with 150 fires every year, nearly all of them started deliberately in derelict buildings. In the words of Mark Binelli, author of *The Last Days of Detroit*, 'Highland Park is the Detroit of Detroit.'

'This one of those T Models?'

I turned around and was met by a trim black woman with pressed white jeans and a big smile, dragging a very noisy trash sack.

'Ain't that something, never saw one before, and I lived in this city since 1956.'

She stooped, picked up a Dr Pepper can, and dropped it into her sack with a reedy clink.

'Got burned out on Grand a few years back and they moved me down here.' Her smile faltered briefly; she turned her head Mike-wards and it recovered. 'What a neat ride. You have yourself a wonderful day.' And she was off, dragging a very different pattern of abundance away into the twenty-first century.

I climbed heavily back in, fired Mike up and eased away down the track that once led right through the heart of Highland Park. This was where Henry and his band of brothers had miraculously translated Piquette's cottage industry into a 120-acre machine that put the world on wheels. And how well he had rewarded them. Peter Martin, 'apostle of the conveyor', was paid an $18,000 bonus in 1913, enough to buy forty Model Ts, and Henry later put him in charge of the River Rouge plant. Promoting Martin to vice president, the old man rather pettily ensured he was paid more than the president – his own son, Edsel. Charles Sorensen, the Danish pattern maker, also wound up as a vice president, and during the war oversaw what must rank as the assembly line's crowning achievement: under his direction, Ford's Willow Run facility turned 488,193 component parts into a B-24 bomber every single hour. Everyone who played a part in the T's genesis found themselves handsomely rewarded. Harold Wills, the engineer who drafted that fabled Ford logo using a script font from a child's printing set, died a millionaire.

Henry wasn't afraid to bear a grudge, but he even did right by the team members who he felt had done him wrong. He fell out with James Couzens, but after his general manager resigned to pursue a political career, Henry purchased Couzens's shares in the company for an astounding $30 million. In the most trying circumstances, he even stood by the wayward Spider Huff – the magneto wizard who had clung to Henry's running-boards in the race that made his name.

Huff had always seemed an unlikely member of Ford's inner circle. Their lifestyles were glaringly at odds: Spider married four times, drank hard and chewed so much tobacco that he had a spittoon installed in his car. He routinely vanished on benders that sometimes lasted weeks. Once, exasperated to find Huff's Highland Park office empty yet again, Henry dispatched an assistant to track him down. It didn't take long. The man went to Spider's favoured bordello, and knocked on every door shouting, 'Huff, you in there?' At last he procured a response: 'No, I'm not.' The assistant flung the door open and found Spider in bed with two female employees.

In 1920, Spider quit Ford and set up his own firm, Huff Laboratories. To no one's great surprise it swiftly folded, leaving him deeply in debt. At this point Huff decided that although Henry had paid him a hefty $10,000 bonus for designing the T's flywheel magneto, he would now be suing his old friend for unpaid royalties: $2.50 per magneto on the 4.5 million Model Ts thus far produced, generously rounded down to $11 million. The court wasted little time in throwing the case out. Henry's response? He offered Spider a senior position in Ford's Experimental Electoral department, where Huff would work until his death. A Ford executive summarised this extraordinary relationship in his memoir:

'Huff was the only man who could tell Mr Ford what was wrong with his cars and not get fired.'

I puttered past a few surviving chunks of the Highland Park plant, cobbled into a half-arsed industrial estate. Then the remains of the world's biggest factory took shape before me: a massive, looming hump of demolished brick and concrete, an Ayers Rock of rubble. It was almost unbearable. So many tales, so much history, and all of it buried in that mountain of masonry. 'Detroit was the birthplace of modernity,' a local photographer told Mark Binelli, 'but it's also the graveyard of modernity.' How right she was. So too was Geoff Dyer, in his essay on Detroit as a modern Pompeii: 'This is what the future will end up like. This is what the future has always ended up looking like.' All that thrilling, vibrant productivity smashed into silence. I felt like Charlton Heston at the end of *Planet of the Apes*, confronted by the beached remains of the Statue of Liberty. And then, because you generally have the Detroit East Side all to yourself, I very loudly sounded like him too: 'YOU MANIACS! YOU BLEW IT UP! DAMN YOU! GOD DAMN YOU ALL TO HELL!'

'*Smooth*, brother – Chitty Chitty Bang Bang, we love yew!'

How good to be back on the open road, heading south-west, reeling in the miles and the redneck greetings under a cloudless sky. Keeping off the interstates meant plotting an Etch-A-Sketch route down backroads that gridded the hot, flat fields of ripening corn: 10 miles down, 10 miles across, 10 miles down. The farms began to look a little scrappy, their barns ventilated by age and neglect. An old guy was selling hay by the road for $3.75 a bale. I crossed back into Ohio, then Indiana, chewing tubes of dried meat, gulping tepid water and taurine, dodging roadkill.

The towns were sleepy and well spaced. Some of the larger ones would be girdled with a scrappy hinterland of gas stations and dollar stores, two or three flat-pack churches, perhaps a Walmart, perhaps a motel, always an assortment of defunct commercial units. If the town had a restaurant, it would be here, and it would be Mexican. Then I'd pass beneath a big water tower on stilts with a union flag and the town's name painted on it, and head down the old main street. This was dead straight and dependably run-down, a memorial to a prosperous past. Half a dozen careworn Victorian mansions, with rotting verandas and the odd crooked turret. A couple of grandly proportioned general stores with decaying Wild West style false fronts, now selling junk and yard-art two mornings a week, or nothing, ever. Peeling old adverts decorously hand-painted on brick and wood, promoting Champion Spark Plugs or American Wire Fence. Right in the centre I'd rattle over a rusty railway line with a flaky grain elevator the size of a moon rocket looking down on it, then repeat the above sequence in reverse.

The names of these towns, I began to note, fell into three categories. Some were evidently christened by homesick settlers (Berne, Warsaw, Antwerp); some in stark reference to a resident industry (Saline, Cement City); and some in tribute to an eventful past that they couldn't wait to share. 'DEFIANCE – On this site, in the center of Indian country, General "Mad" Anthony Wayne ordered a fort built in August 1794. He said: "I defy the English, Indians, and all the devils of hell to take it," and named it Defiance.' 'FORT BINGAMON – Near this fort, established as defense against Indians, stood Samuel Bingamon's cabin. His home attacked and his wife wounded, Bingamon single-handedly shot and clubbed to death all but one of a party of seven Indians.'

Those rare settlements cursed with entirely nondescript names felt obliged to trumpet some homespun claim to fame, generally by painting it in huge letters on the water tower: 'HUDSON – DIVISION 4 WRESTLING CHAMPIONS 2008.' 'WREN – OFFICIAL WIFFLEBALL CAPITAL OF OHIO.' Small-towners really do like to educate and inspire passers-by. And they absolutely love to bemuse and unsettle them, through the medium of front-yard and forecourt placards. 'FLAT RACCOON ANIMAL HOSPITAL – DID YOU KNOW THAT MANATEES CAN LIVE FOR 60 YEARS?' 'LYNNVIEW NURSERY – FREEDOM IS NOT FREE.' 'DO YOU LOVE PLEASURE MORE THAN GOD?'

Mike was hitting his stride now, cruising smooth in the high 30s, knocking out the big miles: 170, 180, sometimes 200 a day as we motored through the fields. The traffic was ever sparser and I began to relax as much as you are ever likely to in a car whose steering wheel needs tightening on the move every half-hour, and which careers madly across the road whenever you drive over an errant speck of gravel. My thousand-mile Model T apprenticeship was now up, and I realised this was about as confident as I'd ever feel driving one.

For the first time I began to take one hand off the wheel, dangling it in the breeze, with the throttle set as a sort of redneck cruise control and my unemployed feet stretched out astride the pedals. On the endless straights it felt more like piloting a narrow-boat down a canal: set your speed, hold a course, steady as she goes. The corners were more art than science, and before tackling one I called all limbs back from holiday. Close the throttle a touch, maybe change down, then coax the car round by feel, hoping the wriggles and slithers cancelled each other out. And all the while the settlements thinned and the landscape seemed to expand around me: the wide-open space of a big country getting bigger all the while.

The motels began to deteriorate as I nosed into the lower Midwest, though the welcoming geniality remained undimmed. One morning a desk manager greeted me with a very different face from the one I'd pulled on opening my room fridge, and finding it stacked with a previous occupant's furry leftovers. 'Good morning, sir,' he beamed. Bet you're looking forward to a cup of our coffee? It's a beautiful day out there!' He was half right. I knew the coffee would be dreadful.

I generally shared these places with long-termers, mostly families who I guessed were on welfare. Their giveaway was a baby gate across the open front door, with laundry draped over it. The bigger kids would always congregate silently around the T, curious but shy, until a harassed-looking mother stuck her head out of a window: 'Jaydon and Leanne, you let that man fix his car in peace or I'll send you both back inside.' Walking into the reception of the Colonial Manor Motel in Bryan, Ohio, I found a fellow guest dandling a pink-vested baby in her lap by the water cooler.

'What's her name?' I asked brightly.

An open smile and a blithe shrug. 'No idea.'

The further south I went, and the more deeply rural, the longer it took to negotiate even basic transactions. These were places with very little experience of people who spoke English, but weren't American. Every time I sat down for my evening meal I'd ask for a glass of water, and every time the waitress would recoil and dart appalled looks at neighbouring tables, as if to say: 'D'yall hear that? Hugh fricking Grant over here just ordered a goddam *hobo's scrotum!*' After several attempts I'd flatten everything into a lobotomised John Wayne drawl: 'A *glaaaaaaaaaass of waaahdur.*' This usually did the job, though one Indiana waitress came back with a frothing schooner of ale and a winning smile. 'And here's your Michelob Ultra!'

I'd often find a copy of the town's newspaper on the table. Every time I did my spirits were lifted. You couldn't leaf through one and not feel warmly smitten by the people who wrote and read it; if my burrito was washed down with a margarita, I might fancy myself living amongst them for ever. The finest example I encountered, in Indiana, introduced itself thus: 'The *Liberty Herald* – the Only Newspaper in the World to Give a Darn about Union County.' Its front-page story related a recent excitement involving the school bus: 'There were no students aboard the bus at the time of the accident, but the collision broke a light at the rear-left side.'

The *Herald*'s centre pages were devoted to Liberty's 4-H club, a defining small-town youth institution whose six million members are best described as farm scouts (the Hs in question: head, heart, hands and health). This was a two-margarita night, and I fear I may have welled up at the wholesome, earnest Union County 4-H Fair Queen nominees beaming timelessly out at me in black and white. 'Alyssa is president of the Hoofbeats Horse & Pony Club ... Olivia is sponsored by Progressive Homemakers ... Madeline participates in cheerleading and the Fellowship of Christian Athletes ... Emily is a member of the College Corner Presbyterian Church where she volunteers at the food pantry.' And on the facing page, their young male counterparts, broad of neck and close of crop, outlining their hopes for the imminent 4-H livestock show: 'My name is Ethan Hornung and I am a member of the Hopeful Homemakers Stateline Farmers Club. Within my ten years of being in 4-H, the only project I have ever done is swine, but do not let that fool you. Showing my hog in the arena is my favourite part. My future plans consist of going to taxidermy school in Idaho.' God bless you, Ethan Hornung.

And so, replete with tortillas and sentimentality, I'd wander out into the warm night. The temperature always seemed to rise for an hour or two after sundown, as the earth and the walls and the asphalt breathed out all the daytime heat they'd absorbed. I nearly always had the streets to myself. Nothing ever seemed to happen in these towns after dark. The only time it did – in Bryan again – was when an auto interiors shop caught fire a mile out of town, filling the night with screaming sirens and my motel forecourt with happy men in wifebeater vests. 'Got five fire departments working down there,' one of them called eagerly out to another, his smiling eyes fixed on a distant orange glow. 'That baby sure is throwing up some smoke.'

But in the main it was just me, the fireflies and a rabbit or two, lolloping about in the breezeless, blood-warm gloaming. I'd wander down main street, inspecting the foreclosed businesses – a drive-thru bank with its ATMs knee-deep in dandelions, a family photographer with a couple of fading fatties tying the knot above a carpet of dead flies – and playing count the flags. Stand in the centre of any American small town, no matter how desolate, and you will always see at least three Stars and Stripes without moving your head. Eight was a typical tally. And I'd cock an ear for the plaintive whistle of a freight-train locomotive, that defining small-town nocturne.

Mike would usually have drawn a fan club by the time I returned to the motel. The local Willie Nelson with a grey ponytail sticking out the back of his bandana, or a couple of white-beards in cut-off dungarees and caps advertising tractors or dog food. A horny hand would be held out: 'My name's Frank J. Weck, and this here's Elway Buckridge. Real purty T you got. Headin' on to that old car show in Revenge?' These chaps always had an endearing habit of sprinkling their own adventures, no matter how peripheral, into the conversation that followed. 'England, huh? One time I been to Anchorage, Alaska.' Or, more effusively: 'Let me tell you 'bout Mike Chapman, he was a Brit, half a one at least, I roomed with him down in Louisville in the mid-Seventies, guy had a stress thing, bit of a stutter, anyways he hooked up with this woman with big titties, I mean they were a green light for Mike, so maybe ten, twelve years ago I'm back in Kentucky, I go to a gas station and there's a guy workin' outside the tyre place next door, and shoot, it's old Mike Chapman, so we have a bit of a hug and a handshake, then a week later I go back, and he's not there, so anyways that's my Mike Chapman story.' Then they'd nod, very slowly, ten or twenty times, and add: 'Elway's just got him one of those hydraulic log splitters. Heck of a machine.'

Some of these old boys were seriously decrepit, and it was extra-ordinary to see them shuffling clumsily back to their pick-ups. I kept wanting to snatch the keys away. The inalienable right to drive is an unwritten small-town amendment, a universal freedom that is blind to age, infirmity or drooling dementia. I suppose that's the legacy of Henry and fifteen million Model Ts. One night a dented SUV pulled erratically into the motel car park and screeched to an untidy halt beside the T's small coterie of admirers. The window buzzed down and a yellowy ghost eased its head out. 'I had me a 1930 Model A convertible,' it croaked. 'Cat got in the roof and ate it all up.' Then the window buzzed back up and the SUV returned to the road, via two kerbs and a flower bed.

When the last old-timer had slalomed away into the dark I'd go back to my room and click on the TV news. After a slow-paced, amiable small-town evening it was always a shock to witness the fresh round of hate and rage that had ravaged the national airwaves all day. Commentators of both stripes raved and squealed and threw up their hands; wild-eyed inter-viewers shouted down guests; panellists ranted over each other, then pulled their mics off and stormed out. And behind it all sat Trump, propped up in bed with his phone and a lapful of cheeseburgers, tossing something soft and whiffy into every whirring news cycle. He'd declare Twitter war on the world's most wayward nuclear power, or replace his communications chief with a ludicrous cartoon mobster, and then – after eleven days – replace the ludicrous cartoon mobster with a four-star Marine general. Attempting to formulate a response to his party's failure to overturn Obama's Affordable Care Act, he completely changed his mind three times in a single day. His only systematic strategy seemed to involve undermining every senior figure in his own administration.

If I had to pick the defining moment from those crazy weeks, I'd probably go for Trump's address to the National Scout Jamboree, when 35,000 fresh-faced teenagers who had turned up expecting a warm homily about comradeship and knots were instead treated to a rambling, vainglorious reminiscence of their president's distant electoral triumph.

'But you remember that incredible night with the maps, and the Republicans are red and the Democrats are blue, and that map was so red it was unbelievable. And you know, we have a tremendous disadvantage in the Electoral College. Popular vote is much easier. We have – because New York, California, Illinois, you have to practically run the East Coast. And we did. We won Florida. We won South Carolina. We won North Carolina. We won Pennsylvania. We won and won.'

This sort of stuff was why you couldn't sit on the fence about Trump, and why the news outlets had now abandoned any pretence of impartiality. Fox News, of course, had never even pretended, and though I did my best to give it a fair crack of the whip, I could never tolerate more than fifteen minutes in one sitting. By then I'd have endured at least ten ad-break idents that shouted 'FOX NEWS – FAIR AND BALANCED!' or 'FOX NEWS – WE REPORT, YOU DECIDE!' and heard at least three presenters pour scorn all over 'the Pravda-like mainstream media', with copybook shit-eating grins. Experiencing all this on a national TV network operated by Rupert Murdoch built up an Orwellian disconnect that soon made my temples pulse and my fists clench and my mouth yell: 'YOU INCREDIBLY STRANGE AND DISTURBING PEOPLE!'

As a liberal elitist I obviously felt much more at home watching CNN and MSNBC, though it was plain that even in the short weeks since I'd set off, both networks had steadily retreated from a position of nominal even-handedness towards one-eyed propaganda. The presenters now switched between two expressions: harrowed disbelief and derisive disgust. Sometimes I'd turn off the sound, and try to imagine what they might be reporting on if I didn't already know. The best fit was that the nation's children had all been lured away by a flatulent, cross-dressing giant. There were fewer and fewer pro-Trump guests, and the brittle courtesy they'd been accorded in the first interviews I'd watched had given way to sneering contempt. This was what Trump did: he polarised, he divided, he compelled you to side with him or against him. So it was now possible – indeed almost unavoidable – for every American to spend his or her life shut in their own echo chamber, only hearing the news they wanted to hear, hardening their prejudices and fostering their fears. You could live either in a world where Trump was forever an infantile narcissist or in one where the fake-news liberal mainstream media was forever foiling his doughty efforts to make America great again.

For many decades, the Federal Fairness Doctrine obliged all US TV and radio networks to cover both sides of every political story or debate, much like the BBC's Charter. But under conservative pressure – there was that hated 'F' word again – the doctrine was repealed in 1987. Rush Limbaugh launched his witheringly anti-liberal radio talk show within a year: soon he was on TV, in a syndicated show that paved the way for Rupert Murdoch's Fox News, launched in 1996. Year Zero, the year America was irreconcilably cleaved in two. By way of example, let us examine the recent electoral history of LaSalle Parish in Louisiana, the thirty-seventh

One dawn a bitter mist came down, and I shuddered through the ghostly fields of southern Indiana, hunched over the wheel with my jacket buttoned right up to the neck. That morning marked my debut dabble with the hefty radio I'd brought along for the trip. For long minutes my chilly fingers fruitlessly worked the dial; then a steel guitar twanged out of the ether and I homed in on it. A man was singing the blues, country style, and these, I swear, were his first clear words: 'If you could see how I'm living in this old car I drive, well you'd probably wonder why I even want to stay alive.' Then the drawled melancholy was swallowed by crackle and pop, and I drove on in wide-eyed silence.

The Midwest's broad, flat sea of green began to gently rise and fall, then abruptly plunged down to the mile-wide Ohio River. This counts itself as the Mississippi's mightiest tributary, and the giant bulk barges battling its midstream currents were shrunk to bath toys. We crossed it rather gingerly on one of those rusty-Meccano girder bridges, the kind that always look as if they're about to be dive-bombed by Stukas. Mike would slither horribly on the gridded steel that typically surfaced these crossings. Driving a Model T, I had by now established, would be a joint enterprise, a pact between man and machine. The best I could hope for was that Mike might do what I asked of him more often than not: start, stop, turn left, turn right, drive over bridges rather than off them. Once resigned to the potentially fatal downsides, I found this a liberating revelation. It was all about giving Mike fewer decisions to make. Modest applications of throttle and wheel. Steady and gentle on the brakes. No more than a rare tweak of the spark lever, to boost power going up hills and enhance engine braking coming down them. Things only unravelled in urban traffic, where the need for more urgent and drastic adjustments reprised the panicky lurching skitters of my early days at the wheel. But towns were now few and far between, and ever sleepier.

Kentucky's storied Bluegrass region was an upscale, manicured dominion of racehorse stud farms and bourbon distilleries, its plump hills accessorised with majestic oaks and smart white fencing. I felt a little homesick: this was like some idealised, epic-scale England, with more money, blazing sun and stronger booze. Mike led a column of placid weekend tourists through the twisty hills of bourbon country, and some rather less easy-going locals in and out of small towns that rang with the cries of competitive dads at Little League baseball games.

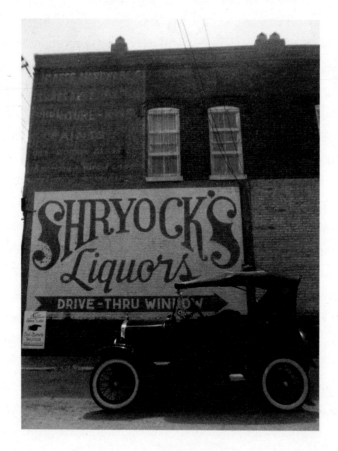

Then, very gradually, we nosed into another Kentucky. There were abandoned farmhouses, the first I'd seen, and a lot of soaped-up shop windows. A family with too many children and not enough teeth sat around a cannonball stack of watermelons under a camping gazebo. Hillbillies were out doing hillbilly things, like sawing a big hole in the side of their house, or rolling vast plastic drums down a steep meadow, or drinking beer in an old wrecked car with a Confederate flag on its bonnet. The pick-up was now undisputed king of the road: one idle afternoon out on the Cumberland Plateau I counted nineteen overtaking me in succession. A front-seat passenger in the last was cooling his bare feet out of the window. People were communicating in what one might charitably describe as measured tones, and my own accent was becoming ever more impenetrable. After Bob Kirk's beaded seat cover wore through the seat of my trousers, I developed a sort of Eliza Doolittle hillbilly training mantra: 'There's a ghastly vast hole in the ass of my pants,' I talk-sang, over and over again, 'and all the daft bastards are laughing.'

It began to feel like the south: hot, lazy and slightly mad. This trinity coalesced at the Super 8 motel in Danville, Kentucky, as I was chocking Mike's wheels on the tilted, sticky car-park tarmac.

'Mah name is Calvin T. Parr Junior,' announced a slightly unkempt old chap in a grimy check shirt and a cap with a bull-dozer on it, 'and I would lack you to give me your wedding ring.'

My faith in small-town America's lawful decency already ran deep, and without hesitation I pulled my gold band off and dropped it in the old man's open palm.

'Now, this is an all-natural product,' he said, tipping a crumpled sachet of chalky powder on top of the ring, before clasping his hands and rubbing them together vigorously. After a few seconds of this he pincered the ring between his thumb and held it aloft with an expression of rapture. 'The Lord just gave it to me in a dream.'

'No, hang on a minute,' I said quickly. 'I just gave it to you in this car park.'

He wasn't listening.

'Look at it glint in the sun! Don't that gold just *shan*?'

I leaned close and took the opportunity to pluck my ring back. It didn't appear to have been switched. It also didn't appear to shan any more than it had.

'It's a shale-based polishin' powder. Recipe between me and the Lord.' He took a quick peek over his shoulder, then dropped his voice to a whisper. 'I had the op-toonerty to go on TV with it, but the Lord told me, "No, Calvin – you need to take this to Japan."'

This seemed a good moment to lug my bags out of the car and prepare to take my leave.

'Ain't just a polish, neither. See how good it makes my hay-ands!'

He held them up. They might have belonged to someone who juggled bricks for a living. I wished him luck and hauled my belongings off towards the reception, accompanied all the way by his fading exhortations.

'I can make three hundred bottles a day! Reckon I'll be needin' to!'

This ingrained rural inventiveness was another of Henry Ford's legacies. Six million farmers saw him as one of their own: they fancied themselves touched by his everyman genius, and some felt vaguely entitled to a slice of the fortune it earned him. Ford's put-upon secretaries opened around a hundred letters from self-styled inventors every day, proposals for everything from electric revolvers to dashboard coffee percolators. A self-lighting cigarette;

a hollow steering wheel that could be filled like a hot-water bottle on cold mornings; a horn that yelled, 'FORD!' Their effrontery was often splendid. 'My price is $250,000 and it is easy worth it. I would like to have the cash by return mail.' 'Would the best transmission in the world interest you? Now listen, boy, I've got the Deluxe Baby. If I come to Detroit, will you promise me a square deal?'

A couple of hours later I was back down at reception, asking its ample young occupant if I might find a restaurant within walking distance.

'You mean, walking *on foot*?' Her eyes widened as she struggled to imagine the unimaginable. 'I don't ... I mean ... just ... well, there's that Mexican place back down the hah-way, food's good and they serve adult beverages, but that's gotta be like ...' She exhaled loudly and shook her head. 'Like, maybe a half-hour?'

This had become a routine reception-desk exchange, indeed a universal one at motels which, like the Danville Super 8, found themselves out on some peripheral highway, clustered between malls and gas stations under a thicket of lofty, illuminated signs. At the Red Roof Inn in Fairmont, West Virginia, the woman at the desk was so appalled when I asked for pedestrian directions to a clearly visible Walmart that she slammed a set of car keys down on the Formica. 'That's my pick-up outside. 'Fraid I smoke.' Coastal Americans might clock up the daily steps on their fitness bands, but in the flyover states no one goes anywhere on foot. One afternoon in Detroit I strolled for almost three miles down a sunny, broad sidewalk in a smart part of town and passed precisely two other pedestrians: a cheery old nutcase collecting pretty leaves in a plastic sack and a black guy asleep in a bus shelter. The discouragement of pedestrian activity – and if that fails, its brutal subjugation – is one of the Universal Car's most prominent legacies.

On the rare occasions you're legally permitted to walk across a hah-way, the flashing red hand of panic bursts into life the second your feet touch tarmac: RUN, LITTLE MAN, RUN FOR YOUR SORRY, WORTHLESS LIFE.

Well, it wasn't even a half-mile to the Mexican restaurant as the crow flies, though a bit more as the crow scrambles up a couple of steep embankments and crawls through a hedge. I would become steadily less critical of the natives' pedestro-phobia. There are only so many evenings you fancy a pre-dinner tramp through marshy culverts and derelict laminate-flooring showroom car lots, getting bathed in sweat and nibbled half to death by blood-sucking buzzers. At any rate, I was sat behind a taco salad, wild of hair and damp of brow, within fifteen minutes.

Given my extensive exposure to US-style Mexican dining, a few related tips seem in order. Here are a couple to be getting on with.

1. Don't order the taco salad, unless you enjoy eating week-old lettuce out of a deep-fried cardboard bed pan.
2. Unless you enjoy tripping face first into gopher holes, don't order a third adult beverage.

In the morning, I raised the hood to give Mike his breakfast quart of oil and saw something was amiss. Something fundamental: the fan belt had, at some unknown point the previous day, shredded itself into a clump of grey spaghetti, wrapped like a rat king around the bottom pulley. It wasn't a great look, certainly not one compatible with a shrug, a slam of the hood and a whistling return to the open road. At least not in any other car. Reasoning that I had covered at least some miles – possibly loads of them – without ill effect, I hacked the fan belt's tortured corpse off the pulley, loaded up and drove away into the sun. It felt like a turning point of some sort. The redneck skill set required to patch up a T on the hoof would hopefully come to me in time, but at least I'd now bagged the gung-ho, fuck-it mindset.

I crossed the Tennessee state line on the Grundy Quarles Highway. Americans just love rewarding local notables with lumps of infrastructure. Most, I assumed, were public servants, though who knows: Grundy Quarles sounds more like someone who might have made his name speed-eating hot dogs. I was forever rumbling over Wilkes T. Thrasher's bridge, or dribbling Outlaw Energy down my chin in Jeff Busby's state-park picnic area, or desecrating a tree behind Hernando de Soto's wildlife refuge. I suppose it's part and parcel of America's cult of the individual, the legend of a land built by great men. What a shame nobody tried buying Donald Trump off with an interstate service station and a couple of long-drop earth closets.

Grundy Quarles did pretty well for himself. His highway wound across some spectacular sandstone bluffs, cut deep and straight through the corky, slab-sided rock. At the foot of its steepest section I picked the wrong gear – that Ruckstell underdrive was a bugger to shift on hills – and willed Mike onwards as the uncooled engine laboured up that big red cleft. The motometer was about to blow its top when I finally crawled over Grundy's summit, half out of the seat, willing Mike on like a jockey in the home straight.

Everything felt more southern at once. Bob Kirk's rattlesnake thermometer nudged up to 110. The roadside ads were all ominous or folksy: 'LEARN PRACTICAL COMBAT IN A REALISTIC URBAN ENVIRONMENT'; 'DONNY'S DINER – IF YOU DON'T EAT HERE, WE'LL BOTH STARVE.' I was finding ever larger and more exotic corpses snagged in the fins of that tombstone radiator, iridescent dragonflies and blue-green beetles. On terrifying occasion, something large and buzzy would inveigle itself through the slender gap at the top of the windshield, and be introduced directly into my face. These incidents induced the least helpful of all human reactions – clumsy panic. If I had come home in a coffin, this would have been why. 'My father died as he lived,' one of my children might tell a horde of weeping mourners, 'swearing at wasps with a sack of crisps in his lap.'

And I was moving ever deeper into the Bible Belt. Even the tiniest towns were bestrewn with churches, most brand new and many enormous. Tennessee is home to sixty-seven megachurches – defined as Protestant congregations with an average weekly attendance of at least 2,000 – the most per capita of any state. I now see that I passed quite close to Jamestown, which has a nation-topping ratio of 230 churches for a population of 1,900. And that I also narrowly swerved Dayton, the Tennessee town that hosted the infamous Scopes Monkey Trial the year after my T rolled out of Highland Park. This was a test case for the teaching of evolution in schools, and though the verdict went in favour of the creationists, the national fallout poured so much scorn over the backward, Bible-bashing hillbillies that the scientific progressives who lost the battle won the war.

Or thought they had. Fuelled by the rise of tele-evangelism, in the 1980s a backlash took hold. Between 1985 and 2005, the number of American adults who accepted evolution actually fell, from 45 per cent to 40. A recent Gallup poll established that an extraordinary 42 per cent of Americans believe humans were created by God 10,000 years ago. Only a fifth think God has played no part in evolution. Since 2012, almost every school in Tennessee and Louisiana has taught creationism alongside evolution, with eight further states considering legislation that would protect teachers who present creationism as a scientific theory.

Across the nation, just 30 per cent of biology high-school teachers take 'an adamant pro-evolutionary stance' in lessons. In the coming weeks I passed several anti-evolution billboards: 'In the beginning GOD CREATED,' they announced, above a circled progression from knuckle-dragging ape to *Homo erectus*, with oblique red lines through all the missing links.

As a pro-choice, pro-science Euro-heathen who doesn't know his Presbyterians from his Pentecostals, I found it overwhelming and a bit scary. Where might the Countryside Church of the Nazarene fit in America's mysterious holy spectrum? Or the Bikers Church, or the Cowboy Church? The signs outside every religious establishment offered few clues to anything except the incumbent pastor's mastery of grammar and passive aggression. 'JESUS LOVE'S EVEN ME'; 'SMILE – YOUR MOTHER CHOSE LIFE'; 'BE GOOD TO EVERYONE. I'LL SORT EM OUT LATER – GOD.'

On a benignly secular level, America's churches have always offered a social focus for far-flung communities. In the pre-T era, going to church might have been the only time you got to meet your neighbours, and had the chance to turn them into friends. This was why Henry Ford walked eight miles to church and back every Sunday. Churches still form the backbone of many small-town civic structures: they run sports clubs and youth clubs, and organise community outings. But as those strident roadside messages suggested, there was something deeper at work. Something more literally fundamental.

America is a land settled by religious dissenters, so I suppose it's natural that they're still making the most of the freedom to worship how they want. The national superiority complex that is such a feature of American Christianity seems almost inevitable. If you emigrated from half a world away in search of free religious expression, you'd doubtless feel an enhanced and lasting debt of gratitude to the nation that granted it, and might forgivably think of your new home as the Promised Land. It certainly looks the part: in almost 2,000 covered miles I had been routinely presented with sumptuous fecundity and scenic grandeur on a scale unknown in Europe. The landscape artist Thomas Cole memorably described America's mighty wildernesses as 'the undefiled work of God'.

We should also appreciate just what an awful lot America has to feel proud of: saving the planet from dictatorship, putting the world on wheels and man on the moon. But with all those real-world achievements receding, the conflation between patriotism and Christian belief really does seem to have been cranked up in recent years. Both, I suppose, are leaps of faith, and in the small towns those leaps landed smack in the middle of every other front yard and car bumper. 'GOD, GUTS & GUNS MADE AMERICA'; 'BLESSED IS THE NATION WHOSE GOD IS THE LORD.' I saw a fair few crucifixes painted up in Stars and Stripes.

The nation's flag is revered with religious devotion: for days Fox News pursued a 'totally sickening' incident wherein some small paper Stars and Stripes ended up in a trash sack during a clear-up after a veterans' parade in somewhere like Minnesota. After an outcry the authorities agreed to retrieve the flags and 'retire them' with due reverence at a special ceremony. 'Mamaw always had two gods: Jesus Christ and the United States of America,' writes J. D. Vance of the grandmother who raised him. 'I was no different, and neither was anyone else I knew.' So many small-towners believe, quite plainly and passionately, that they've been born and bred in God's own country, that they're the chosen ones. In this context, making America great again seems less like a campaign slogan than the battle cry of a righteous crusade.

It was swamping, and often surreal. With 1,600 religious broadcasters in the US, it must be very difficult to spread the word in a way it hasn't been spread before. I'd tune in to a radio station and hear a man comparing human temptation to a broken dishwasher, in tones laden with dramatic foreboding. One night I flicked on my motel telly to be met by an evangelist with an easy manner and extremely bright teeth holding smoothly forth about marital repairs: 'If you feel your marriage is broken, give all the pieces to God and he'll make something beautiful out of it.' Then the camera panned back and behind him, stuck on a plinth, was a life-sized great white shark.

Here's the rub, though. Small-towners, judged as an entity by their Christian fundamentalism, their electoral decisions and their personal armouries, filled my bleeding metropolitan heart with dread. But on an individual level, there were just lovely: cheery, mellow, hospitable, polite, helpful, enthusiastic, informative, fun. At Cookeville, a youngish janitor in a baseball cap and huge sunglasses ambled over as I was loading Mike up in his motel car park. 'That Model T of yours is quite the deal,' he drawled, before casting a glance at the terraced hutches lined out around us. 'Kinda weird to think that little old car started all these places, the whole auto touring thing.' The Virginia plates were beginning to speak for themselves, marking me out as a visitor from a faraway realm, a man on a mission. At a flyblown gas station near the Alabama state line, a posse of truck drivers came over and shook my hand with jaw-rippling intensity:

'Coast to coast, huh? Ain't that something.'

'Name's Bubba Merryweather the dooce, real good to meet you, sir.'

'My granddaddy had a Model T, put in a little fuel hand-pump to get up the hills. I was in the back one time in the rain, he's working that little hand wiper on the windshield, Grandmammy is pulling hard on the fuel pump, both of 'em jacking the car off like crazy!'

Every time I pulled over, motorists would stop to ask if I needed assistance. Grumpy hardmen, toddlers, hip teens, young mums, old men and all in between – never have I been so universally loved. No one even laughed at the vast ghastly hole in the ass of my pants, at least not until I'd left the room. Anyone suffering severe self-esteem issues might do well to consider a trans-continental journey in a Model T Ford. The comedown's pretty rough, mind you.

I drove footloose and fan-belt-free for 500 miles, suffering occasional steamy alarums up long hills or at red lights that took too long to change. We were into the Sun Belt now, and the heat was relentless and astonishing. It messed with my head, my mouth and my limbs. I started pushing the throttle lever the wrong way. Incredibly, twice I nodded off at the wheel, hypnotised by the temperature and the stroboscopic shadows of telegraph poles laid across the softening tarmac. Both times I was mercifully roused to full alert by fortissimo contributions from my back-seat symphony: the wind-whipped snap of the ugly blue tarp I'd tucked in over my bags and boxes, or the clatter of energy-drink cans and oil quarts in the rear-footwell empties' bucket.

Long into the evening, as I sat slumped before a steaming tortilla, the world around me still seemed to shimmer and pulse as it had done all day through Mike's shuddering windshield. Then one night I took out my Trumpland route map, laboriously brought it into focus and understood that I would soon be passing into the deepest south, where Model T guys seemed very thin on the ground. And that I'd then be hitting Texas and heading due north, a proposal that shook a lot of heads and sucked a lot of teeth: 'Sir, you are headed for the hottest part of the US at the hottest time of the year.' That fan belt would need sorting before then, and if I wanted any help with it I had better start looking now.

The MTFCA worked its magic and directed me to Bill Robinson's workshop in Gurley, Alabama, not far from the space-race city of Huntsville. Skirting it I caught a glimpse of the 360-foot Saturn V rocket that towers over the centre, like a cathedral spire to American achievement. The rocket that put man on the moon was designed in Huntsville in 1963 by ex-Nazi aerospace whizz Wernher von Braun and his team. It was made up of three million parts – all of which had to work – and in thirteen launches never lost a payload. I simply couldn't get to grips with the brain-bending fact that less than forty years separated Mike from the Saturn V. It occurred to me that the two machines neatly bookended America's gilded pomp. No matter how long mankind may survive, we will surely never again witness such astonishing progress in such a stunted time frame.

An encounter with a cruel and discouraging T guy seemed long overdue by the law of averages, but it wouldn't be happening in Gurley. Bill was another splendid fellow, a tall, ponderous retiree with a grey beard and an air of cheerful bemusement that may be the lot of those who live on Salty Bottom Road. A home-made sign on his shop wall wished me a 'Happy Hillbilly Christmas'. One of the five Ts in his fleet was a tourer the same age as mine: with a wink he flipped up the hood and jabbed a thumb at the spark plug leads, which I noted were fashioned from barbed wire.

'Any partickler reason you ain't put a new belt on yourself, Teeum?'

That detached half-smile tugged at the corners of Bill's mouth. It was a fair question: I'd just watched him fit one in around three minutes. Any auto spares store could apparently have offered me a spare of the correct diameter. Another must-do-better stamp on my obliterated report card.

We were presently joined by two further T men, Dave and Seth, each driving a stripped-down, two-seat, topless speedster. Seth was the youngest old car guy I would meet, a Huntsville mechanical engineering student whose bright yellow T offered a technological counterbalance to his research into 3D printing applications for the aerospace industry. The car had been in his family since his great-great-grandfather bought it new in 1914 – a wonderful story, but one that barely surprised me: the supporting role played by the Model T in the history of almost every small-town American was now taken as read. I was considerably more taken aback by the revelation that Seth's performance modifications – an additional carburettor, a high-compression cylinder head, everything slavishly period-correct – had endowed his T with a top speed of 75mph. 'Guess I ought to consider uprating the brakes,' he chuckled wryly.

Dave and Seth had come to induct me into the fellowship of the antique roadshow. It was a giddy affair. Bill led us out of his yard in a 1921 Model T 'depot hack', to all intents and purposes a quaint bus shelter on wheels, and for three splendid hours we trundled nose to tail through the soupy heat of the high Alabaman summer. Up and down red-earthed hills, over the wide Tennessee River, between fields and yards alive with crops and colour: carpets of green studded with fluffy white cotton, garish blurts of bougainvillea and crepe myrtle. How strange to find Mike hemmed in by fellow centenarians, to no longer bear sole responsibility for that huge rearward queue of traffic (though to be fair I still bore half of it: both speedsters jockeyed impatiently about in my juddery mirror, straining at the oily leash). And what a relief that nobody had proposed such an outing before: playing follow-my-leader in those cack-handed early weeks would have swiftly stoved in somebody's pride and joy. After eight states and 2,300 miles, I had finally mustered a decent approximation of cruising competence.

Approaching the steepest incline, Bill stuck a hand out of his window and made an urgent beckoning gesture. I knew what this meant: hit full gas now, or feel gravity's dead hand grasp Mike by the tail pipe, then struggle all the way up to the brow at walking pace. I complied and was touching 45 by the time the road tilted up. Piloting a T at such speeds meant a deafening, buffeted flirtation with terminal velocity, but looking ahead at Bill's depot hack pulling away from me and thus going faster still, there was no indication of the clattering frenzy I knew he would be enduring. With a sigh I understood that no matter how fast I went, no matter how raggedly I heaved the car around, to every other road user I would always look like some pootling old fart. With a deeper sigh I realised they'd be at least half right.

Our convoy pulled in for refreshments at a remote little diner. Over several beakers of iced tea we put the four-wheeled world to rights, agreeing that if every motorist was required to spend an hour behind the wheel of a Model T, they would become vastly superior drivers. 'Read the road better, allow safer distances, keep an eye out for dangers and escape routes.' Then agreeing that several of them would perish during this experiment, and changing our minds. Stopping for gas an hour earlier, Dave noted with interest that one of his tyres had almost completely detached itself from a wheel rim. And we'd all been obliged to speed through a couple of red lights, a routine flirtation with tragedy for which I now adopted a special 'brace face': pursing my lips tight and turning my head sharply to one side, an expression ready-made for smearing across the tarmac.

The presence of four parked Ts drew a procession of passers-by inside. A very old man shuffled up to our table, took out a very old cellphone and spent a long time silently scrolling through fuzzy images of a dim barn filled with car-like shapes. Halfway back to the door, he turned, fixed me with a look of perfect blankness and said: 'You got a accent.' Soon after, a more excitable and slightly younger chap all but burst through the door. 'Sure is good to see all those Model Ts outsad! My brother un me used to go out moonshinin' in my uncle's T when we was young and dumb as bricks. Why, one night we gone broke most every bone in our damned bodies. Woooh!'

'You are deep in moonshine country,' confirmed Seth, after he'd gone. His girlfriend was a teacher, and at her first parents' evening one of the more rustic mothers had sidled up with a gift. 'My husband said I oughta give you a jar of coffee, but that don't seem fittin' for a teacher, so I got you this,' she'd said, and plonked a big mason jar of bathtub spirit on the desk.

A deadlier narcotic scourge had now reached Alabama, as I learned when Bill took a brief call and reported it in his default tone of incredulity. 'That was a friend of mine, she's about fifty years old, got that Crohn's disease, they put her on those opioids for it, and she got *addiction*.' He shook his head. 'She just *overdosed*. For the *third time*.' In testament to the appalling epidemic sweeping the US, this wasn't even my first brush with it. A few days after starting, shopping for oil-drain pans at a parts store in West Virginia – the epidemic's Ground Zero – I overheard a customer freely discussing his son's oxycodone habit with the guy behind the till: 'Don't know how he's still getting his hands on that shit, boy never seems to leave his damn apartment.'

The statistics are shocking beyond belief. In 2016, 42,000 Americans died from opioid overdoses, victims of an epidemic that has so far claimed more than 200,000 lives. Drug overdoses now kill more Americans than cars and guns combined. Indeed, overdose is now the leading cause of death for Americans under fifty.

Most of the more downbeat motels I'd stayed at had a tattered flyer in reception giving details of the local opiate addiction support network, and there were billboards everywhere. The most common featured a steely-looking middle-aged, middle-class woman beside the slogan 'STAND. FIGHT. WIN. TOGETHER WE CAN BEAT PAIN MED ADDICTION.' There were even stickers on police cars, giving the number of an opiate-addiction helpline. And almost every CNN commercial break featured an ad for the Addiction Clinic, in which a pretend doctor in green scrubs delivered grim-faced deadlines: 'A million people have called us already. Don't leave it until you've lost your job or worse.' What a very American circularity: the opioid crisis, a prescription-drug scandal created by criminally cynical pharmaceutical corporations and doctors with dollar signs in their eyes, would now be conquered by fee-hungry private clinics.

The authorities had belatedly woken up to the crisis, yet enough opioids were still being annually prescribed to give each and every American – man, woman and child – a full month's supply. An estimated two million people in the United States now suffer from 'substance use disorders' related to prescription opioid pain relievers. Opiates did seem grimly well suited to the zeitgeist: doomsday drugs, blotting out pain and bleak reality and allowing you to retreat into your own little cocoon. The age of Trump just doesn't lend itself to good-time, yee-hah moonshinin'. McDowell County in West Virginia, now cursed with the highest overdose rate in the US, recorded one of the highest swings to Trump in 2016, and did so with a record turnout.

Beyond that, I'm pointing the finger at the nation's hard-wired consumerism. Americans like buying their way to health and happiness. The TV ads promise a pill for every ill, and if one pill is good, ten must be better. I was flabbergasted by the pharmacy section in the Walmarts I went into to bulk-buy quarts of oil. There would always be an entire aisle devoted to painkillers, many in industrial-sized drums. In England, supermarkets won't let you buy more than thirty-two painkilling tablets at a time. At Walmart I could have bought 1,000 ibuprofen for $12.97. So I did.

I'd have happily stayed all day shooting the breeze with my convoy buddies. In fact, I'd have happily just sat and listened to them take turns reading out some of the more appealing names from the state map that Bill had laid across the table: Tuscaloosa, Alabaster, Eclectic, Loachapoka, Splunge. Social bonding, I had learned, was a firm and instant process with Model Ts. They tapped into some sort of communal folk memory, and seemed to stir up a warming nostalgia for a cheerier, slower, more optimistic age. An age of rose-tinted, apple-pie afternoons at Granddaddy's farm. An age when America had a future, not just a past. And that, I suppose, explains why almost a century since the last one was built, almost 300,000 Model Ts still survive in one form or another.

Collecting old cars was an inherently conservative hobby, indeed literally so, but it shared nothing with the divisive mean-spiritedness of Trumpism. As curious as I always was about their politics, it was very plain that these guys got into their Model Ts to escape from all that crap, exchanging the grim, intractable conflicts of the modern world for a simpler time when everything could be put right with some baling wire and a hose clamp. And so I patted my new, old friends on their hot, damp backs, and watched them walk across the gravel to that wobbly old wooden truck, and the two antique warm-rods beside it. Bill climbed into his open-sided cab, then called out, 'Teeum, I gotta ask you ...' The corners of his mouth eased upwards. 'When are you going to get a damn haircut?'

Alabama was poor – the road out of Tennessee shrivelled and fell apart as soon as I crossed the state line – and I now broached some of its neediest counties. The settlements were scratchy and underpopulated, with plenty of dead grocery stores and gas stations, many of which appeared to have gone under during the last surge in the price of oil: the rusted pump dials were set at $4 a gallon, double what I'd been paying. Those claims-to-fame painted on the water towers grew ever more daft and desperate, stuff along the lines of 'DRY PRONG – BIRTHPLACE OF CARSON FUDGE, ALABAMA'S MR BASKETBALL 2003' or 'VIGILANTE – HOME OF THE RUSTLIN' VARMINTS.' Tina Turner wrote 'Nutbush City Limits' about her childhood home, a declining, unincorporated town a couple of hundred miles north-west of me, and those lyrical snapshots of one-horse, parochial banality sprang from my blistered lips for days, generally in a sun-crazed bellow.

The heat really was daft, and now came accompanied with wilting, claggy humidity. A bag of sink-laundered socks and under-wear steamed for three days on the engine-room floorboards, before I abandoned all decorum and dangled its fetid contents up to dry, wedged in the breeze-catching roof hinges. The mirages that loomed on the road ahead were very often actual patches of shiny, melted tarmac.

And the accents were going all to hell. A guy in a pick-up truck pulled alongside me at a stop light in Russellville, surveyed Mike with deep appreciation, then opened his window and said: 'Compass back you rack-toot and spurs root up cork now, sir.' His young son leaned over and shyly added: 'My daddy misshapen my beard-flag.' I would be doing a lot of wordless, smiley nodding from this point onwards.

One afternoon I drove into Hackleburg ('HOME OF THE PANTHERS, STATE BASEBALL CHAMPS 2007') and was mildly diverted by a vast new factory-like structure that rose incongruously from the cornfields just out of town. I asked the cashier about it when I filled up at the Shell station down the road. 'Randall Jane's whorehouse,' she told me, but I was pretty sure she hadn't meant to, so I persisted. It took a while to decode the whole story, and a lot longer than that for it to sink in. The building was a Wrangler jeans warehouse, built to replace a predecessor that had been destroyed in 2011 by the deadliest tornado in Alabaman history. Seventy-two people lost their lives – nineteen of them in poor little Hackleburg, including an employee at the warehouse. 'Bluejanes fell right out the sky in Courtland,' she said, distantly. 'That's 50 miles from here.' In an appalled moment I understood why I'd been seeing storm shelters – reinforced concrete Nissen huts – in every town I'd passed through, and why that grain elevator I'd driven past an hour before had lain crumpled like a giant beer can at the edge of a roadside field.

A gas station full of bereaved survivors didn't seem a diplomatic forum to satisfy morbid fascination, so I transmitted my sympathies to the cashier, then went straight outside and Googled it on my phone. As I read my jaw steadily lowered. The mile-wide Hackleburg tornado, one of a dozen that ripped across Alabama on 27 April 2011, was clocked at 210mph. Those who heard its approach – 'like a very loud, very low organ note' – dashed into the storm shelter, then watched through its porthole window as cars and hunks of masonry flew through the air outside. In fifteen seconds, 75 per cent of their town was destroyed. Proceeding north-east – the exact route I'd just driven down – the tornado carved a 90-mile gouge in the earth and hoovered up long slices of road. Three million chickens were killed on the region's many poultry farms. Thousands of pine trees were snapped in two and thousands more bent double: their trunks had been twisted around five or six times, pulping the innards to plasticine. People were killed in their homes by flying furniture, then sucked out of windows, their bodies carried to faraway places that were in some instances not located for days. Across the state, 236 people died that day – America's deadliest twenty-four-hour tornado toll since the year after Mike rolled off the Highland Park line. What a haunting juxtaposition with the slow-paced, slow-voiced rolling tedium of southern small-town life. The people of Hackleburg had probably only just got over winning that 2007 baseball championship.

Yet Alabama was once a veritable hotbed of violent death, mostly caused by the deadly game of historical consequences that played out across the southern states in four terrible decades. In central Alabama I drove right over many branches of the Trail of Tears, those death-march expulsions of Native Americans ordained by the authorities in the wake of the 1830 Indian Removal Act. Of the 21,000 Creek Indians forced to walk 700 miles from their Alabaman home territories to Oklahoma, 3,500 died en route. The principal motive? To open the land up for cotton plantations, where in the coming decades more than two million slaves would be put to work in murderous conditions that afforded a life expectancy of twenty-one. And which in turn begat the US Civil War, whose southern killing fields I was now entering. The conflict that ended when Henry Ford was a toddler claimed more American lives than both world wars and Vietnam combined: 4 per cent of the male population was slaughtered, amongst them 30,000 Alabamans.

In apt sympathy, the car was now filled with fire and fury. Just after crossing into Mississippi, I inadvertently established it was possible, via the fickle miracle of Bluetooth, to transmit the live audio content of TV news stations from my phone to my giant radio. This discovery just happened to coincide with perhaps the angriest, shoutiest news week in recent memory. The brief but memorable tenure of Anthony Scaramucci as Trump's press spokesman was a paranoid, ranting *Scarface* interlude that marked the discordant, self-destructive low point of the whole Trump circus thus far. Its absolute nadir was hearing 'the Mooch' reference one of the Trump regime's most unappetising personalities – and by some margin its most repulsive physical specimen – in an image that has been blighting my life ever since: 'I'm not Steve Bannon, I'm not trying to suck my own cock.'

CHAPTER 9

'Recreational hauling only. No commercial vehicles. Speed limit 50. Patchy signal on your phone, it's like a Mooch-free zone, all of your own.' What a tremendous relief to find myself welcomed on to the Natchez Trace Parkway by a sign which said at least most of the above, in a jolly old script font that recalled the credits from an early Hanna-Barbera cartoon. For the thick end of two days I burbled serenely along in a reverie, living the motor-tourist's dream as Henry would have dreamed it. The sky was blue and the breeze delicious, the velvet tarmac beneath me winding its graceful way through dappled forests and over vivid green meadows. Every curve swept, and every gradient was thoughtfully tempered by a cutting or embankment. Some of the bridges were breathtaking, slender concrete ellipses that vaulted valleys in a single dainty leap.

A deer and a chipmunk skipped gaily across the road together. White egrets took lazily to the air. It felt like driving through one of the more dreamily bucolic sequences in *Fantasia*. I didn't even see any roadkill, because there was almost no traffic. Nor, by stern and hallowed decree, was there any commercial intrusion: no gas stations or motels, not even a single snack stall. I stopped at every historic marker and interpretation board, learning that the 'trace' the road followed was left by generations of migrating bison. I unsheathed Slim Jims at picnic tables scattered decorously with pine needles, and relieved myself at rest facilities that seemed to have been spaced apart with a single kind of motorist in mind: quite an old one who drinks a gallon of water a day and drives at 34mph.

Mike was in the form of his life, purring along as smoothly as he ever would, like a so-so sewing machine. The inclines were gentle, and there were no junctions or stop lights or people to flag me down and shout: 'WHAT YEAR?' These felt like free miles. Perhaps Mike just felt at home: as betrayed by the Natchez Trace sticker Bob Kirk had affixed to one of my wind deflectors, this was the first road that I knew for certain he'd driven down before.

The National Parkways are a legacy of Franklin D. Roosevelt's Depression-fighting, federally funded Public Works Agency. From 1933 to 1942, the PWA embarked on an extraordinarily ambitious infrastructure programme, spending $7 billion on the construction of dams, bridges, airports, tunnels, schools, hospitals and homes. But mainly on building 11,428 roads, some of them extremely long ones. The Natchez Trace Parkway – Europeans may like to sit down at this point – runs for a stupendous 444 miles. A brand-new road, longer than the distance from London to Edinburgh, built with public money and purely for public recreation. As I tooled cheerily along I felt my heart soar.

What a bold project, and what a noble intent. Drive the Natchez Trace and you can almost hear America – the America of Henry Ford and FDR – rejoicing in its own good fortune. To be blessed with such a surfeit of space and beauty, and then to summon the public-spirited self-confidence to bring this 444-mile joyride into being. The Natchez Trace picnic areas and side trails were built by some of the three million young men who enrolled in FDR's Civilian Conservation Corps, working like Trojans in exchange for board, lodging and $30 a month – $25 of which they had to send home.

You may not be completely astonished to learn that the National Parkways – there are ten of them, and the Natchez Trace isn't even the longest – are now under threat. The parkways are maintained by the National Park Service, which has lost a third of its workforce since 2002 and is currently burdened with a $12 billion maintenance backlog. One of Trump's first actions on taking office was to slice 15 per cent off the NPS budget. His administration is also keenly exploring the privatisation of many National Park services, so it's a decent bet that the next time I drive down the Natchez Trace those leafy picnic areas will have been replaced by Taco Bells.

If you had to ascribe the National Parkways with a single founding characteristic, it would be sincerity. From planning to realisation, it was such an earnest and well-intentioned project. From FDR to the CCC, everyone involved was inspired by the selfless hope for a better future for each and every American. All my old car guys exuded this sincerity: they were straight-up, genuine folk. In fact, I'm struggling to think of anyone I met who came across otherwise. Yet most of these people, as dictated by the polling data that informed my itinerary, had voted for one of the modern world's most drippingly insincere personalities. Trump failed even the entry-level tests of heartfelt good faith. He only ever sounded like he meant it when he was doing people down or bigging himself up. A few weeks later, arriving in Houston to inspect the catastrophic aftermath of Hurricane Harvey, Trump delivered a tub-thumping address that came across like a campaign speech. 'What a crowd, what a turnout!' he yelled gleefully into the mic, in an address that made absolutely no mention of the death and devastation the city had endured. (Later that day, asked to comment on the inundation that had left hundreds of thousands homeless, he offered this classically Trumpian response: 'Nobody has ever seen this much water. The water has never been seen like this, to this, to the extent. And it's, uh, maybe someday going to disappear.') Why could none of his supporters hear it? It was bewildering beyond words.

I ducked off the Natchez Trace at Jackson. This was the first city I'd driven through since Detroit, and by curious coincidence followed Motown as the metropolitan area with America's second highest black population. After all that parkway velvet, it was painful to readjust to deeply crevassed urban asphalt. The camber was extreme and the potholes depthless; I had repeated cause to thank Henry for the flexible chassis that allowed the top-heavy T to right itself just as it felt set to topple. (A week or so later, rereading the original Mike's life story more attentively, I learned that Ts did in fact tip over all the time, even in cities and at low speed, and that Dib Fewer's Mike had suffered precisely such a fate in the incident that broke Pinky Robinson's arm.)

Downtown traffic was the one environment where the T didn't get a free pass, with indulgent waves replaced by honked irritation. My mood and road manners were not improved by one of those hair-shirted radio exposures to Fox News, an ordeal which always seemed to infect me with shouty over-assertiveness. That night I kicked up a truly unedifying fuss at a nice family-friendly restaurant. 'Yeah, well I *wanted* to order that second glass of wine before the happy-hour deadline,' I heard myself snap at the craven waitress who brought me the bill. 'I suppose it's my fault that you took so long to come over to my table. Tim Moore – I report, you decide.'

I'd come to Jackson – an off-piste, deeply Democratic city – to pop in on an old school friend. Richard Grant is a travel writer, would you believe, albeit one of a much bolder stripe, whose missions have involved Mexican drug barons and previously uncharted African rivers. It was twenty-seven years since we'd last met, and he'd spent nearly all of them in the US; Jackson has been his home long enough for him to say 'Miss'ippi', the preferred local styling. I left the T dribbling hydrocarbons all over a suburban driveway, then knocked on a door, shook a hand, and watched a man who was two inches taller than me attempt to squeeze himself behind a very old steering wheel. 'This is ridiculous,' wheezed Richard, and indeed it was: he looked like a dad wedged in his toddler's Cozy Coupe. What a blessing that my dimensions tallied with the stunted farmers Henry had designed his T to fit: in the last century, American men have grown by an average 2.5 inches.

Richard effortfully extracted himself, then showed me into the cool, well-shaded ranch house he shared with his wife and their young daughter. How deeply I envied that spacious and uncluttered office at the end of Richard's garden, and the age-appropriate diversification he'd masterminded within it, composing thoughtful, prize-winning books on Mississippi's kaleidoscopic culture and history, and erudite features about jaguars and trees for the *Smithsonian Magazine*. 'Struggling to get anything done in the last few weeks, though,' he said, handing me the first decent cup of coffee I'd had since setting off. 'Just too much crazy Trump shit going on.'

We talked about this shit – his neighbour, who kept a collection of colossal military trucks in his yard, was unamazingly a big Trumpite – and then, in what didn't seem a jarring progression, we talked about racism. 'It's pretty ingrained in the south,' said Richard. 'There are people on my Facebook feed who have some dreadful opinions, which freaks out a lot of my British friends.' I was slightly surprised by this, and mentioned that the restaurant I'd shouted in the night before had been conspicuously mixed: black families, white couples, groups of multiracial friends. I hadn't seen that in Detroit (and in fact I wouldn't see it anywhere else). 'Well, racism is pretty ingrained in the north, too, but there's a difference. Up there, white people are happy for black people to have equal economic status and opportunity as long as they don't have to be friends with them. Down south it's the other way round. The saying here is that when a white guy puts his arms round a black guy, it's just another way of holding him down.' Not for the first time or the last, I appreciated what a very different trip I'd be experiencing had I been even a bit less white. Or indeed had I been driving an electric Nissan, with my boyfriend.

Race seems to get entangled in everything that's ever happened down south. The Confederate battle insignia is still incorporated into Mississippi's state flag. Richard asked if I was aware that a number of Native Americans had kept black slaves; I told him I wasn't, and he related the tale of Greenwood LeFlore, a nineteenth-century half-French, half-Choctaw go-getter who straddled both worlds, winding up as chief of the Choctaws and a Mississippi senator, with a parallel career in cotton planting. LeFlore kept 400 black slaves, lived in a huge mansion full of French antiques, and seriously aggravated his tribe by cooperating with their expulsion from the state following the 1830 Indian Removal Act. In consequence, after he died, furious Choctaws exhumed his body and buried it face down in an unknown location.

And we talked about crime. It's what city-dwelling Americans do. Richard's stories were even more awful than my cousin Marshall's. Two months before, a mother had been carjacked in a local gas station by thieves who drove off with her six-year-old son in the rear seat. Nine hours later the police found the abandoned car, and also the boy, dead in the back with a bullet in his head. Then there was the retired jeweller who answered his door to find a gun in his face, and in due course pressed to the back of his neck as he drove the two assailants to the nearest ATM. When they got there, the old man very boldly whipped out a 9mm pistol he'd had hidden under the driver's seat: he shot one attacker dead but missed his fleeing accomplice. The accomplice was arrested the next day after posting a detailed account of his evening on Facebook (a British criminal defence lawyer of my acquaintance says this is much more common than people might believe, on account of the typical miscreant's extremely high stupidity levels). The kicker: both assailants were prison officers.

I had two more proper coffees – all those insipid diner refills still linger miserably in my mind – then took my leave. As we shook hands Richard thoughtfully pointed out that if we allowed the same amount of time to elapse before our next meeting, we would both be eighty when it took place. And with that dread reflection pinging about in my caffeinated brain, I fired Mike up and set off into the thuggish midday heat.

South-west of Jackson, heading towards the Mississippi, I soon broached the dishevelled, depopulated heartlands of the former Plantation Belt. Weeds spread eagerly in from the edge of the road, and the bayous cleaved deep through the orange mud were clogged with last autumn's leaves. There was barely any traffic and the few people about were all black. This was the only part of my route where it had proved impossible to find a red way through: the counties clustered along the lower Mississippi are some of the most deeply Democratic in the US. If you're poor and black and hope for a better future you vote blue. If you're poor and white and pine for a prosperous past you vote Trump.

A gang of stripy-trousered prisoners collecting roadside litter cheerfully mimicked me as I creaked past them, wobbling their hands about on imaginary steering wheels. 'I like it, man!' cried one, showing me several gold teeth. 'That's *clean.*' They didn't seem busy and I wasn't surprised. Even in the scabbiest, most run-down areas I barely saw any rubbish blowing about. That's just not the small-town way. When a rural American opens his car window, you don't need to worry that he's going to throw litter out of it. But you do still need to worry, because he's about to point a shotgun through it and pepper a road sign.

Americans need to be house-proud about litter because they really do produce an awful lot of it: 2.5kg per head per day, more than anyone else on earth. Every motel breakfast ended with a small mountain of plastic and Styrofoam being tipped into the buffet area's giant trash bin: fork, knife, spoon, juice and coffee cups, bowl, plate. Even Italy, where fly-tipping is a national sport, recycles more. The food-waste stats are a particular scandal: the US throws away roughly 50 per cent of its produce, $160 billion-worth every year. Once again Donald Trump leads by example. Nearly everything he eats arrives in a disposable fast-food container, and Air Force One is loaded to the gunwales with little sealed packets of Oreos, pretzels and potato chips, few of which are ever fully consumed as the president will only ever graze from a fresh, unopened package.

In this regard Trump is truly the anti-Ford. Henry despised waste, with a passion that bordered on phobia. At his factories, he had floor shavings processed into formaldehyde and creosote, and used the slag from his steel furnaces to surface roads. Every day, seven tons of garbage from the River Rouge plant was distilled into heating oil and gas. He processed the plant's sewage into soap. In 1930, the *New York Times* said that Ford threw nothing away from his factories, 'not even the smoke'. Everyone sneered at his parsimony back then, but from a twenty-first-century perspective Ford looks very much like an environmental pioneer.

It all derived from a fanatical quest for efficiency, the Model T's defining principle, and an increasing preoccupation for Henry after his company found itself manufacturing Universal Cars by the million. He obsessed over economies of scale and production techniques in the drive to pare down unit costs. 'In one case we found that by using two cents more worth of material in a certain small part we were able to reduce the total cost of it by 40 per cent,' he droned to his long-suffering ghost-writer, Samuel Crowther, in 1925. 'That is, the amount of material under the new method cost about two cents per part more than under the old, but the labour was so much faster that, under the new method, the cost which was formerly $0.2852 was now only $0.1663. On a 10,000-a-day production [this] meant savings of $1,200 a day.' It's said that Henry went right off James Couzens after calculating that his general manager's $150,000 salary added 50¢ to the price of every Model T.

A parallel mania propelled Henry's lust for vertical integration – ever deeper control of the Model T's supply chain. Ford started manufacturing its own windshield glass, roof canvas, artificial leather, wire and batteries. Henry acquired 400,000 acres of Michigan woodland to provide the Model T's timber frame and floorboards, then sold the offcuts to a cousin in the charcoal business (Kingsford briquettes remain the US market leader). In due course Henry would run his own iron mines and coal mines, even his own merchant fleet and a railroad. But he spectacularly over-reached himself trying to make his own tyres. In 1927, Ford acquired a concession for 2.5 million acres of Amazonian rainforest, with the intention of creating a rubber plantation and a fully featured city for the people who would work there. Fordlandia – the scheme reeked of hubris from its name down. Some 10,000 workers dutifully built hospitals, schools, railroads and an airport out in the remote jungle, but the crucial rubber-growing side of things proved an agricultural disaster, and the venture was swiftly abandoned. The incurred losses would have ruined many a business, but not one owned by the ninth richest man in human history.

Presently the world around me was smothered by a heavy green blanket. It was draped over the ruins of old cotton gins and old cotton mansions, over abandoned school buses and houses, over every living thing in sight. Shrouded trees struggled up from stifled meadows; an electricity pylon stood like a mighty green phallus. At length the canopy of shiny leaves leapt over the road, blotting out the sun and trailing tendrils that flicked my windshield. And all because in 1935, somebody decided to tackle soil erosion in the neglected former cotton fields by sending FDR's Civilian Conservation Corps out to plant a few Asian vines. What could possibly go wrong?

Kudzu grows a foot a day and is currently annexing 150,000 acres of southern Mississippi every year. 'The vine that ate the south' has been shown to thrive when treated with most herbicides, and the few that do kill it take ten years to finish the job. The reckless introduction of invasive species was a bit of a thing in the south around that time. In 1938, Edward McIlhenny – son of Tabasco's founding deity – elected on some fathomless impulse to import a few pairs of the hideous dog-sized guinea pigs we call coypu (and the Americans call nutria) from Argentina to his family's Louisiana estate. In one deathless assessment of this whim's aftermath, 'McIlhenny was surprised both by their prolific breeding and the difficulties in confining them to their pens.' As we speak, some twenty million nutria are busily devastating Louisiana's rice fields, sugar fields and coastal vegetation.

It was Bill Robinson who told me to visit the Grand Gulf military park. I found his dented, cigar-shaped reason propped on the lawn outside the park's clapboard museum: a home-made, one-man bootlegger's submarine, powered by a Model T engine. 'Someone found it in the Sixties on an island in the Mississippi,' a curator told me. 'Whoever ran whiskey under the river had hidden it pretty well.'

Henry Ford was always tickled by stories of Model Ts put to weird and wonderful use: it tapped into the vein of rustic inventiveness that had inspired him. But as a hardcore liquor-loather he would have been deeply unamused by this application. Henry railed against the demon drink with such passion and regularity that early Prohibitionists urged him to run as president on a temperance ticket. In 1923, three years after Prohibition became law, a reluctant Ford found himself as the adoring public's favourite for the upcoming presidential election. He eventually gave his endorsement to Calvin Coolidge – on condition that if elected, Coolidge would enforce Prohibition with draconian intensity. Coolidge promised, won, and failed abysmally.

For America's Spider Huffs, Prohibition cast a miserable shadow over the late Model T era; for its Henry Fords, the booze ban promised to bathe the nation in a healthy, golden, God-fearing glow. 'The noble experiment' was actually a rather Trumpy phenomenon, and not just because the Donald – no matter what that reckless, ranting small-hours Twitter habit implies – doesn't drink. The driving force behind Prohibition was the Anti Saloon League, a small-town movement whose alco-phobia slotted into its reactionary hatred of urban growth and the spread of corrupt and ungodly metropolitan culture. The traditional, church-based values that still held Protestant rural America together were a bulwark against all those factories full of immigrants, and those office-ponces with their jazz and straw boaters and cocktails. And because rural America, then as now, held the whip hand, in 1920 the Eighteenth Amendment was abruptly enshrined, proscribing 'the manufacture, sale or transportation of intoxicating liquors within, the importation thereof into, or the exportation thereof from the United States'. Though not, conspicuously, banning consumption – an oversight that heralded a plague of lawlessness which would soon make the temperance movement pine for the wet old days.

Bootlegging got its name in the 1890s, when entrepreneurs smuggled booze into dry Indian reservations by hiding it in their tall boots. Prohibition-era bootleggers operated on a rather grander scale. Detroit's proximity to Canada established alcohol smuggling as the city's second largest industry after car manufacture, employing an estimated 50,000 people. Al Capone is thought to have made $60 million from bootlegging and underground drinking dens; New York's speakeasies paid out an estimated $150 million a year in bribes to city officials and police. Two-thirds of the fifty million gallons of whiskey that were locked up in government warehouses when Prohibition was declared were found to have vanished by its end. The nation's murder rate rose by a third.

Loopholes were eagerly exploited. After doctors found they could prescribe whiskey legally, they did so with abandon, treating ailments from anxiety to influenza and earning $40 million a year in the process. The number of registered pharmacists in New York State would triple during the Prohibition era. Enrolments also soared at churches and synagogues, which had coincidentally been licensed to obtain wine for religious ends. Home brewing was rife, though retailers hawking the raw materials had to cover themselves. Grape growers cleaned up selling 'grape bricks', boxed slabs of dehydrated juice that came with splendid nudge-nudge anti-instructions: '(1) Do not dissolve contents in a gallon jug of water. (2) Do not leave jug in cool cupboard for 21 days.' So successful were these kits that the price of grapes rose by almost 4,000 per cent under Prohibition, and the grape-brick boom begat many of California's best-known wineries. And moonshining thrived, though amateur dabblings came at a price: tainted home-made liquor killed 1,000 Americans every year.

Dib Fewer's dad was a cop, but he still brewed beer in his base-ment, and Dib's mom had sent them on their way with a bottle of bootleg bourbon. The original Mike boys made conspicuous detours into Canada and Mexico, and made no bones about the rationale in their letters home: 'Went into Ontario and bought 4.4 beer at a station (20¢ pint)'; 'You ought to see Tijuana, what a wide-open place. Every store and stand has a bar. Old Judge whiskey, ABC beer.'

It's thought that per-capita booze consumption fell by no more than a third under Prohibition. And the expected upsides largely failed to materialise, crowded out by a welter of unanticipated downsides. Court rooms and jails overflowed with bootleggers and moonshiners, obliging the judicial system to clear its backlog with plea bargains – virtually unknown before then, and one of Prohibition's most prominent legacies. Countless restaurants and theatres went bust as customers deserted them for the mush-rooming speakeasy clubs, at least 50,000 of which sprang up in New York alone. As well as all the redundant brewery and distillery workers, the Depression's endless dole queues were swelled by Prohibition's knock-on effect into the haulage and catering industries.

Most significant of all, the loss of alcohol-related taxes kicked an unexpectedly huge hole in government revenues. New York discovered that almost three-quarters of its state income had been derived from liquor levies. The federal authorities found that a ban they'd paid $300 million to enforce had simultaneously deprived them of an extraordinary $11 billion in tax and duty. A challenge under usual economic conditions, maintaining this state of affairs in the Depression was arrant lunacy, and in 1933 FDR turned the taps back on. But small-town values are never sacrificed without a fight, and a rearguard action played out in the fundamentalist boondocks. Mississippi remained booze-free until 1966. There are still 500 dry counties in the US, largely in the south, and several thousand 'moist counties' with their own bespoke restrictions. A couple of days down the road, I asked for a beer to wash down my enchilada and was asked to fill in a club membership form. And the age of alcoholic consent – at twenty-one, the highest in the world – remains an unsettling obsession. Half the bars I went into had a booze-watch LED calendar on prominent display, showing the birthdate of the youngest legal drinker. Most Americans can buy an assault rifle three years before they can buy a beer.

CHAPTER 10

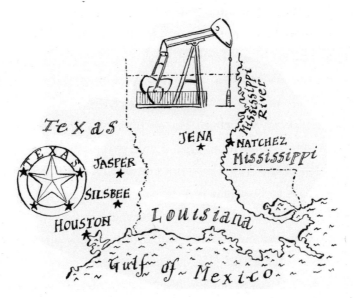

Heat and clouds coagulated into ominous darkness as I approached the Mississippi at Natchez, and by the time Mike got his front wheels on the gangly girder bridge to Louisiana, the oncoming headlights were pushing bow waves of rain before them. I could barely make out the end of my bonnet, let alone the storied waters beneath, which was a shame as it isn't every day you get to see an old man rolling along.

Mike's stifling, porous side curtains went up for what would be the last time: their pointless erection still left me soaked, as it were, as well as suffocated, so to speak. Enclosure really locked in the T's body odour, a challenging pot pourri of petrol, old trousers, old leather, solvents and dust. The smell of hot shed. My nose was put through its paces but my eyes had nothing to process beyond 20 feet of grey smear. All I really saw of Louisiana was the inside of the Burger and Brisket House in Jena.

'Man, you talk just like Doctor Who!' said the girl at the counter after I placed my order. 'What's that thing you folks say?'

She looked at me promptingly.

'Um ... Glass of water? Tickety-boo? Fortnight? Wanker?'

'"Gents." Yeah – that's it. Gents.'

Jena was the capital of LaSalle Parish, previously referenced in my intriguing study of small-town America's polarisation: 86 per cent white and 89 per cent Trump. The dominant local employers were a detention centre for immigrants, a police maintenance depot and a national guard armoury. The dominant local pastime – as it would be for the balance of my journey – was shooting animals. Glass-eyed trophies cluttered the diner walls, interspersed with photographs of extremely young boys posing with rifles beside their first kill. A poster by the door offered local hunters a 'deer processing' service. Louisiana doesn't really have gun laws. An unlicensed vendor can sell you an assault rifle without asking any questions, and you won't need to register it. Anyone can walk into a New Orleans bar with a loaded gun. Unastoundingly, the state has America's highest rate of death by gunfire, twice the national average.

So LaSalle subscribed to the Trump Belt work/play trinity: Huntin', Shootin' & Incarceratin'. All washed down with wristy lashings of Louisiana's liquid fire. As I doused my Cajun dirty rice in hot sauce, a young man on the next table revealed his own troubled relationship with the devil's condiment. 'Man, I used to love that shit. In the army we had these little Tabasco bottles in our meal packs, and one evening my drill sergeant got bored and challenged me to a contest.' A sort of proud wince annexed his features. 'He drank seventeen, I did twenty-one. Kind of lost the taste for it after that.'

I slooshed west on a wide, empty highway cut through the Portuguese pines. So many of these once bustling arteries had succumbed to Route 66 syndrome, their traffic sucked away by the opening of a nearby freeway. Authorised in 1956, the Interstate Highways System evolved into the largest public works project in human history: 47,000 miles of controlled-access freeways, constructed at a cost of $500 billion in today's money. In its way the IHS was as much a symbol of American might as the space program. It's now possible, in accordance with the stated aims of that 1956 declaration, to drive from coast to coast – and from Canadian tip to Mexican toe – without encountering a single stop sign or traffic light.

A quarter of all American vehicle miles are now clocked up on interstates, and an awful lot of native drivers know no other way from A to B. 'You didn't come in on I-10?' asked a nonplussed motelier a few days down the line. 'So how d'you get around the swamp?' The rise of the interstate has probably done as much as anything to kill off motor touring as a leisure activity. Freeways are very good at crushing distance, but crushing distance isn't much fun. Parents no longer bung their kids in the station wagon every summer and hit the open road. So many of those local attractions that depended on this holiday institution – the Wonder Caves, the Dinosaur Canyons, the Funtown Mountains – were now just fading billboards along my route, their passing trade siphoned away by an interstate and a related shift in vacation habits. Family road trips were what your parents went on, or maybe just your grandparents: Americans now expected more glamorous holidays, flying out to the coast or to Vegas, or Mexico, or the Bahamas. Motels that had clearly been built for family road-trippers now announced their struggle for solvency with drifts of leaves in drained swimming pools, pining for responsible, respectable guests who didn't steal the hairdryers and the remote batteries or use the ice bucket as an ashtray. Plenty more – generally one or two in every sizeable settlement – stood boarded up. I invariably had picnic areas to myself, even on the splendid Natchez Trace Parkway, deserted on a beautiful afternoon in the school holidays. It sometimes felt as if I alone was driving the American Dream as it was first dreamed.

I left Louisiana on Highway 8, a little two-lane blacktop that crossed the Sabine River and became Highway 63. 'Drive Friendly – The Texas Way!' read the first sign. The second: 'SPEED LIMIT 75.' Almost at once a truck overtook at lunch-loosening close quarters, demonstrating that this monstrous 'restriction' was open to all. Texas would duly present Mike with his stiffest non-urban traffic challenge.

Crossing state lines meant an instant change in the road surface and a Forrest Gump chocolate-box adventure: you never knew what you were going to get, or get done for. I was welcomed into Ohio by a stern reminder that transporting non-coniferous firewood from Michigan carried a $5,000 fine. Whatever 'jake brakes' might be, using them in West Virginia would have gone down even worse than my 'fake brakes'. Almost every state seemed to have conflicting regulations on the wearing of crash helmets and seat belts. In Texas I could use my cellphone to talk at the wheel but not to text, with neither permitted in a demarcated school zone; in Louisiana, all cellphone use was granted to drivers with at least one year's licensed experience (Massachusetts allows drivers to use phones as long as they keep one hand on the wheel; Florida, splendidly, allows the same 'as long as the sound goes through only one ear'). In Oregon, you can't pump your own gas (unless, as I would discover, the attendant doesn't fancy sticking his hose under your antique seat). State sales taxes are all over the place. So are can and bottle deposits. A packet of cigarettes that costs $5 in Kentucky would set you back $13 in New York. And – hold on to your Pilgrim-father bonnets – twenty-five US states impose no minimum age limit on marriage. In 2001, three ten-year-old girls in Tennessee were married to men aged twenty-four, twenty-five and thirty-one. Across the nation, 985 fourteen-year-olds have pledged their troth in the last two decades.

One night I watched a dramatised documentary about Bonnie and Clyde and was amazed to learn that the FBI couldn't pursue the pair for armed robbery or murder, which weren't covered by federal jurisdiction, and had to wait until they transported a stolen vehicle across a state line, which was. The programme offered an instructive insight into lean and desperate times. When W. D. Jones joined Clyde Barrow's gang on Christmas Eve 1932, he didn't even own a pair of shoes. The local police who tailed them had to supply their own weapons, pinging small-calibre revolvers at a gang that had relieved a military depot of several enormous machine guns. Small wonder that two-thirds of US murders went unsolved in the era, as did 90 per cent of all serious crime. County police even had to provide their own cars, quite often Model Ts that were embarrassingly outrun by Barrow's half-inched Ford V8s.

of barns and elevators; I barely saw the Stars and Stripes. When I opened my mouth people said, 'Well, you sure ain't from Texas,' a styling conspicuously absent from encounters in other states. The tropical colours of the south – those purple crepe myrtles and bright red cardinal birds – gave way first to dense, green forest, then the sandy-soiled scrub that is the default Texan landscape. The sun came out and didn't go away. Everything seemed bigger and more open. I very often found myself without a phone signal.

Texas had been Mike's home for at least the last half-century, and I awoke in Jasper – a beat-up hunting town in the Deep East woods – to find an exciting related mission flashing on my phone. Antony, an MTFCA member from southern Houston, had sent a message letting me know that Bob Kirk, Mike's ninety-three-year-old previous owner and a fellow Houstonite, was keen to meet up. I redrafted my route accordingly, and gave Antony a rough ETA that allowed for breakdowns and another kind of service: it was Sunday, and I was heading into the Bible Belt's last holes. Michael, take me to church.

It seems fair to assume that almost every single one of those fifteen million Model Ts would have been driven to church at some point, and most on a weekly basis. Churchgoing, like the T, was a predominantly rural institution. And so it remains. Since the 1970s, the proportion of Americans who go to church every week has dropped steadily in the coastal cities but increased in most flyover states. Weekly attendance at Alabama's churches alone is now twice that mustered by the Church of England across the entire UK. More than half of Texans go to church at least once a week. Across the Bible Belt, regular worshippers pay a tithe to their church that typically totals 10 per cent of earnings: in 2016, US churches received a remarkable $123 billion in donations. Pertinently, a detailed analysis of recent presidential contests has shown that frequency of church attendance is now the strongest demographic predictor of voting behaviour, much more so than income or age, and rivalled only by race.

Until around 1980, nobody spoke about 'the Christian right'. As late as 2008, three-quarters of the Republican party's presidential candidates proclaimed a belief in evolution; by 2012 it was a third, and last time around Jeb Bush was the only non-creationist out of sixteen Republican runners (and even that came with an asterisk: 'Yeah, but I don't think evolution should actually be part of the school curriculum, to be honest with you.').

Donald Trump has offered few convincing suggestions that he truly believes in any power higher than himself, and let forth an especially muddy torrent of Trumpism when asked to volunteer his favourite passage of scripture: 'Well, I think many. I mean, you know, when we get into the Bible, I think many. So many. And some people – look, an eye for an eye, you can almost say that. That's not a particularly nice thing. But you know, if you look at what's happening to our country, I mean, when you see what's going on with our country, how people are taking advantage of us, and how they scoff at us and laugh at us.' The interviewer chose not to point out that 'an eye for an eye' only appears in the Bible as a course of action specifically repudiated by Jesus in his 'turn the other cheek' riff. Seventy per cent of Americans believe in God, but Trump just didn't convince as one of their number. It was certainly difficult to imagine him saying what I heard his chief of staff, Reince Preibus, say after he'd been ousted during the Scaramucci debacle: 'God is good and everything works to good in the end. I believe that. I live for God, my family, my kids, and I know everything is going to be just fine.'

But Trump's dubious faith – not to mention his studiously unchristian egomania and pussy-grabbing pastimes – seemed almost irrelevant to the evangelical right. All those dark doubts were bleached out by the hopes and values they projected on to him with blinding intensity. 'Millions of Americans', declared Robert Jeffress, a Texan tele-evangelist whose programme is broadcast on 1,200 Christian TV channels across the US, 'believe the election of President Trump represented God giving us another chance – perhaps our last chance to truly make America great again.' Electing Trump was another act of faith, and one that must have come pretty easily to the church-going millions who had already put their trust in God, guts and guns.

And so I headed south on the super-heated US-96, assessing my ecclesiastical options via the message boards posted outside every church. 'ETERNITY – IT'S YOUR DECISION' – hmm, bit heavy for a Sunday morning. 'SEVEN DAYS WITHOUT PRAYER MAKES ONE WEAK.' Too cheesy. 'TOO HOT TO KEEP CHANGING SIGN.. SIN BAD, JESUS GOOD, DETAILS INSIDE.' Now that I liked. But there weren't any cars in the lot behind it, so I was either too early or too late.

What I really wanted was a Pentecostal service, which Richard Grant had recommended for the full-fat experience. Pentecostalists spoke in tongues and laid on hands. Some of their pastors handled rattlesnakes to prove their faith, and more than one had died after being bitten and opting to leave the outcome in the hands of the Lord. On the outskirts of Silsbee, I passed the First Pentecostal Church, a large, brown building of recent construction, with a lofty pitched roof and a packed car park. The sign outside didn't pull any funnies, but it did name the resident preacher as Pastor Homer Looper. That would definitely do. I swung Mike round and pulled in.

You can never make a surreptitious entrance in a 1924 Model T, and by the time I'd installed myself in the very back pew, most of the 150-odd worshippers – very smart, very white – had come up to welcome me. Word seemed to travel back through the ranks of pale grey suits and crisp, demure dresses, so that the last ones who held out their hands were very fully informed.

''Preciate you stoppin' by in your antique vee-hickle, Mr Moore.'

'Now, I ain't ever been to London, but I would be mighty tickled if you wrote your address down here. Visited Aberdeen one time, though. You happen to know Ann and Steve McCarthy?'

'That's a beautiful Model T, Mr Moore. God bless you. Now we get noisy sometimes, but don't be alarmed.'

Nobody else needed a haircut or had a T-shirt with pink cats on. I doubt too many were silently urging themselves not to blaspheme either.

A Hammond organ whirled and began to swell, then a ten-piece band and a gospel choir kicked in. Homer Looper was a personable and mellow character who didn't seem the snake-charming type at all, but when he picked up the mic and held restrainedly forth about glory and grace and God's salvation, a number of middle-aged men and women rose erratically from their seats and began to sway, eyes closed, arms aloft, pulling guitar-solo gurns. Prayers were said on behalf of an ancient and very frail parishioner who was pushed up to the altar in a wheelchair and at once engulfed by worshippers. Somebody called out to give Sister McDaniel a touch from heaven, and I supposed that deep in that ruck of bodies, hands were laid on. Then she was wheeled away.

'My, it's good to be in church,' said Homer, beaming, and the tubby family in front of me all warmly embraced each other. 'I'm so happy I've been converted, that I've been down to the water.' I looked about and saw big, lazy smiles smeared across every face, arms clasping shoulders, everyone acting the way I only ever do after five pints. These people hadn't turned up as an automatic act of duty. They were here because they *believed*. It was all a very long way from the mist-breathed Eleanor Rigby muttering that defines the British churchgoing experience.

'I'm so happy to hear we've got a brother all the way from the UK with us today.' A hundred and fifty faces turned towards mine, and with a wan smile I noted that Homer had given way to a younger preacher, a more intense chap wearing the suit and glasses Kevin Costner wore in *JFK*.

'And that's interesting, because I got up early this morning and was praying and talking with the Lord before I had my sausage biscuit, and I heard something from Him, I heard there would be somebody here for me today. A-MEN!'

I did my best to croak along with the amens that chorused stridently out around me for the next half-hour. The young pastor steadily ramped up the tremulous, soaring intensity of his words, periodically muting them to a dramatic whisper, all the while concentrating his focus on that malleable sceptic the Lord had promised him over breakfast.

'JESUS-uh, I do LOVE him-uh. I'm preaching to somebody here today-uh that doesn't have the holy ghost-uh. Somebody who needs a helping hand with their family, their marriage, hallelujah, in their home, in their body, because they're in the right place, there's peace here ["YES, SIR! A-MEN!"], peace of mind, peace of soul, salvation, LIFE ETERNAL!'

A shaft of multicoloured sun speared dramatically in through the garish stained glass beside me. For a moment I was caught in two minds. Sneak out the back or jump to my feet, cheeks wet with tears, and beg to be taken down to the water.

'We all hear these people asking why do I need Jesus-uh, I'm a pretty good person, I don't steal, I never killed anyone, I only drink sometimes, I only smoke dope at the weekends, I'm not that bad, I gave a five-dollar bill to that bum at the stop light. Let's hear from Timothy! What does Timothy have to say?'

My eyes widened. What did Timothy have to say? Before I had a chance to put him straight about the stop-light charity, and if we're going lifetime full-disclosure the theft, he opened a bible.

'First Timothy chapter 2, who desires all men to be saved and to come to the knowledge of the truth he will allow all men to be saved, willing that none shall perish-uh. I am not sufficient, I am not adequate. There is nothing God hates more than feeding man's arrogance. Everyone that is proud at heart is an abomination to the Lord, HE SHALL NOT BE UNPUNISHED-UH!'

Then the organ swirled and everyone chorally exulted in the name of Jesus-uh and suddenly the young pastor was right at my side, sweating freely, offering a hot embrace. I leaned woodenly in and he began to murmur urgently into my ear about the Lord, the details lost in the hubbub of exiting worshippers. 'Um, congratulations,' I said when he released me. 'That was, you know, quite a performance.' Then I considered these words, and blurted: 'Obviously I don't mean to, ha-ha, feed anyone's arrogance. Definitely not yours. Christ no. I mean, not Christ like that, but the actual Lord Jesus. Amen.'

The pastor's damp brow furrowed; I clapped him briskly on the side of the arm and scooted out to the car park. 'Coast to coast, huh?' called an elderly Pentecostalist, opening the door of his Buick as I jabbed the T's starter. 'Hot as heck and dry as a powder-house out west; you better take an up and a right or you gonna *die*!'

I would hate to accuse Silsbee's hospitable Pentecostalists of casting a wrathful curse upon me, especially as their church sent a very sweet postcard to my home which my wife read out over the phone a week later. Nonetheless, my soul began to sweat a little that day. An hour down the road I somehow endeavoured to inhale a mouthful of chilli vinegar from my lunchtime Hot Head pickled sausage, and pulled messily on to the verge, gasping and blind with tears. Shortly afterwards my winged motometer acquired a strange tilt, which became a lot stranger after I clattered over a cattle grid. The entire radiator neck had snapped off; I wedged it vaguely into place with strips of cardboard, crossed my fingers, and praised the good Ford that a Model T could always limp on after mishaps that would stop most cars in their tracks.

Then, with Houston's forest of silvered chimneys taking shape on the hazy blue horizon, Antony called: poor Bob Kirk had been rushed to hospital with a chest infection. Happily he later recovered, but by then I was far, far away. So I never did get to meet the man who was as old as the T he had owned for fifty-one years, one of the last living links with the age of Henry Ford and his Universal Car.

Houston offered some solace: I sold it to myself as another living link, wellspring of the oil boom that powered the Model T boom. At the dawn of the auto age, petroleum was an obscure commodity that you typically had to order from a chemist – motorists tended to run their cars on cleaning fluid, which was both cheaper and more readily available. The cost and scarcity of fuel was such a serious issue that for a while the internal combustion engine seemed likely to lose out to the electric motor. All that changed on 10 January 1901, when a surveying team at Spindletop, in south-east Texas, broke through a 1,000-foot-deep salt dome, unleashing a gusher that blew thirty-six million gallons of oil 150 feet into the air before it was brought under control. Spindletop was the first of a series of vast Texan discoveries that would see the oil price plummet to 3¢ a barrel, cheaper than water in some areas.

In short order the fortunes of a dusty ranching state were utterly transformed: by 1940, the GDP of Texas had increased by 24,000 per cent. The state rode out the Depression, and still prospers, courtesy of a hundred-year oil boom that doesn't know when to quit. Every time it seems US oil production has peaked, some lucrative but contentious reserves come to light – Alaska, offshore fields in the Gulf of Mexico, the frack-fest shale sands. Almost half of America's oil still makes its way down to Houston, the world's largest petrochemical cluster, where 100,000 Texans refine it and store it and hose it into tankers. An astonishing panorama opened out as I crossed Burnet Bay on a little ferry, every shoreline cluttered with gleaming flare stacks and cranes and gantries and pylons that marched right across the water. For an hour thereafter I puttered through a petrochemical dystopia, the T dwarfed by hissing, rumbling, chrome-plated Pompidou Centres that filled the air with an eye-stinging miasma of solvents, eggs and burning rubber. Crossing over an interstate I gazed out at the smog-rimed Gulf of Mexico, my journey's southernmost tip and an unantici-pated sea between the seas, and thought: Wherever I eat tonight, hold the shrimp.

The *Guardian* recently declared Houston 'one of the last places you can live the American Dream', which in native terms just means it's getting bigger and richer. The shale-oil boom has pushed the population of Greater Houston up by a third since 2000: it now stands at 6.3 million, larger than half the countries on earth. I drove for long and harrowing hours up US-6, the second outer-most of Houston's four ring roads, an eight-lane, 90-mile strip mall whose every last gap was being busily filled in by men in yellow hard hats. After all that decay and dereliction this was a realm where everything turned to gold, no matter whether it deserved to or not (exhibit A, above a packed car lot: 'SMOKES, LINGERIE, NOVELTIES – YOUR ONE-STOP SHOP').

Even at 8 p.m. on a Sunday the traffic was relentless, jockeying about, cutting me up, weaving right alongside for a suicidal selfie. I ploughed on, rigid and vacant, shooting helplessly through a good half-dozen freshly red lights at the kind of intersections that really didn't lend themselves to such behaviour. The light began to fail and I still only had one headlamp. Prosperous, bustling, big-town America is no place for a Model T.

'That your car?'

It was gone eleven and I'd stepped out of my motel room for the now traditional driver's-seat night-cap: Mike was parked directly outside the door. This wasn't the seediest place I'd stayed at, but it was by a long chalk the sleaziest. After flumping on to my bed I'd opened my eyes to find my reflection staring down at me from a huge ceiling mirror.

My questioner was a middle-aged black guy with very red eyes and the smouldering stub of a cigar in his teeth, leaning back against the door next to mine. I nodded; he pincered the cigar out of his mouth and spat emphatically into the gutter before us.

'You a millionaire?'

I supplied the answer and he spat again.

'Well, you might wanna put a tarp over that shit in the back, this ain't a real good area.'

This sentence, delivered as a continuous wayward sound, made me aware that my companion was extremely drunk. If it had taken a while to realise, that's because I was too. All I'd found to eat in the gas station across the street was a long-life cream-cheese crois-sant, so colossally repulsive that I'd only managed two bites. But that didn't seem to matter now, and nor did anything else, because I had also purchased and fully ingested a can of Lime-a-Rita. I say can but it was more of an aluminium pillar box: 25 fluid ounces of 8 per cent citric-flavoured malt beverage that had really done the job on an empty stomach and a weary soul, hitting the spot so hard it went completely out of focus. An alfresco tooth-mug of bourbon seemed the obvious sequel.

'So izzat your car, then?'

I flicked a matey finger towards the ostentatious vehicle parked beside mine, a very shiny, low-slung white saloon with black glass and the most extraordinary wheels: long chrome spikes jutted a good ten inches out from the hubs, in the fashion of a *Ben-Hur* chariot. It was the most compelling car-lot double-act Mike would star in, an era-spanning display of the Texan showmanship that had inspired Bob Kirk to paint Mike's wheels purple.

His derisive snort segued into another extravagant expector-ation. 'Not mine, man. Them wheels are swangers, they're *nasty*. Cost you 'bout two or three grand a set. You ride on swangers, you better be strapped.'

I took a sip of bourbon and gazed placidly into the warm breeze. The crown of a palm tree rustled gently above the reception office; each of the streetlamps around it sported a fuzzy halo of flying insects.

'You better be what?' I drawled at length.

'You better have a gun. Guy I know got shot for a set of swangers.'

A rather bigger sip seemed in order.

'Now I don't know who owns that car, man, but I can tell you he sells drugs. Betchoo he's got a TV in the back to watch butt-naked movies. Those guys will fuck you up. That's Houston, man. That shit is just the way it is.'

I waited for him to spit into the gutter, which he did with immense feeling, twice. Then I nodded wearily, in attempted emulation of a man who knew all about that shit, maybe too much, who if anything was pretty bored with it being the way it was. As casually as I could, which was much less casually than I hoped, I drained my tooth mug and set about transferring Mike's waist-deep rear-seat accumulation of tools and spares and quarts of oil into my room. On the final and noisiest trip – in one spec-tacular action I dropped the oil-drain pan and punted it straight in through the door – my companion took a step forward.

'Hey,' he said, his voice low and suddenly sober, 'you gotta woman in there witchoo?'

I slept like a baby. A baby with third-degree nappy rash and five teeth coming through.

From Houston I struck out north by north-west, away from the swangers and palms and into Texas proper: a lonesome, prone land-scape of ranches, corn and cotton, the horizons steadily stripped of trees and pulled taut, distant pick-up trucks trailing plumes of dust across a flatness sparsely studded with grain elevators and nodding-dog oil derricks. This would be my default backdrop for a thousand miles, along with those blurts of yee-hah Texan exuber-ance that sporadically enlivened it. A 12-foot revolver erected barrel-up in a front yard; the gates to the Deep Shit Cattle Company; a state-wide anti-litter campaign sloganed 'DON'T MESS WITH TEXAS!' Texan motorists had a habit of honking their appreciation as they overtook me, but because they generally did so at around 90mph I often felt a few internal organs change place.

'What have YOU done for your marriage today? NOW is a great time to do something EPIC.' I will never know what inspired a rural

Texan to paint these words on a billboard, and erect it in their front yard. Nor can I explain why my wife phoned about a minute after I'd passed by it, to say she was planning to fly out and join me for a few days, in a fortnight's time. It took her a while to transmit this proposal: I'd pulled over to take the call, but my ears still rang with the echo of all those accumulated roars and creaks and grinds. 'No, a fortnight. Can you hear me? Two weeks. TWO WEEKS. Hello? Hello?' My deafened plight offered its own compelling testimony of just what my wife was letting herself in for. But in two weeks I'd be approaching my journey's bleakest, loneliest ordeal, up in the wind-torn badlands of Montana, and the last thing I wanted was to put her off. 'It's a terrible line,' I said. Then, as I'd already started lying, I added: 'Seriously, it'll be fantastic. You won't regret it.'

College Station, halfway between Houston and Waco, was another Texan boom town, this time built around its eponymous attachment to the ever-swelling Texas A&M University. The enormous stadium that dominates its centre is apparently the fifth largest sports arena on earth, fitted with a 163-foot video screen as part of a recent billion-dollar refit. Every year, it hosts precisely six games of college football. The scale and economics of the US college system are difficult to grapple with. Texas A&M, which I'm afraid I'd never heard of, educates 68,600 students, each of them paying an average $27,200 a year for the privilege.

On the town's arid outskirts, I pulled up by vague appointment in front of a great big metal shed with 'FORD – THE UNIVERSAL CAR' emblazoned across its lofty gable. A distantly familiar figure rolled out from under a pick-up, stood up and greeted me with distantly familiar badinage. 'Bloody hell, not you again. Never expected you'd make it this far.'

I would spend two days with Ross Lilleker, sleeping in a trailer pitched halfway between his vast workshop and the house he shared with his wife Jennifer and their two extremely sweet young daughters. Their sprawling property was bestrewn with animals – chickens, dogs, cats, a sullen donkey – and shipping containers full of Model Ts in various states of repair. It was an environment that almost demanded idle pottering, an activity to which Ross seemed constitutionally allergic. He was up at 5.15 a.m. every morning, and long after flicking off my trailer's bedside light I could still hear him restlessly out and about, feeding livestock and banging away at old metal. 'I can sleep when I'm dead,' he told me.

I did my best to keep up, filling the days watching Ross re-solder the radiator neck and fix my broken headlamp, failing to befriend his donkey, and shooting stuff. He was most insistent on this latter activity. 'I'm the only man I know who doesn't own a gun, but they're such a big part of life down here. I'd say 70 per cent of the locals have one on them at all times.' A customer had recently offered a barter deal for a Model T engine rebuild: 'He led me out to his car, and there was a belt-fed machine-gun on the back seat.' Ross rolled his eyes. 'But, you know, I can get my hand on a gun when I need one. Had a black Labrador, lovely dog, but he was old and got sick with a tumour. The wife asked what we were going to do for him, and I said, "What d'you mean? We're going to shoot him."' On the face of it, Ross made an unlikely Texan, but his blunt Derbyshire banter seemed a decent fit with the regional mentality.

The Champion Firearms Indoor Shooting Range sat at the edge of a shopping mall, in a long beige building shared with a cell-phone store and a Starbucks. I walked through its doors with an air of sombre disapproval, the face of a pinko Yurpean federalist appalled by this gung-ho firearms free-for-all. The range's shop was flogging AK47s for $495, and a Barbie-pink .22 'My Little Rifle' for a lot less.

I flashed my driving licence and the range cashier tossed us some ear protectors and school-lab glasses, then waved an airy hand across a shelf stacked with pick-and-mix handguns: 'So whaddya wanna shoot, guys?' I tutted gravely as Ross made our selection. Forty deafening minutes later, I shuffled stiffly out into the sun with adrenalin drooling from the corners of a rictus grin.

'Every Texan thinks he's a crack shot,' Ross had said as he loaded up our introductory weapon, a 9mm pistol. 'But they're all full of shit. I was brought up on Friday-night punch-ups in Chesterfield, and I reckon I could land a good English smack in the mouth on any idiot with a gun before they got an accurate round off.' I nodded without paying much attention, already hopelessly in thrall to the macho theatrics: the little boxes of gleaming ammo, the deft click of rounds being slotted into the cartridge, the deeply satisfying whack as it slammed home. And above all, that dead-weight heft of the gun in your hand, and the shock-and-awe tumult that raged out when you let the distant paper target have it, from whip-crack sonic boom to the delicate tinkle of spent cartridge on concrete. Ross notched up bullseye after bullseye – 'Not bad for a bloke with one eye,' he said after scoring three in a row – but I barely cared where the bullets went. BANG-BANG-BANG! Fire came out of the barrel and everything.

'Just keep the guns pointed down range, guys,' said the cashier, marching in to interrupt the intemperate, whooping aftermath of my final salvo with an Eastwood-grade Magnum, evidently witnessed on his CCTV monitor. 'Not cool to wave loaded weapons about.' It was, though, which may have been the problem.

Yet this was merely a ballistic warm-up for the die-hard, full-bore main event. Half an hour later we were parked up by a warehouse-sized workshop out in the sticks. 'GUNS ARE WELCOME ON PREMISES,' read the largest of the many signs neatly affixed to the shop's stout steel doors. I politely scanned the others while Ross rapped his knuckles on the metal. 'DUE TO INCREASE IN PRICE OF AMMO, DO NOT EXPECT WARNING SHOT'; 'HEAVILY ARMED – EASILY PISSED'; 'HIPPIES – USE BACK DOOR. NO EXCEPTIONS.'

The door clanked ajar and we were met by a man with a thin silver moustache, metal-framed glasses and a blue T-shirt pulled taut over a round belly. Mark was a machinist who bored out, skimmed down and reground large pieces of car for Ross and others, using the lathes and drills lined up in the workshop shadows around us. But he was also a doomsday-ready firearm fanatic with a number of deep-seated grudges that trickled from his lips as we followed him through the heavy-metal gloom. 'Mike Pence can kiss my ass … Hillary, let's not go there … College Station city council … That royal family of yours.' Ross had pre-warned me about this one, and its improbable chief focus. 'Don't get me started on Camilla,' muttered Mark as he led us through an office littered with double-take still-lifes. A sheaf of invoices paper-weighted with a desert-camouflaged assault rifle. An open flight-case on top of the printer, home to four Magnums neatly ensconced in foam cut-outs. A desk tidy with compartments full of paperclips, ballpoint pens and shotgun cartridges.

*

'Never counted, guess three hundred or so.'

We were in Mark's inner sanctum, a survivalist chamber secreted behind the office, and I'd asked him how many guns he owned. It seemed a conservative estimate. In the corridor that led to this windowless bunker we'd squeezed past an array of wardrobe-sized gun safes; Mark had opened one and I saw it stacked with at least thirty rifles, below a top shelf laden with sidearms and ammo. There were another two safes here in the sanctum, along with a bed, a petrol generator, a chest freezer, a microwave and boxes and boxes of bottled water, dried food and cookies. There was also a pool table, which would give Mark something to do in the post-apocalypse – something other than killing people, which he evidently expected to do a lot of, and at short notice. A rack on the wall above the bed was home to three assault rifles and a cavalry sword. Two crossbows lay ready on a chair.

I was already a bit too scared to ask Mark questions he might find over-stimulating: how he felt about Donald Trump, what on earth Prince Charles's second wife could possibly have done to incur the wrath of a Texan lathe operator, and above all any investigation of scenarios that might lead to him taking his last stand here. And that was before he opened the gun safe and effortfully extracted the largest firearm I ever hope to see in paranoid private hands. 'When those SWAT teams come,' he grunted, propping the stock of a 5-foot black-and-tan machine gun on the concrete floor, 'I'll pull up the shop doors, and they'll see my bad-ass Browning and turn tail.' His jaw tightened as he stood beside that outrageous weapon, pike bearer in a one-man army. Then he looked at me over the top of his glasses. 'Now that I've shown you this place, I will have to kill you.'

Mark's shooting range was an expanse of browned pasture behind his workshop. We went out and took turns with an Army-issue M4 assault rifle, slamming shoulder-punching rounds into a stack of railway sleepers and water-cooler bottles. Conflicting emotions coursed through me: this ranked amongst the manliest experiences of my recent life, and the most childish. Then Mark lugged out his monstrous Browning, set its bipod support feet on a camping table and sat down on a swivel office chair behind it. It was quite the incongruous spectacle.

'There's been jets shot down with these,' he said, feeding a bullet the size of a frankfurter into its chamber. 'Got a five-mile range, and will go straight through half-inch steel plate.' We all pulled ear protectors on and Ross and I retreated a good 10 feet back. Mark tilted his head, eased his right eye towards the telescopic sight and unleashed hell. The ground trembled beneath my feet, splinters of railway sleeper flew high into the air and I blasphemed severally and at immense volume. It was all I could do not to leap into Ross's arms like Scooby Doo into Shaggy's.

'I don't know if you can appreciate this,' said Mark, casually plucking off his ear protectors and easing himself back in his typist's chair, 'but firing that is a lot like being punched in the nose.' He took off his glasses, briskly rubbed his face with both hands, then swivelled round to face us. 'Who's next?'

'Too much gun for me,' said Ross. I conveyed my own reluctance through a ridiculous bleating giggle. Then a distant rattle grew into a hefty clatter and a freight train trundled slowly across the end of Mark's property, passing directly behind his target-stack at a range of perhaps 150 yards. As an infringement of the most basic protocols of health and safety this demanded explanation, and when the train had disappeared from view Mark stood up, frowned pensively, and said, 'What's real fun to do is find something you can blow up. I got twenty-one acres out in the country and a *lot* of tannerite explosive.'

On the drive back, Ross told me that Mark and a lot of other people he knew had begun to stockpile serious weaponry in the aftermath of Barack Obama's reaction to the Sandy Hook massacre, an especially dreadful mass shooting which cost twenty six-year-old schoolchildren their lives. 'When he said there was no need for anyone outside the military to own an assault weapon, a lot of guys took that to mean: "The government is coming to take all my guns away."' There it was again, that blind, deaf hatred of federal authority, the same pioneer-pattern phobia that underpinned the Trump phenomenon. In a curious conflation of constitutional amendments, gun ownership had evolved into a currency of individual freedom: the more guns you had, and the bigger they were and the faster they shot, the freer you became.

'Guys like Mark, he's doing pretty well, no money worries or whatnot, but you're just hoping their lives don't take a bad turn.' I struggled to keep my imagination in check as we drove on in silence. 'That enough shooting for you, then?' asked Ross after a while. ''Cos if it ain't, I know a guy who'll take you up in a chopper with an AK47 and fly over a herd of wild pigs.'

Mike seemed reinvigorated by his halfway service, and for my part I drove away from Lilleker Antique Restorations almost dangerously enthused by a surfeit of human kindness, ballistic bravado and deadpan English snark. We raced a three-loco Santa Fe goods train to Temple, where I did boisterous battle with a cockroach in the door seal of my motel fridge. I hit 48mph sweeping through the largest military base on earth, Fort Hood, 215,000 acres of huge beige sheds and huge beige vehicles – sand is now the standard backdrop for America's military might. And mile by noisy, north-west mile I found myself easing away from swelling, wealthy Texas into shrivelled old clapboard towns on the slide, past boarded-up laundromats and dry goods stores strung out along yawning, empty main streets, places that once had oil or cotton but now had little left but a name that conjured their glory days: Gunsight, Rising Star, Energy. Rich Texans vote Republican. Poor Texans vote Trump. Inching towards the northern panhandle, I was headed into my electoral map's very reddest blots.

Breakfast is the only meal small-town Americans get excited about, a communal institution for local old-timers. It's the only meal I got excited about too, because a US breakfast is really a million meals in one, a groaning, greasy smorgasbord of enticing fried options. Five types of toast, eggs a hundred ways, potatoes any style, bacon, bacon, bacon. You can't go wrong. Actually you can. Never, ever have biscuits and gravy, unless this seems like a tempting three-step start to the day: (1) Moisten two scones. (2) Stir one cup of meat gravel into one cup of magnolia emulsion. (3) Combine, serve, tip into bin.

Richard Grant had advised me that even if the only restaurant left in town was a McDonald's, the boys would still meet up there for an early McMuffin. He wasn't wrong. One morning I stopped in Breckenridge, an old oil town with a few rusty derricks about, a drive-thru 'Beverage Barn' and a scattering of used needles in the Walmart car-park undergrowth. The Breckenridge Maccy D's was decorated with framed photos of that Mike-period black-gold boom: ranks of derricks and clapboard hotels, earthen streets messily log-jammed with Model Ts and their owners, men in shirtsleeves and straw hats, staring into the camera with hands on hips. A caption told me that in 1920, the town's population rose from 1,500 to 30,000 (it's now 5,700). Fox News was playing on a wall-mounted telly, and a dozen seventy-somethings were gathered beneath it: ironed polo shirts, trucker caps, a couple of Stetsons and a lot of neatly marshalled moustaches. These elderly breakfast buddies invariably seemed in fine fettle: most were pretty trim, and none of them nipped outside for a smoke. It took me a few weeks to realise that their podgy, puffing friends were all long dead.

'That your T? Fine little outfit.'

Mike always gave me an in.

'So, ah, what do you boys think about your new president?' These studiously non-judgemental words would do me yeoman service in the deep-red Trump Belt. (Breckenridge is the largest town in Stephens County, where the Democrats had attracted just 10 per cent of the votes – comfortably their worst ever result.) The discourse that followed set a durable template: for a good ten minutes, my grey-'tached companions took turns to denigrate Trump's predecessor and his election rival in the most vitriolic and often flatly deluded terms, without ever once mentioning the man himself by name.

'He's a whole lot better than the last one. That man Bay-Rack Obama put us thirty trillion dollars in debt, and he was gonna steal our guns! Woulda been a war down here if he'd tried to take even one pistol.'

'I think he's a Muslim. I really do.'

'I *know* he's a Muslim.'

'Hillary Clinton, she's just a crook, plain and simple. She's lied, she's cheated, she's corrupt.'

The subtext: Trump might not be a great president, maybe not even a good one, but come on – what choice did we have? I never really did find out why Hillary Clinton was quite so universally reviled. I've no doubt that for a certain slice of the electorate, a female president would have seemed like the last straw after eight years of a black one. But even the handful of Democrats I met couldn't muster a good word for her. I suppose she represented the establishment that so many people on all sides seemed desperate to reject.

'How long you taking on this drive?'

I flipped my half-drunk cardboard cup of Ronald McPisswater into the bin by the door and turned to face a weather-beaten chap in a lilac checked shirt and a bright yellow cap. A lot of these old dudes really went balls-out with their colour combos, possibly in reaction to the ever-beiger landscape. I told him I had just under two months before my visa ran out.

'Nah, they'll let you stay,' he said, with a cheerily dismissive sweep of the hand. 'You're one of the good ones.'

This was the same man who a minute earlier had told me that 'Obama blackened America's name.' In fact, he'd said it twice, to make sure I got the point.

'That's what you think,' I replied, and walked out into the blinding sun.

Henry Ford, as I've said, was a more racially tolerant employer than most. He paid blacks and whites equally. It was not unknown at Ford for black foremen to take charge of an all-white crew. In 1939, when Ford was no longer the dominant force in Motown, the firm still employed two-thirds of Detroit's black car workers. But all these apparently heartening initiatives in equal opportunity – Ford was also unusually keen to offer jobs to ex-convicts and the disabled – were founded on a dismaying principle.

'I could not do the same thing day in and day out,' he wrote. 'But we have to recognise the unevenness in mental equipment. To other minds, perhaps the majority, repetitive operations hold no terrors.' The Highland Park assembly line was intended as a death blow for skilled industrial labour, a workplace fit for even the most brainless prole. Even the blind. Even the black, because

Ford was at best a benign racist, who believed white people were duty-bound 'to give philanthropic service to subordinate races'. Of course there was a lot of it around back then, and still is. When MTV started in the 1980s, they were too scared to play Michael Jackson for fear of upsetting the Midwest. A recent survey found that white patients are twice as likely to receive pain medication as black patients with the same symptoms (which may partly explain why opioid addiction is an overwhelmingly white problem). Some 45 per cent of Trump supporters say that the word 'violent' describes blacks 'extremely' or 'very' well. An old re-enacting chum of mine who lives in Kentucky tells me that the accepted rule of thumb counts 15 per cent of the US electorate as fundamentally racist. I even heard a Fox News presenter concede that the figure was at least 5 per cent. My Kentucky friend has absolutely no doubt about the dominant reason for Trump's victory: 'Revenge for eight years of a black president.'

'The Ford Company has no use for experience, in the working ranks anyway,' wrote an admiring editor at the *Engineering Magazine* in 1915. 'It desires operators who will simply do what they are told to do, over and over again, from bell-time to bell-time.' Ford's $5 day made his workers prosperous, but it came at a price. The repetitive, soul-crushing toil – unbearable for so many staff at $2.34 a day – now had to be endured. 'We all moved the same, like marionettes, like a living machine,' an old Highland Park hand told a documentary team decades later. Every human need, from sustenance to excretion, had to be squeezed into a single fifteen-minute lunch break. 'Without the most rigid discipline,' said Ford, 'we would have the utmost confusion.' In this spirit, spotters were recruited to enforce endless and draconian rules: no squatting, no whistling, no smoking, no leaning against the machines. Above all, no talking. Workers had to master the 'Ford whisper', muttering to each other through frozen lips like ventriloquists, as they tightened the same bolt 5,000 times a day. This was work at its most relentless and inhuman. In the broiled Detroit summers, half a dozen overworked, under-watered line assemblers might drop dead in a single day. Charlie Chaplin did much of his research for *Modern Times* at Ford's assembly lines, and it's no accident that the actor he cast to play the hellish factory's dictatorial boss was a dead ringer for Henry.

But Ford's hold on his workforce stretched way beyond the factory floor. No one had established any ground rules for the new relationship between generous boss and beholden staff, and Ford's $5 day was duly accompanied by the creepiest, most intrusive employment regime in industrial history. More than 200 investigators from Ford's Sociological Department visited workers at home, quizzing them on their diet, social outlook, recreational habits and living arrangements. To qualify for the new wage, husbands needed to show they were 'taking good care of their families', and bachelors were required to demonstrate 'thrifty habits'. Those who gambled, drank to excess or refused to attend mandatory English classes (in 1914, two-thirds of Ford's employees had been born outside the US) were expelled from the profit-sharing scheme and given six months to reform, or face the sack. So too, with a broad stroke of the scary brush, was any worker deemed guilty of 'malicious practice derogatory to good physical manhood or moral character'.

Somebody persuaded Ford to give his Sociological Department a moderately less Orwellian branding, but in 1921 the re-named Education Department was disbanded after its director quit, traumatised by his superiors' insistence that 'fear is a greater incentive to work than loyalty'. Henry, however, was soon keeping his men in line with a much blunter instrument. The swiftly notorious Ford Service Department was headed by Harry Bennett, an ex-boxer with underworld links who Henry had first met in New York, after a friend of his bailed Bennett out of jail following a bar brawl. 'I could use a man like you,' said Ford. 'Can you shoot?'

Nominally head of security at Ford's River Rouge plant, Bennett would be Ford's right-hand man and enforcer for more than twenty years – the boss of a 3,000-strong army of hoodlums and ex-cops that one newspaper called 'the largest private para-military organisation in the world'. He stood 5'6" and always wore a fedora and a bow tie – neckties, he explained, were liabilities in a fight. Bennett kept two pet lions, and sometimes brought them into work. He was never without a gun. Staff became attuned to the explosive retorts from his office as he let loose his .32 target pistol, with Henry often in active attendance. When asked what his job was, Bennett would smile and slowly answer, 'I am Mr Ford's personal man.'

His Service Department kept brutal order at River Rouge, deploying informers and intimidation to quell resistance to Ford's 'speed up' policy, in which assembly lines were run ever faster, by surreptitious weekly increments. 'Spies and stool pigeons report every action, every remark, every expression,' noted a *Time* journalist, revealing the 'hatred and fear' that hung over River Rouge. In 1932, Service Department thugs and the police opened fire on a hunger march as it approached the River Rouge gates, killing four people. Five years later, forty of Bennett's men viciously broke up a union meeting outside the plant, kicking workers down two flights of stairs.

Staff at every level suffered nervous breakdowns and an anxiety-induced ailment known as 'Ford stomach'. Even the toilet attendants lived in fear, never knowing if they'd polished enough porcelain that hour. Nor were the top brass spared. Edsel began to notice men in fedoras and big suits were following him, even staring out from deep in the woods when he played golf. He was told it was for his own protection. Edsel's eldest son, Henry II, once made the mistake of telling Bennett that some shady character had been threatening him. 'Later on,' recalled Edsel's youngest son, William, 'the guy was found floating face-down in the river.' In 1945, with old man Henry enfeebled, Henry II finally plucked up the courage to fire Bennett, wisely delegating the task to his own enforcer, John Bugas, a former head of Detroit's FBI. The meeting in Bennett's office ended with both men pointing large-calibre handguns at each other. 'Don't make the mistake of pulling that trigger, Harry,' said Bugas, 'because I'll kill you. I won't miss. I'll put one right through your heart.' They don't make board-room disagreements like they used to.

Ford's achievements in low-cost mass production had been hailed around the world, but the working environment he fostered drew a very particular kind of admirer. A mighty human machine kept running at maximum capacity by a network of informers and the threat of violent retribution ... hmmm. Stalin was quick to praise Ford as 'one of the world's greatest industrialists', and adapted Henry's techniques to force through his demanding and ever more brutal Five Year Plans. Anyone nicknamed 'Man of Steel' was all right in Henry's book, and the appreciation became mutual. By 1926 Henry had shipped 24,000 Fordson tractors to the Soviet Union, and in 1930, Ford dispatched Charles Sorensen to Russia to help set up a series of factories that would build over 100,000 Ford-derived vehicles. All this in a nation whose existence the US government wouldn't even acknowledge until 1933. Russian parents named their children Fordson, in honour of the machine that would cultivate the steppes, and Henry's ghost-written autobiography, *My Life and Work*, was translated and reprinted five times. 'Incredible as it may seem,' wrote a visiting journalist after a two-month tour of the country, 'more people in Russia have heard of Henry Ford than of Stalin.'

The *New York Times* referenced a different breed of totalitarian Ford-fan in 1928, when it dubbed Henry 'an industrial fascist – the Mussolini of Detroit'. The doctrine of 'Fordismus' was roundly praised by certain elements of the German political scene, and Henry Ford won his most unfortunate cheerleader in 1923, when Adolf Hitler, then in prison after his foiled beer-cellar coup, came upon a translation of *My Life and Work*. Ford would earn a glowing namecheck in *Mein Kampf*, and after becoming Führer, Hitler always kept a photographic portrait of Henry in his office. In 1936, Hitler sent his motor supremo Ferdinand Porsche to meet Henry in Detroit, where the pair toured Ford's factories and discussed the Führer's plans for his Volkswagen – a 'People's Car' project wholly inspired by the utilitarian Model T, and the brutal efficiency of its mass production. River Rouge workers had already dubbed Bennett's Service Department 'the Ford Terror', and many commentators would later wonder if Hitler borrowed it as the model for his Gestapo.

I would like to say this concludes Henry's besmirching association with Nazism, but regrettably we shall be returning to it later. While we're here, though, this seems as good a place as any to note the prominence of Ford and the Model T in Aldous Huxley's *Brave New World*, published in 1932, with its T-shaped crucifixes and pious reflections on 'the time of our Ford'. The Year Zero of Huxley's dystopia, the After Ford age, aligns with the year that the first Model T rolled off the Highland Park lines.

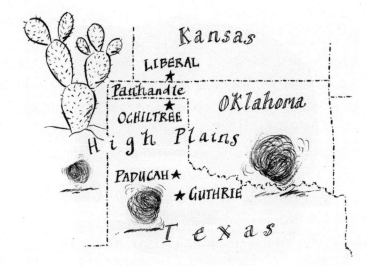

Mike and I were now heading into proper horse-with-no-name country, through cowboy panoramas of boulder-strewn, deep-red plains and dried-up orange creeks. Clusters of morose dark brown cattle jostled for shade under spindly mesquite trees. I swooped into burnt-ochre canyons, then laboured deafeningly back up to the Martian bluffs and mesas. The hot, dry air seemed to extrude this landscape's immensity: the grain elevators of the next lonely settlement always stood clear and sharp and imminent, before a signpost revealed it lay ten or more miles distant. Behind me, that two-lane blacktop juddering about in the mirror seemed to exist in a very different dimension of time and space. No sooner did a mobile glint take distant shimmery shape than it shot by at three-digit speed, with the slamming whoosh of an express train. And then I was once more alone, reeling in hot, straight miles with a sack of Walmart trail mix between my knees, a gallon jug of water warming on the passenger seat, and a soaring heart. What a thrill to be pitting my frail old car against this muscular, hostile vastness. What a relief to be doing so now that I could vaguely control it.

I bagged my first 'howdy' at the liquor store in Old Glory, its solitary shop, and saw my first roadrunner – long fanned tail, silly little crest, hot-footing it down the shiny tarmac past a coyote-tempting roadside inducement: 'TNT – BUY ONE, GET FIVE FREE.' Every few hours I'd pause at a plaque or monument blasted half-smooth by sand and the West Texas wind, and decode some of the T era's more unfortunate language and attitudes. 'In honour of Major General Mackenzie, who defeated the Comanches in Tule Canyon and ended Indian power in Texas.' 'First white child born in Motley County was Nora Cooper, born here in 1882.' Native Americans were still being killed in armed encounters as late as 1918, and the Indian Plains Wars didn't officially end until 1924, the year of Mike's birth, when a gang of Apache horse thieves surrendered in Arizona.

Guthrie looked big on the map but not in the dusty flesh, little more than a high school and a courthouse (every half-horse town seemed to have one of these). The gas station I'd anticipated was conspicuous by its absence, which very nearly cost me dear – when I stuck my measuring stick in the tank by the pumps in Paducah, 30 miles up the road, it came out dry as a bone. For some weeks henceforth refuelling opportunities were routinely spaced 80 or 90 miles apart, and I learned to top Mike up whenever I passed one.

Guthrie was the gateway to King County, number two in my pack of Top Trumps, a district where precisely five people voted for Hillary Clinton. There were few signs of life, and fewer still of productive potential. A dozen longhorns stood up to their haunches in a pool of brown water. Beyond them, a scattering of little tin-bladed water-pump windmills poked out from the scorched earth. Not a derrick in sight: nobody was making money from 'ahl', as they pronounced it round these parts. This was ranching at its scrappiest and most marginal. The pick-ups that now sped crazily past were dwarfed beneath some perilous, monumental load, a bale of hay as wide as a tube tunnel, or a shed-sized plastic tank.

'Where you come from, and where you headin'?'

A pleasingly ageless greeting in the 'Crossroads of America', as at least a dozen towns I'd already been through had already styled themselves, most with no better justification than Paducah, which happened to find itself at the nexus of two not especially significant highways. I provided my answers, and without appearing to process them the elderly manageress of the town's last surviving motel launched into an unprompted, freewheeling history of the rise and fall of Cottle County and its seat. 'Now, this was cotton country but the wind and the boll weevil took it away. Back in the Thirties we had sand storms so bad folks had to hide in the jailhouse. Ten thousand of us in Paducah in those days, and I just heard we're down to nine hundred. Only thing growing here is the cemetery.' This last sentence rolled out with the mannered ring of a catchphrase. In the minutes ahead I learned that the original Marlboro Man, a blue-eyed cowboy named Clarence Long, was a son of Paducah; that the town's retailers had taken a fearsome hit when Walmart opened a store 30 miles north; and that after voting Democrat for most of its incorporated life – an uninterrupted run, I later established, from 1928 to the 1990s – Cottle County had now placed its trust very firmly in Donald Trump. 'He's trying to get things done. I just wish the media would give him a chance instead of baulking him at every turn. It's such a shame, that poor man has only got his family left to support him.' She sighed with such sincere empathy that I thought better of grabbing her by the shoulders and shrieking like a chimpanzee.

Paducah was something else: no Mexican restaurant, no crickets or cicadas, no purple-shirted seniors clustered around Mike. Dinner was two cheeseburgers at a sticky-tabled shack where my place setting included a fly-swat encrusted with trophies. Then I went out in the low, gold sun and walked on empty, lightly grassed sidewalks to a town square that encapsulated my mission, more starkly and sadly than anywhere else I would visit.

At its centre towered Cottle County's magnificent 1930 courthouse, a four-storey civic temple in the Gotham City mould, graced with stylised eagles and fiercely angular representations of Liberty and Justice. The four broad streets that framed this stirring monument were edged with perhaps forty red-brick buildings of commercial aspect, their facades topped with geometric chevrons and other art deco architectural cues. In the absence of any modern accoutrements, not even one parked or passing car, it was easy to picture Bonnie and Clyde's Ford V8 sidling into shot. The 1967 movie was largely filmed in north Texas towns just like this. I now irresistibly recalled the couple's abortive raid on a Farmers State Bank, speeding away after the cashier told them it had failed three weeks before and he didn't have a cent in the safe. Except here in Paducah, the failure was more profound. Of the forty establishments around me, not one – not a single one – remained open for business. The shuttered Palace movie theatre, its marquee board forever promoting 'JOHN WAYNE – RED RIVER'.

The windowless Cottle Hotel. The soaped-up offices of the *Paducah Post*, born 1906, died 2014. J. F. Norris & Co Furniture – no roof. Jordan Fashion – no doors. M. E. Moses Five and Dime – very hopefully for sale. Every other store front betrayed a weird retail death-spiral: 'FLOWERS GIFTS BALLOONS AND MORE!' above a window display that comprised a single traffic cone and a very dead pot plant. There wasn't a soul in sight.

I gazed up at the mighty courthouse. Its monolithic portico was topped with an engraved inscription: 'TO NO ONE WILL WE SELL, DENY OR DELAY JUSTICE.' Noble words above all this forsaken squalor. The courthouse was erected at the high-water mark of that agricultural boom that swept across the Midwest and far beyond in the early T era, a green-rush that brought flocks of immigrants and unimaginable wealth to remote, unlikely places like Paducah. On cue, the rains came, and the desert bloomed with corn and cotton. Good weather and soaring productivity –

irrigation, Ford tractors, railroads to deliver supplies and take away produce – led to record harvests and bumper prices.

Then, quite swiftly, everything went wrong. The market was glutted, and in the three years up to 1924, commodity and livestock prices plunged 85 per cent, bankrupting 600,000 farmers. When the price of corn dropped to $9 a ton, farmers started burning it at home instead of coal, which was twice as dear. A barter economy kicked in. A farmer's wife in Maryland complained that a dentist had billed her a ton of tomatoes to do twenty minutes' work on her daughter's teeth. Lawyers billed farmers 150 bushels of corn to draw up their remortgage documents. Then the boll weevil, a pest that had been spreading north from Mexico since the turn of the century, marched north at speed. In the mid-Twenties, boll weevils destroyed half the US cotton crop, a loss folksily audited as 500 shirts for every man in the land. The rains stopped and the dust storms came. Then the Great Depression pitched up to apply the *coup de grâce*.

Paducah had been bled dry for ninety years, but at least it still had a faint pulse. The next day I drove past a grand red-brick ruin set far back from the road in the mesquite trees and wispy grass: a roadside board told me it was Whiteflat high school, opened in 1922 and closed twenty-four years later, the only surviving trace of a town that had once boasted three churches, three gas stations, four grocery stores and a cotton gin.

The agricultural recession propelled Henry Ford's small-town popularity into the stratosphere. He had made the car that had changed their lives, and made a fortune doing so. In 1919, Ford danced a jig around his office after buying out every minority Ford shareholder – a ballsy move that cost him $106 million, but delivered complete control of the company. Ford was the people's tycoon, not beholden to the money men who were busily repossessing farms, or the politicians who stood by and let them do it. Americans seem to have a hardwired weakness for confusing business success with political potential. But in the 1920s, the millionaire they put their faith in at least made a worthy saviour: a hard-working, self-made man of simple tastes and old-fashioned values.

In 1916, Henry Ford inadvertently won a presidential primary in Michigan. Somebody had put his name on the ballot without telling him, and when he heard the news he thought it was a joke. After that accidental victory he withdrew from the contest. In 1918, he was persuaded to contest the Michigan Senate primaries, but endeavoured to do so on both tickets, beating his Democratic rivals but losing to the eventual Republican victor. Yet despite all this ambivalent reluctance, as the agricultural recession wore on a Ford-for-president bandwagon got rolling and picked up speed. A national organisation, snappily dubbed the Give Henry Ford an Opportunity Club, was swamped with donations. 'Which side are you on?' asked one club leaflet. 'Wall Street or Henry Ford?' 'No more politicians or lawyers for us,' declared another. 'Ford is our Moses.'

By the summer of 1923, with a presidential election looming, Ford was acknowledged across the nation as the strongest candidate. Every opinion poll suggested a comfortable win. He hadn't aligned himself with either mainstream party – no bad thing in terms of his popularity – and nor had he yet declared an intention to stand. He never would. In August, President Warren Harding abruptly dropped dead from a heart attack, and Ford announced he would be playing no part in an unseemly fight for succession. (He should have waited: Harding was soon posthumously exposed as a corrupt womaniser who openly flouted Prohibition in the Oval Office – red meat for Henry's old-fashioned, anti-establishment fanbase.) Thereafter Ford withdrew from politics, and drifted to conservatism as the old are wont to do. He came to despise FDR's New Deal, and cursed the unions. In time he was swept right-wards to a very dark place indeed.

The motel manageress had already gone to bed when I let myself in. A stout cardboard notice stood propped on the reception desk: 'No refunds for ANY reason.' I hadn't noticed it before. But then I also hadn't noticed the little plastic dishes that I now spotted under each leg of my bed, nor the number of beady-eyed little reasons that were marooned in them, mired in some deathly fluid, antennae twitching feebly. Just before dawn I went for a pee, turned on the light and watched several very much larger reasons scuttle with hideous alacrity into every corner of the bathroom. Two terrible hours later, as the sun rose above Paducah's gap-toothed, residential wastelands, I heaved my bags into Mike's back seat, scraped crushed brown legs off my soles on a weathered kerbstone, shielded red eyes behind tinted lenses and clattered off into the derelict silence.

My ascent to the High Plains had begun, a surreptitious process only betrayed by the elevation signs posted outside each town: Paducah, 1860ft; Matador, 2,380ft; Pampa, 3,238ft. These russet flatlands, clotted here and there with prickly pears, aromatic tufts of sage brush and world-weary cows, receive less than a foot of rain a year, and are subject to the extraordinary daily temperature swings that are the lot of the lofty desert. Mornings began to bring me out in goose pimples, though by noon the sun beat down so brutally that I seared my forearm flesh on Mike's black bodywork.

Buzzards circled high above. A debut ball of tumbleweed skittered across the road and lodged itself under a headlight. It became ever easier to believe that only 2 per cent of the United

States is classed as built-up. Every desolate town was home to a one-stop oasis serving gas and groceries to lonesome old ranchers from far and wide, standing in line before me with 2 gallons of milk and a slab of beer. Goodnight, Rule, Tuxedo ... these settlements were blessed with such tirelessly quaint names that when I passed a sign for 'SANITARY LANDFILL', first word above the second, I read it as a two-town direction post.

No bends and no traffic meant distance was measured in driving hours out here: I'd ask the cashier how far it was to the next gas station, and be told how long it would take to get there, an estimate that required trebling to bridge the gap between the locals' cruising speed and mine. I wasn't surprised to find every fellow motorist tackling this hostile enormity hoist a fraternal, encouraging hand out of the window. But then almost every single driver I'd encountered in 3,500 miles had hailed me in some fond and approving manner. By this stage I was reflexively lifting a finger or two off the wheel at every approaching car, in pre-emptive acknowledgement.

Every High Plains morning, at whatever plucky settlement found itself in the right place at the right time, there was breakfast, a great convivial round of bacon and bonhomie, with Mike and I as the talk of the tiny town. My challenge: to get to the bottom of the Trump phenomenon before dying face-down in a fry up.

'Vern, Dave, this here is Tim Ball, and that's his keen little deal outside ... Maylene, give your daddy a call – this gentleman is taking a 24 Model T coast to coast and he needs to meet him ... Hey, Merle! Merle! Stop starin' at that old Bonnie and Clyde car out there, get yourself in and talk to this crazy Brit who's driving it to the Pacific.'

And soon enough I'd be sharing my table with every oldie in town, shooting the shit over sunny-side-ups and hash browns and endless cups of bitter, brown water. These diner gatherings kicked off like a very good-natured job interview – the firm hand-shakes, the exchange of names, the preludial pleasantries about the weather and your chosen route into town. Then we were off on a free-roaming exchange of gossip, bullshit, old-school cheers and fears. 'Read about a guy back in the Eighties, he lost 175 pounds and all he ate was bacon … I just can't keep up with all this L.G.B.T.Q.M.O.U.S.E., whatever the hell it is today … Well, long as you're not killing or hurting someone, I say you should be allowed to do it. What *you're* doin', Teeum, well, ain't that a kick. Me, I ain't never been out of Texas.'

With varying degrees of finesse, I'd introduce a certain flabby old narcissist into the debate. 'See, he's a businessman who won't follow the rules, and if all those self-serving politicians and the media hate him for that, then he's gotta be doing something right … Left wing and right wing are part of the same bird … I'm not strictly pro-Trump, I'm just anti-politician, anti-federal … And hey, congratulations on your Brexit!'

I must have heard these last four words a hundred times. As cheerfully ignorant as most Americans remain about events beyond their borders – in the realm of broadcast news, the outside world simply doesn't exist unless an Islamic terrorist attacks it – the EU referendum result had burned itself deep into the small-town consciousness. The Limeys had flipped the finger at federalism – woo-hoo! It was such a self-evident cause for universal celebration that they simply blanked out my protestations, no matter how bluntly I expressed them, which by about the eightieth time was extremely sodding bluntly.

Such was the split personality I encountered every day, the small-town yin and yang. On a personal level, these rural oldies were just so irrepressibly upbeat, so open and positive. At the Main Street

Café in Matador, a well-built guy with a 'Vietnam veteran' lanyard round his neck insisted on paying for my breakfast. As I climbed on to Mike's running-board, the sprightly old proprietor trotted out and flicked a smart blue Main Street Café trucker's cap on to my head. 'Not too often we get visitors,' he said. Yet their world view was a bundle of darkness, a doom-laden, paranoid bunker mentality. Just outside Matador, full of hash browns and humanity, I was confronted by a big black sign that read: '9/11 – WORSE THINGS COMING – FIND JESUS!' Fiercely anti-governmental sentiments wobbled up out of the heat haze in half the towns I drove through: a giant metal pig with 'COUNTY ASSESSOR = GREED' painted on it in a front yard, 'TO ALBANY TAX PAYERS: CHECK YOUR LIGHTS, KNOW YOUR RIGHTS!' daubed on a barn in vast letters.

Speed limits and other roadside notices often carried a rider that spoke of ingrained rebellion: 'OBEY SIGNS – STATE LAW.' In some US states a third of drivers still refuse to wear seat belts, in defiance of mandatory regulations.

From now on the default farewell urged me to 'stay safe' or to 'have a safe one', a perception of peril entirely at odds with the ever more harmless reality. These guys rarely locked their front doors. I was leaving more and more stuff in the car overnight, and no longer bothered to take my phone out of the windshield mount when I went into gas stations to pay. The obsession with lawless murder that held urban America in its morbid thrall at least had some foundation in fact (though not much: violent crime has been steadily falling across the nation for more than twenty-five years). But to encounter it out in the benign, studiously law-abiding boondocks was a source of deep bewilderment. Perhaps it was a hangover from the lawless Wild West, like the courthouse in every town. Perhaps they cultivated it as justification for all those vast domestic arsenals. On my first night in Texas, I walked past a pick-up truck with a sticker on the door that read: 'NOTHING IN THIS VEHICLE IS WORTH YOUR LIFE.' Its windows had been left open and the keys were in the ignition.

The landscape crisped up and sandy grit began to drift across the road. Ahead, beyond my motometer gunsight, a long and empty strip of undeviating asphalt bisected the ochre plains, a view that began to appear on the inside of my eyelids as I stood blinking at every gas-station urinal and motel reception. James Dean, who had taught me how to start a Model T, met his end on a dead-straight desert road, and I found myself scanning the hazy funda-ment of every flat brown vista for inattentive rustics like the one who drove into his path one broiled afternoon in 1955.

Dean was going faster than I'd ever go when he crashed, but speed was rarely a factor in the appalling toll of road fatalities that accumulated in the Model T era. In 1927, the T's final year, 24,470 Americans died on the nation's roads: well over half the current annual total, with a tenth as many registered vehicles. Road safety wasn't even a consideration back then; indeed, reports of fatal accidents were recorded with graphic relish. 'Mrs McCormick's head was impaled upon the maple tree's lowest branch,' reads an eager newspaper account of a 1912 crash in Connecticut, 'and a great rent was torn in her side by a blow from the steel wheel of the wrecked machine.' After Mr McCormick – flung into a neighbouring field – died in hospital the same evening, doctors found a clipping in his pocket describing a previous accident in which he had cheated death, just five miles away. 'Since he married the Poughkeepsie beauty,' the article concluded, 'he and she have been in no less than a dozen auto wrecks, ranging in territory from Maine to Missouri, and in seriousness from explosions to mutilated legs and arms.'

McCormick was estimated to have been driving at no more than 40mph when his car left the road for the last time. A century of material fatigue was hardly an encouragement to push Mike any faster. In 2011, a Model T on a tour of Minnesota suffered a suspension collapse at 30mph on a flat, straight road that pitched the car into a double roll, killing the driver and badly injuring his wife. Two years later, a Model T driving four-up on a state highway in Utah pulled over to allow traffic to pass; on crossing into the rough verge, the right-hand front wheel disintegrated, again throwing the car into a roll that left a fifty-one-year-old passenger dead. Without seat belts, it didn't seem to take much. The MTFCA forums were full of harrowing close shaves: one member reported that his car had completely fallen apart, Laurel and Hardy style, while crossing a cattle grid at unremarkable speed. As much as these reports concentrated the mind, they also infused me with a sense of helpless fatalism. Something fundamental might give way without warning: there was nothing I could do to stop it doing so, and nothing I could do if and when it did. Stay safe.

That fierce south-westerly wind was a bullying menace in the days ahead. When it blew me onward it also blew me about, requiring a new stability-control technique in which I braced both elbows against the bottom of the steering wheel as my whitened fists grasped the top. Through slitted eyes and flapping wisps of grey fringe I watched the motometer nose high into the red zone: when a T is outrun by a tailwind, there's nothing to cool it down. More than once I had to pull over and park Mike up to chill out with his face to the oncoming blast. His flanks, so durably glossy, were now dulled by an ancient orange dust that forced itself deep into every crevice.

I did a lot of scary High Plains drifting when the road weaved around on the desolate, dust-bowled moorland mesas. Wind scooped into the big front fenders, knocking them up and about. Fat crickets shot into the cabin and pinged about like bullets. Twice my sunglasses were blown clean off my face and out into the sand-blasted, sundried tussocks. I battled to keep the car on the road, on occasion forcing my knees up against the steering wheel for a six-point grip. It felt like a bumpy fairground ride that just wouldn't stop. Every few hours I tottered across a gas-station forecourt on wobbly legs, my stomach lurching. The tousled, ruddy survivor that stared vacantly back in the restroom mirror might have just been airlifted from a storm-shattered raft.

Yet there was evidence of a long-rooted human determination to brave this environment and make it home, described by historical markers that sang and quivered in the gusts. Over 15,000 years ago, some of America's earliest known humans chased mammoths over these windswept plains. And in 1919, the 300 citizens of Ochiltree showcased the T era's boundless get-up-and-go in the most literal fashion: a new railway had been laid across the prairie 8 miles north, so they hitched every single building – post office, church, the works – to a fleet of tractors and moved the whole town to meet it. They could have just nailed sheets across their chimneys and sailed there.

The sign that welcomed me into Oklahoma had been shot to shit by exiting Texans. It didn't take long to establish that residents of surrounding states really don't care much for their Lone Star neighbours: too shouty and uncouth, too full of themselves, and maybe – though nobody admitted this – just too irksomely prosperous. The road shrank to half its Texan girth as I passed from one geographical panhandle to another. If there's one thing

Americans love more than a belt – Sun, Bible, Rust, Corn, Snow – it's a panhandle, no matter how stupidly stubby.

Until 1890 the Oklahoman panhandle was a bona fide no man's land, an ungoverned free-for-all that attracted only outlaws and the very wariest settlers. The state itself was only admitted into the union in 1907, the year before the T, and still looked like a hayseed latecomer. Wooden farmhouses sat hunkered into hollows, many reduced to a dishevelment of bleached planks strewn about the totem pole of a stone chimneybreast. A trail of weeded ballast marked the route of a defunct railway. The towns were palpably forlorn, littered with abandoned cars and dusty, bill-posted requests for roustabouts that flapped against lamp-posts. And that was it for Oklahoma. After my thousand-mile trans-Texan epic I went through the next state up in a couple of hours.

Liberal, the gateway to Kansas, sat right on the dark-red Trump spine that ran north from Texas to the Canadian border. This incongruity delivered such appealing juxtapositions – 'LIBERAL POLICE'; 'VISIT THE LIBERAL RODEO' – that on a whim I decided to stay there, even though doing so meant a night in the kind of motel I had vowed to shun after that terrible dawn scuttlefest in Paducah. The Budget Host La Fonda sat behind a drained pool and a row of scabby haci-enda arches, somewhere a C-list mobster might end up under a witness protection scheme. I was applying a veneer of aerosol insecticide to every suspect in-room surface when knuckles rapped my door.

'We just love everythin' about your antique,' said a man in a suede bucket hat after I opened up, showing me a crescent of tiny, jet-black teeth. Beside him stood a woman in a smock dress with a smudged blue tattoo on her neck. Beside her was a freckled girl of about ten. All three were wearing wire-framed spectacles, and had teamed socks with sandals. 'Look, baby-girl,' said the father, pointing a nicotine fingertip at the legend stamped into Mike's radiator. '"Made in USA." Don't see that much no more.'

I glanced at the Honda saloon behind them, its wan blue paint sandblasted here and there to scabby bare metal, a tattered sheet of opaque tarpaulin standing in as a rear windshield.

'Damn hailstorm took that out,' he said, following my gaze. 'Stones the size of softballs.'

'Three years ago,' added his wife, neutrally. 'Gas gauge don't work neither.'

His name was Trent, and he told me he'd lived in Liberal all his life. The town had earned its appellation, he explained, courtesy of a nineteenth-century homesteader famed for offering free water to passing pioneers: '"That's mighty liberal of you," they all told him, and when the town was incorporated it seemed as good as any. Kind of a funny story, right?'

Before I had time to agree Trent fixed me with a sudden and threatening glare. 'This place is a trap and I want to get out,' he said, his voice scaled down to an urgent, bitter whisper. 'Been over a hundred all summer and it's colder than hell in winter. So damn flat you can watch your dog run away for three days. Had no work for six years. I can weld, I can paint, I can drive a truck and do all kinds of shit, but the only place hirin' is the meat-packin' plant, and they wouldn't take me on because I don't speak fuckin' Spanish.' He put his hands on his hips and let out a bull-like snort. 'I want to go as far away from here as I can get without a passport. I want to go to *Florida*.'

This tirade seemed to drain Trent as much as it alarmed me, and I watched him shuffle back to the Honda with his head down. His family, though, had evidently heard it all and more before. 'My daddy wants to live on a boat,' said his daughter in an amiable sing-song, sounding at least six years younger than she was. And then they were gone.

An hour passed. I was just about to crack open a cheeky Lime-a-Rita and start swearing at Fox News when there was another knock at the door. It was Trent again, this time alone.

'My wife and I been talkin' about that story of how our town got its name, and we thought, well, it would be kinda fittin' if we could invite a traveller over for a bite to eat.' He took off his suede hat and cradled it humbly, revealing a thin mat of damp grey hair. 'She makes a mean burrito.'

It was the most touching invitation I had yet been offered, and the most shriekingly ominous. Ten minutes later, Liberal's Friday-night pedestrians watched an ancient black car turn off the main drag and follow a partly glazed Honda down one of their town's least promising residential side streets.

The hours ahead presented an invaluable insight into the Trump phenomenon, something I kept having to remind myself. Trent ushered me into a clapboard shack of interwar appearance, with a lot of missing shingles and wooden walls I could have pushed my thumb through. The tiny, low-ceilinged front parlour was hemmed in by teetering stacks of VHS tapes and magazines, most topped with a brimming ashtray. Decades of tobacco-tipped fingers had left broad yellow smudges around every door handle and light switch. A framed pencil sketch of Kenny Rogers hung on the wall. Two small, tubular dogs yapped half-heartedly at me from a collapsing sofa. 'That's my police scanner,' said Trent, indicating a clunky black box with about ninety buttons on the front. 'Friday nights are pretty fun. We got a lot of Mexicans here and they sure like to fight.'

I was led into the kitchen beyond and met by his wife, his daughter, and a very complicated aroma. Everything below chest height was Jackson Pollocked with hard-baked matter. Everything above it was lacquered in nicotine. The fridge might have been dragged out of a canal.

'Hope you like sweet tea.'

Trent held out a chipped beaker and bid me sit at the little table. Then his wife withdrew a sweating platter of rolled tortillas from the ancient enamel stove, adding a top note of cheese-grease to the miasma.

'I honestly couldn't eat more than one,' I said, theatrically patting my stomach.

'Ain't no need for those Briddish manners here,' she protested, tipping three on to a liver-spotted plate. In a panic I forked one and crammed it whole between my lips.

'Pretty good, huh?' said Trent, winking. I took aboard a desperate gulp of sweet tea and managed a gurgle of assent.

'I'm told I'm extremely antisocial,' he continued, with a mirthless laugh that I would be hearing a lot of. 'And it's true – I just don't like people. Been in this house thirteen years and I know two people on the whole block. Rest of them I don't care to know. They're mostly Hispanic. If you don't speak Spanish they won't speak to you.' He took a thoughtful swig of tea. 'I hope Trump does build that wall. I truly hope so. I would volunteer to help him build it.'

'And Mexico will pay for it,' added his wife, bisecting a flaccid burrito. 'Everywhere you look here it's Mexicans. We got 22,000 people in this county, and 86 per cent of them are Hispanic. Can you believe that?' (I couldn't, and was right not to. The actual ratio, I later established, is just under half that.)

'At least this president has the balls to do somethin'. The last one was against this country from the start. He admitted being a Muslim, and said he would open the doors for his brethren. He openly said if there was a war against the Muslim countries, he would stand with them. Sorry, but that's just not president material.'

Sorry, but that's just not true, I might have said, possibly even yelled. But I was a guest, and one with half a mouthful of acrid pulp to get down. In any case it was already abundantly plain that America's polarised politics were now fully tribal: dissent would achieve nothing but ill-feeling and the further entrenchment of views. A couple of nights earlier, CNN had broadcast the results of a poll revealing that 62 per cent of Trump supporters – a third of all Americans – said they would never criticise anything he might do. *Anything.* And didn't he know it. Almost a year before he was elected, Trump famously announced he 'could stand in the middle of Fifth Avenue and shoot somebody and I wouldn't lose a vote'.

Trent gave good hate. As I forced ragged, weeping hunks of burrito between my teeth he revealed that along with Mexicans he despised Walmart, doctors, drug companies, the National Beef company, nasty teenage bastards, Haitians, unions and cars with plastic body panels. It would have been much quicker to catalogue things he liked, namely his police scanner, Donald Trump and the worst food in the world. Though this list took no account of the one thing he loved, now revealed in a scene I was pleasantly surprised to survive.

'Hey, come out here, got somethin' for you.'

Trent had left the kitchen and was hailing me from the parlour. With one-third of my dinner still unfinished, I wasted no time in leaping to my feet. Three sticky steps later I rounded the corner and came nose to nose with Trent, breathing hard, his features alive with an excitement that I quite swiftly connected to the samurai sword he was holding aloft in both hands.

'This is my baby,' he cooed, jumping with unexpected grace into the stance of a ceremonial executioner. The sword's honed blade shimmered before me. Trent was blocking the front door, but that Kenny Rogers wall looked pretty fragile and there seemed a decent chance of running straight through it. 'It certainly is a beauty,' I said, in a level, slow, keep-him-talking voice.

'Full tang,' he breathed, holding it lower. 'Steel goes all the way down.'

'Let me … let me take a look,' I whispered promptingly, holding both hands out very slowly and fighting a grisly bolus of Tex-Mex back down into my stomach.

'Swapped a long-bed GMC pick-up for her,' he said, reverentially passing it to me, grip first.

'Good, that's good.' I took the sword in my hands and with great deliberation lowered it on to the balding carpet. 'Let's just leave her to rest there.'

That was that. Or so I vainly hoped, and kept on vainly hoping as Trent repeatedly darted from the claustrophobic parlour and burst back in brandishing a succession of terrible weapons. 'Now *this* is for intruders!' he cried, re-entering with what looked very much like a Dothraki scimitar. 'Keep it under the mattress, so when someone sticks a hand through the window – wham! – that's comin' off, it's *my* property now!' Next up was a vast broadsword. 'This has a real good weight, could do you a *lot* of damage.' He clanged it hard against an old iron stove. 'Nice ring to it, too.'

'My daddy done broke his phone with that one,' piped up his daughter. The minute she joined us in the parlour, I'd manoeuvred myself into a position that employed her as a human shield.

Trent let out that mirthless laugh. 'Cellphone screen went black and the store said it was out of warranty. So I came home, gave it the chop, took it back to 'em in two halves. Their faces!'

After a dagger and two further swords, he made his final reappearance with a double-barrelled sawn-off shotgun. 'Accuracy by volume,' he wheezed, aiming it at the front door. 'Someone comes in, they're getting this up the nose. I got rock salt in one barrel and a tube of dimes in the other and we're gonna play a game.' Trent was dangerously animated as he ran through this well-rehearsed routine. 'Which barrel you gonna pick, huh? Huh? You chose the wrong house, dude. The door you kicked in was for *your* protection, not mine.'

It was gone eleven when Mike creaked to a halt outside my door at the Budget Host La Fonda. I went in, opened the fridge and downed 25 fluid ounces of margarita-flavoured malt alcohol in several consecutive gulps. Then I lay down, waited for tranquillity to take hold, and tried to make sense of the last few hours.

Trent had asked me to drive him around the block a couple of times in the T before I left, and while touring the dark streets he'd told me that his first wife had died fourteen years earlier, after a three-day illness that had set him back $38,000 in hospital fees. We also established that he was exactly two months younger than me. At once I had an empathetic hold on Trent's embittered plight. First a tragedy that wrought emotional and financial ruin, then the twenty-first-century's new midlife crisis: hit fifty, and you might well find your work is done. Half the jobs you want have disappeared, and the rest have gone to younger, hungrier men. People who will work harder for less. Who would up sticks and emigrate to follow the money. Who were still enthused by the pioneering determination that drew all those settlers west on wagon trails, and inspired the citizens of Ochiltree to tow their whole town 8 miles north. If Trent was so set on moving to Florida, why didn't he just do it? For the same reason that I still haven't painted over the stain in the sitting-room ceiling where the bath overflowed six years ago. We were baby boomers, a generation that came of age in an era of plentiful jobs and easy money, when determined application didn't matter. Now that it did, we couldn't be arsed.

When a couple of Hispanic guys fixing their car waved at us, Trent had waved back. 'It's actually a pretty safe area,' he murmured. 'I only lock the door when I remember to.' Poor Trent. He'd fallen out of love with life, and with Liberal, but still wanted to do right by the kindly-minded homesteader who gave it the name. Suddenly I was disgusted by my own disgust. What an ungrateful snob. I stared at the ceiling, impatient now for a surge of alcoholic forgiveness to bathe this traumatic evening in a kinder light. Then I picked up the empty can, inspected its small print, and established that in Kansas, Lime-a-Ritas carry an almost pointlessly feeble 3 per cent kick. 'You're not in Texas any more,' I sighed, and switched off the light.

CHAPTER 13

Kansas went flat on me in every sense, a greyscale table-top under thick, low clouds. At length these exuded a thin, hanging drizzle that smudged everything into an incredibly basic Impressionist landscape that went on for ever. Such vistas irresistibly conjured up the fanatical, brain-boiling boredom of American rural life in the pre-T age. What a place to call home.

On occasion the fuzzy cornfields were interrupted by a gigantic and malodorous feed lot, where thousands of unseen cattle lowed and crapped in the fog. Americans really are relentlessly carnivorous. The average consumption of meat equates to three quarter-pounders per head every single day. Even in farming towns nobody seemed to eat fresh produce: the fruit and veg section in the supermarkets was no more than a token rack or two of oversized apples and tomatoes, looking glossy and artificial in plastic boxes. The average American obtains just 1 per cent of their calories from vegetables, a proportion that continues to shrink. Even Icelanders eat more fruit. In such a fecund nation it seemed extraordinary.

Every hour or so some vast agricultural machine festooned with rakes and blades trundled out of the gloom, easing me off the tarmac. Great mouldering stacks of baled hay were piled up like lost cities along the road. We were now close to 3,500 feet and the corn was giving away to bleak stretches of full-on prairie, a whole new level of prostrate, tussocky nothing. A lot of wagon-train pioneers died out here, most from thirst and cholera, though the roadside memorials naturally focused on more eventful bereavements: 'In Commemoration of Jedediah Strong Smith, 1798–1831, a Great Plainsman Who Was Killed Near This Spot by Comanche Indians.' Deep into the 1930s, the lonelier prairies were still strewn with shallow graves and the charred remains of wagons.

The rain intensified, and without the curtains up, Mike and I took a number of proper Stan and Ollie drenchings as cattle trucks slooshed past. There are 15.5 million trucks in the US – more than in Europe, a continent twice as populous – and truck driving is the most common profession in almost every state I passed through, even Texas. It's hard to believe because most American trucks appear to drive themselves. Everything about them – their steel-toothed radiator grilles; their shiny, belching dragon-breath exhaust chimneys; their implacable, thunderous progress and sheer enormity – seems consistent with gleaming, brutal automation. They are routinely burdened with outrageous loads, like a two-storey house or a blast furnace, that no sensible human would ever consider a suitable candidate for road trans-port. The cabs stand about 10 foot above the ground, so you never see a driver, and the top halves of their windshields are sheathed in a stainless-steel sun visor that perfectly tops off the RoboCop vibe.

Mike, by contrast, was busily exploring his animal side. The warm, wet steam that rose up through the floor; the capricious bucks and whinnies; the cheeky squeaks. Cars aren't supposed to dither. Either they work or they don't. But Mike increasingly ran on his own terms, in a realm of gaiety and sulks that lay way beyond mechanical logic. He'd lumber along all morning like a malingering donkey, all fitful huffs and shudders. Then, without rhyme, reason or warning, I'd be thrown back in my seat and suddenly find us galloping smoothly across the plains for hours. He growled. He farted. He liked the wind in his face. Sometimes I'd plant my full weight on the brake and find a STOP sign approaching at undiminished speed; sometimes I'd dab the pedal and Mike would noisily dig his back hooves in. E. B. White, who as the author of *Stuart Little* and *Charlotte's Web* was well versed in zoomorphism, composed a delightful elegy to the Model T that makes fond and repeated reference to the car's animal qualities. 'The T trembled with a deep imperative and tended to inch forward,' he wrote. 'There was never a moment when the bands were not faintly egging the machine on. In this respect it was like a horse, rolling the bit on its tongue, and country people brought to it the same technique they used with draft animals.' In the early Twenties, as a young writer fresh out of college, White had crossed the US in search of work, driving an old T that he dubbed Hotspur. This was a crank-started model that would roll gently forwards after he fired it up from the front: 'I can still feel my old Ford nuzzling me at the curb, as though looking for an apple in my pocket.' Poor Henry. He'd set out to make a machine that would render the beast of burden obsolete. But his horseless carriage was really horsey.

Mike had cantered up northern Texas like a stallion, a very old stallion, but out on the prairies he'd begun to wheeze and toil, a pit pony fit for the glue works. On my last night in Kansas, a terrific small-hours thunderstorm blew so much sideways rain in through the bonnet vents that when I went to tip in the morning quart of oil, I found the spark-plug wells abrim. It took a dozen attempts before the engine fired, and something still wasn't right: as I puttered across the peaty moorland into Nebraska, Mike laboured miserably, struggling up every rare and gentle incline. Deep in the usual tumult of progress I detected a persistent hiss, the sound of a steam locomotive coming to rest.

I stuttered into Imperial, coaxed Mike to a motel at the windswept edge of town and phoned Ross. 'Head gasket,' he said as soon as I'd described the symptoms. 'Piece of piss, you can do that.' I could. Of course I could. I had a spare gasket. I had the required tools (all three of them – a flat-head screwdriver and two wrenches). The elderly manageress had taken a bit of a shine to me – 'From Virginia? In that? Holy smoke!' – and probably wouldn't press charges when I spilt 24 pints of coolant across her immaculate forecourt. I would get out there at first light.

It was probably second or even third light by the time I did get out there, and instead of pulling the bonnet off I threw my bags in the back and brought Mike to feeble, wheezy life. At breakfast it had suddenly occurred to me that I didn't have any gasket sealant. Shortly afterwards, sweeping bagels from the buffet into my open backpack, I glanced over my shoulder and was met by the manageress's disappointed gaze. The answer to both these issues was to cajole Mike to the auto parts store I'd passed half a mile down the road, buy the sealant and do the gasket job in their parking lot.

'You don't want to work on a car like that outside, back it into my shop.'

A very old man had emerged from the parts store, and was waving his walking cane at me. 'Casey won't mind. Well, it's my store and my shop, so he can't.'

As it had just begun to rain I wasted no time in accepting this splendid offer, though I can report that Casey did mind.

'I run a tidy shop,' said a stern young man with the requisite name embroidered on his crisp grey overalls, after I creaked to a halt in his commodious covered realm. Casey had a crew cut and tightly folded arms. 'Don't make a mess.' With that he disappeared into the workshop shadows.

I'd helped Peter remove the cylinder head in his sweltering Dearborn garage, and set about recreating the procedure as best I could. The first stage was to drain those 24 pints of coolant; I kicked my bucket under the radiator, dropped to the floor, and opened a filthy little brass drain tap. A single drop of green fluid slowly swelled, and after fifteen seconds plopped into the bucket. Fifteen seconds later so did another. I frowned, removed the radiator cap, then stooped down and rammed the tip of my smallest screwdriver into the drain hole. After much twisty probing with this tool and a length of wire I had raised the drainage rate to one drop every twelve seconds. This was hopeless. Something drastic had to be done. I surveyed the neighbouring equipment and saw exactly what that something was.

'You makin' a mess back there?'

I was beneath the T, with the nozzle of an air hose in my fingers. A healthy stream of coolant was now tinkling from the drain hole I had just wedged this into. On the downside, the jet of compressed air that had unclogged the orifice had also sent forth a towering geyser of luminous fluid straight up through the opened radiator cap, the last spatters of which were still dropping on to the spotless concrete all around me.

Well, it happened again. There was just something about Mike and I – his sad old eyes, my blithering incompetence – that seemed to melt even the hardest heart. When Casey clomped out of the shadows I prepared myself for fearsome retribution, perhaps combining that air jet and the hole in the ass of my pants. Instead, after sating his anger with a tut and a single shake of the head, he assumed executive control of the entire operation. How glad I was that he did so. Towards the end of what became a four-hour process, one of the head bolts stripped its thread; he went off into the darkness and returned with a replacement. Then one of the bolt holes did the same, a more complex fix that Casey remedied by screwing in a threaded insert. He even began to smile, and recoiled in offended horror when I tried to fold a couple of twenties into his embroidered pocket.

I bumped out of Casey's shop with a farewell ahoooga, but grateful relief soon gave way to very different emotions – the sort that came accompanied with this word: arsepipes. Mike wasn't better. That sputter returned and so did the hiss. I was definitely missing a cylinder, maybe two. Heading out across the Colorado cornfields I slammed into a headwind so punishing that my enfeebled car struggled to make progress. The 50 miles that followed were brutal for all concerned. The road kept making right-angle turns, abruptly shifting the gale into a crosswind that whipped my neck about and blew that back-seat collection of empty cans and oil bottles to kingdom come. Sorry, Colorado. Oncoming trucks full of cattle and hay delivered a split-second of windless calm, then a terrifying rifle-crack storm-blast that flung Mike right into the verge. Ragged cries of alarm were blown back down my throat or torn half-formed from my flapping lips.

Route 59 plunged under an interstate, over the South Platte River then topped a brow and lowered me mercifully into becalmed scrubland. My head hurt, my arms hurt and so, most of all, did my windward inner ear. I could tell, by touch alone, that my hair had been blown and set into a deranged Phil Spector afro. Mike was crawling along in a death-putter, The Little Engine That Couldn't. The first town we inched into, Sedgwick, had three surviving commercial operations along its broad and desolate main street. One was a bed and breakfast. One was a bar. One was a marijuana dispensary. I pulled nose in to the kerb and climbed woodenly out.

The Sedgwick Antique Inn B&B had begun life as the Farmers State Bank, a name picked out in smart blue tiles across a four-square 1920s facade.

Its Hispanic proprietor, Lupe, was a voluble, hyperactive force of nature: a retired elementary school teacher who had almost single-handedly brought this town back from the dead. 'If you see a white wall out there,' she told me, 'it's because this woman put on her pants and painted it.' Sedgwick, yet another rural settlement in decline since that T-era agricultural boom, was flat broke and down to its last 191 citizens when Lupe pitched up in 2002. She bought the old bank, converted it into a cheerily homespun guesthouse, and then acquired a derelict general store across the street. In 2012, following the controversial implementation of Colorado Amendment 64, she sold this to a pioneering entrepreneur. 'I want you to know that I was raised Pentecostal, so I'm not down with those marijuanas,' she told me next morning, pouring coffee in the sepulchral bank hall. 'And this is a deeply conservative town. But we needed money, and that dispensary is now paying us $50,000 in tax every month.'

The dankly herbal smell of success that wafted out through the net-curtained doors of Sedgwick Alternative Relief and all the way down Main Avenue would become very familiar to me. So too would the creaky boards and dusty chintz of the Antique Inn, the regulars who lined up at the bar of RD's Tavern, and the 3.2 per cent beer that was all they were licensed to serve. But the bulk of my next three waking days was spent getting down and dirty with a bespectacled young man with a ginger beard.

'Charles Toyne out of Sedgwick.'

I don't think I've ever heard a phone answered so appealingly. Lupe had given me Charles's number after I showed her Mike and explained his malaise. She said he had an old car a little like that in a barn. She was half right. Charles had four, and they were exactly like that. Sedgwick, to remind you, was a town of 119 souls that I had pitched up in entirely at random. A century on, out in its rural heartlands, Henry Ford's Model T remained the Universal Car.

Charles was a farmer, as were his elder brother and his father. But Charles was a very particular sort of farmer. He had a llama, which he'd bought as a goatherd, and appeared to make most of his money selling hay on Facebook for five bucks a bale. He lived alone in a ramshackle farmhouse girdled with rusty machinery and cats named after the seven deadly sins. He largely expressed himself with a two-tone variant of the sound Bugs Bunny makes before he says, 'What's up, Doc?' And of course he had a barn full of Ts. I kind of fell in love with Charles Toyne out of Sedgwick.

'Ee-huh.' Charles raised his head from the pitted, sooty surface of my engine block. 'You burned a couple valves out real good there.' In the hour that had elapsed since our first call, he'd trundled down Main Avenue in a decrepit pick-up, introduced me to his piebald mongrel Richard ('He's a bit of a dick') and whipped off Mike's cylinder head. Ross had already suggested this hypothesis: I now phoned him again, ordering four new exhaust valves and another sodding head gasket. 'Should be with you in two days,' he said. 'Ever lapped a valve?'

'Not since the court order.'

'It's a world of fun,' said Ross, with leaden sarcasm.

Charles drove away and presently returned at the wheel of an even more decrepit tow truck. 'Blimey,' I said, kicking cobwebs from a rust-ravaged arch, 'you did well to get this through the test.'

'Ee-huh,' said Charles, meaning he hadn't even tried to. I spent a lot of time decoding this gnomic utterance. Sometimes it was an obvious stand in for 'yes' or 'no'. But quite often, in my case at least, it seemed a polite euphemism for 'Please, please tell me you didn't just say that.' We winched Mike noisily aboard, drove a mile out to Charles's farmyard, unloaded and pushed him into an earth-floored barn. Familiar silhouettes took shape in its depths, though it was a while since Charles had fired up any of his Ts.

He asked me how I intended to occupy the next two days. I asked him how he did.

'Farming.'

'Um ... can I come?'

'Ee-huh.'

So quite suddenly there I was, heaving hay on to the back of some old cowboy's huge trailer, baling cord cutting deep into my dainty steering fingers. The cowboy's three sons roared with laughter when a hurled bale knocked me clean off the side of the trailer, then whooped their approval when I hauled myself doughtily back on deck, white faced and straw haired, a winded scarecrow. We waved them off with a hundred bales aboard, then climbed into Charles's pick-up and bumped around the perimeters of his parents' shiny green cornfields, turning irrigation valves on and off, dragging big lengths of piping around silos in the ochre dust. Old Man Toyne's corn largely ended up as ethanol vehicle fuel, I learned, which provided an excuse to delight Charles with some related history: it was Henry Ford who first proposed the use of corn-derived ethanol.

Henry, always a rum character, went impressively dotty in his dotage. He developed a firm belief in reincarnation, and would regularly hold forth about a 'queen cell' that passed from body to body. He proposed setting fire to deep-seam coal mines so that heat could be piped across the land. He told a friend who fainted to stop drinking milk, and asked a severely sunburned guest if he'd eaten too many eggs. Doctors at the Ford Hospital came to dread him dropping in. One patient recovering from a heart attack was ordered to get out of bed, lie on the floor and eat celery until he felt better. But in the field of agricultural technology, old man Ford mustered some remarkably prescient proposals and insights, precisely none of which were appreciated in his lifetime.

Everyone knew that the oil would someday run out, but Henry was one of the very few to propose a sustainable alternative: alcohol was both a menace to humanity and an unlimited man-made resource, a future fuel which could be distilled from almost any crop. In 1938, Ford gave researchers $1 million to refine motor fuel from potatoes and corn, but at the end of the project they regretfully reported that the process could never make economic sense. He gave another team of scientists another million to explore his deepest agricultural passion: the soybean. Soya thrived in poor soil and dry weather, yet was almost unknown in the US. Henry was thrilled by the crop's potential: his scientists found that extracted soya oil made an excellent basis for car paint, and that soya meal could be processed into a Bakelite-type material. You could feed soya to livestock, make it into linoleum, soap and glue, even spin it into fabric. At the height of his fixation, Henry showed up at a trade fair wearing an entire outfit made from soya fibres – shirt, suit, socks, everything but his shoes. He invited his staff to a dinner party where every course – soup, bread, pie, ice cream, coffee – was made from soya beans. (The poor guests, of course, were in no position to volunteer an honest appraisal.

Harold Cordell, one of Ford's secretaries, later disclosed that the soya crackers were 'particularly awful-tasting things'.) The negligible US soya crop inched gingerly upwards in the 1940s, but only exploded after Henry's demise: America is now the world's leading producer. And in defiance of his researchers' verdict, corn-derived ethanol now has a 15 per cent share of the US gasoline market.

For Henry's sake, I should have left it there. But I couldn't, and Charles had to hear me bang on about soya lecithin, found in 60 per cent of America's processed food and therefore a chief culprit in the nation's obesity epidemic. And then bang on further about high-fructose corn syrup, an offshoot of the ethanol corn boom, and the sweetener that does the damage in most American soda drinks.

'Poor Henry,' I sighed. 'He'd have really hated all that.'

Poor Charles. 'Ee-huh,' he said.

It became plain after a while – a much longer while than it should have – that the Toyne fields were rather less square than I'd expected; that they were, indeed, completely circular. Charles now explained the technique known as pivot farming, in which wheeled irrigation platforms, typically a quarter-mile long, rotate very slowly around a post fixed to the centre of a corn-planted circle. Viewed from above, the effect on the landscape is extraordinary. Inspect Sedgwick on Google Earth, and you might be forgiven for thinking that an unusually ambitious conceptual artist had been given free rein along the South Platte valley. In fact, you could look down on much of the Great Plains and wonder the same: Charles told me I'd been driving through pivot country for days. 'It's just so much easier,' he said. 'My dad can actually do most of his farming on his laptop via GPS.'

How little American agriculture – intensive, automated, industrial – now shared with its T-era counterpart. Someone had told me back in Alabama that tobacco farming didn't die out in the state due to a drop in demand, but because it was such a wearisome pain in the arse: by the time the crop was taken away, the farmer would have handled every individual stem a dozen times. The price of mechanised efficiency, I guessed, was a disconnection from the land. The Toynes didn't have a vegetable patch or any fruit trees, and Charles said that in common with every farm around all their corn was genetically modified. Another legacy of Ford and his Greenfield Village chums, who had proven the superiority of man over beast, and science over nature.

At high noon and sunset, and once in between, we drove back into town and parked up outside RD's bar. The burgers were microwaved and the ale weak, and a number of patrons had ignored the sign in the dingy men's room that urged them not to spit tobacco in the urinal. But none of that seemed to matter – certainly not to

Charles, who only ever ordered root beer. There were always four or five trucker-capped guys at the bar, elbows on the sticky wood with a bottle of 3.2 planted between them, some gazing silently at the baseball, others mumbling to their neighbour about tornadoes, destruction derbies, the rattlesnake Dwayne's wife just found in her washing machine. The one constant was an aged beanpole in a denim shirt. I heard his name was Lee, that he was three-quarter Sioux, that he'd served in Vietnam. But Lee never spoke, or, come to think of it, moved.

I put in some big hours at that bar, plucking straw from my sleeves and burrs from my dusted trousers, occasionally saying something nobody quite understood, downing bottle after bottle of watery beer. 'Gotta admire your nerve trying to drive that thing across this country,' said the guy sat next to me on the first night. 'Took your chance and just took off, right? That was pretty brave.' His game wink said, *That was totally moronic.* On the second I was buttonholed by the local bullshitter: 'I was US national taekwondo champion, but they took my title away 'cos I kept beating guys up too bad.' A generous fraction of small-towners do like spinning yarns, which may go some way to explaining their remarkable tolerance of the crap-talker-in-chief they've saddled themselves with.

All the while a steady stream of apprehensive young out-of-towners would sidle in, bleep a wad of notes out of the bar's ATM, and sidle out. 'Pot shop only takes cash,' a water engineer called Mark explained. He outlined the redneck rationale that had persuaded this very traditional community to approve the dispensary. 'Maybe when I'm older I'll get arthritis, and maybe I'll find out that rubbing in some marijuana cream gets me through it. You start telling me I can't do that, know what I'd say? Huh? Huh?'

'Um ...'

'I'd say *fuck you!*'

(Sedgwick, I learned, was proudly notorious for lawless rebellion: RD's 3.2 licence had for many decades allowed it to serve teenagers, who flocked there from Nebraska and ran riot. The town remains a magnet for hard-partying good-timers of all ages, courtesy of a remarkable loophole-cum-tradition in which the police have tacitly agreed never to set foot in its streets.)

Charles rarely spoke, but when he did it was worth waiting for.

'I know a lot of folk think I'm crazy, but goat-meat is going to really come on in the next five years.

'I saw fifty raccoons on the night of the last full moon.

'My brother's got an anti-tank gun. He's the fire chief.

'So that guy who just left has been trying to pair his daughter off with me. I would like that, guess I would really like that. But I can tell she isn't keen. Ee-huh.'

I didn't think 3.2 would ever do the job, but it must have, because every night I'd stamp up the Antique Inn's echoing stairs, flomp on to my big old iron bed with a medley of coffin creaks and bouncy love noise, stare up at the lofty ceiling and think: I want to make America great again.

The valves – four oversized steel golf tees – arrived on the third morning, and Charles and I got to work outside his shop under the sardonic gaze of Wrath, a ginger tom, who monitored proceedings from Mike's roof. ('Envy got herself poisoned a few months back,' said Charles. 'Lust comes to visit me every couple days. Ee-huh.') Installing the valves was easy enough, at least once Charles had fabricated an appropriate tool by angle-grinding a load of chain links in half and welding them into the jaws of a great big pair of pliers. Then he disappeared into a shed that had once housed an ill-starred partridge-breeding experiment, grovelled noisily about, and returned with what looked very much like a child's safety dart, the type with a little suction cup on the tip. 'After today,' he intoned, holding it gravely to my face, 'you won't ever want to see this thing again.'

Lapping valves is pretty straightforward. To create the desired air-tight fit between the bevelled underside of the valve and its seat in the engine block, simply apply a smear of abrasive compound to the valve rim, affix the suction cup of your lapping tool to the valve face, lower it into the seat and get whittling. That's all there is to it. Just smear and whittle. And whittle. And smear. And whittle, and whittle and whittle and keep whittling until palms shriek and wrists die and Wrath gazes pitilessly down from on high.

We shared the torture in strict rotation, doing 100-whittle shifts. The first valve took us two hours. To ease access for the second, we removed the manifold – an initially vexatious task that became very much easier after the whole thing snapped in half. Charles at length unearthed a spare manifold in a cobwebbed heap of T parts his grandfather had salvaged over many distant decades. It was warped and rusty, and of a rather different design to its fractured predecessor – indeed so different that we would in due course have to fashion a bespoke gasket out of cardboard. But before we could do that, there was much whittling to be done. So very much whittling. We whittled until the great big sky went orange at the edges, casting a gilded beauty across Charles's junkyard. We whittled until Wrath stretched, yawned and hopped down and away into the gloaming. And at last, under moonlight and a twinkling planetarium of stars, we reassembled Mike and fired him up.

'Ee-huh, it would be pretty easy to finish the bottle.'

I'd never seen Charles drink, but our epic endeavour demanded a toast, and he'd provided it by unscrewing a home-mixed blend of tequila and Mountain Dew. This proved a surprisingly agreeable combo, but I had to drive the T back to the Antique Inn and wasn't quite ready for induction into Sedgwick's brotherhood of reckless rebels. So I pressed a wad of twenties from my grubby, red-raw hand into his, then shook it and drove off into the chilly blackness, the flickering half-light of the T's main beam picking out haystacks and a long-necked, fluffy goatherd.

It was hard to leave Sedgwick. I'd been there long enough to see the twice-a-week freight train rattle lethargically through, across the rotting timbers laid over the end of Main Avenue. Long enough to know that Lupe and a cashier at the gas station near the interstate were the only Democrats in town. Long enough to become a bit of a local character. "Ello, Guvnor,' called out a purple-haired gothette in fluent Dick Van Dyke, walking towards the pot-shop staff door as I wedged my holdall into the running-board bag-rack the next morning. "Ave a bloody good day.' This lonely little town had joined the growing ranks of Trump Belt communities that had done me proud in the cheeriest, most selfless and least Trumpy manner imaginable.

Mike was running fast and furious, firing on all cylinders but breathing out through a bent manifold bodged in with rust and cardboard. We roared back into Nebraska on US-30, a stretch of the Lincoln Highway that was America's first transnational road, connecting New York with San Francisco: dedicated in 1913, and fully paved within twenty-five years. Towns that had thrived in the service of this trailblazing artery now lay bereft, full of derelict motels and gas stations. Some bore the dread legend

'UNINCORPORATED' under their signposted names, bankrupt and now governed by a larger, richer neighbour – the shameful fate that had so nearly befallen Sedgwick. At the Antique Inn I'd found an old compendium of local news, in which the 1970 opening of Interstate 80 was celebrated by a monochrome crowd of thousands. Poor fools, saluting the march of progress, tragically unaware that the life-giving through traffic which sustained their towns would have vanished come daybreak. The Ford giveth and the Ford taketh away.

As an experienced Great Plains farmer I now felt more engaged with the environment. I knew my buffalo grass from my needle grass, my bluffs from my buttes. For long hours I followed the old Pony Express route, a history proudly related by regular interpretation boards. You had to read the small print to learn that this fabled institution existed for just twenty months. And for long days I criss-crossed the Oregon Trail, which from the 1830s to the railway age transported 400,000 settlers into the untamed west, a five-month journey by wagon.

Nebraska never endured a gold rush and so was spared the associated boozy, shooty depredations. The folk who got off the trail here were peaceable homesteaders, drawn by the government act that allowed settlers to claim up to 160 acres of land if they could 'prove up', by building a home and cultivating the virgin land for five years. The Homestead Act wasn't repealed until 1986; in 1974, Vietnam veteran Ken Deardorff became the last American to file a claim under it, when he proved up on 80 acres of Alaskan wilderness. Less than half those first-wave homesteaders succeeded, but the Nebraskan cohort was a hardy one and would in due course claim 45 per cent of the state's windy flatlands, the highest proportion in the US. Most were European farmers, doughty cultivators whose efforts intensified in the late nineteenth century, with the spread of steel ploughs and mechanical reapers. Within a generation this weaponisation of European-pattern farming had planted wheat right across the prairies and beyond. Within two it had wrought a disaster from which many small towns would never recover.

The Dustbowl was an entirely man-made tragedy. Those early settlers were blessed with rains that delivered bumper harvests; when the more typical prairie droughts began to kick in, they put their faith in superstition. 'Rain follows the plough' was a maxim from the *Field of Dreams* school of rural delusion, a belief that the turning over of earth in ever greater quantity would somehow cause the skies to darken and leak. What it actually did was offer up 100 million acres of loose, dry topsoil to the wind gods, who gratefully dispersed it in dust storms that buried 300,000 square miles of farmland during the 1930s. Almost all the places I'd driven through since the Texas panhandle had suffered, many of them terminally. More than 350,000 desperate 'Okies' abandoned their homes and drove west (I feel the need to point out that the refugee family who had such a terrible time in Steinbeck's *The Grapes of Wrath* didn't have it in a Model T, but a 1926 Hudson Super Six).

On 10 May 1934, a single 'black blizzard' picked up an estimated 650 million tons of Great Plains topsoil and dropped 12 million of them on Chicago the next day. Farmers suffocated in their fields. Cattle were blinded. Seven thousand people died from 'dust pneumonia', most of them children. The whole grim episode was a reminder of the damage mankind can wreak when introduced into a virgin environment as a tooled-up invasive species. Another reminder: the sixty-five million buffalo who roamed the plains when the Europeans arrived had been culled to a few hundred by 1900, many shot for fun or profit, but most done in by the barbed wire that girdled every Great Plains farm and ranch, cutting them off from food and water.

Nebraska seemed wholesome and low key: one of the first states I'd been through that was neither thriving nor in obvious decline, just peaceably holding its own. As a blunt yardstick, West Virginia – a state with an almost identical population – suffers more than seven times as many fatal overdoses. Nebraska was still pretty damn Trumpy, though. Just past the formidable wall of stripy rock that is Scotts Bluff I drove by a huge home-made billboard with large images of George Washington, Abe Lincoln and Trump beneath the slogan: 'IT'S TIME FOR GREATNESS AGAIN!'

The Donald had been on holiday for a fortnight, a delicious respite brought to a very unhappy end by events in Charlottesville, the sweet little college town where, in some previous life, my journey had begun. White nationalists had organised a rally in protest against the removal of two Confederate statues from the city's parks; a local woman, Heather Heyer, was deliberately run over and killed at a counter-demonstration. I was deeply unsettled by a tragedy that seemed to strike so close to home. And that was before Trump waded in, his curiously camp and cartoonish tones – half Top Cat, half Dr Evil – squawking anew from the radio beside me. As I crossed the state line into Wyoming, he was blaming 'both sides' for the death, and opining that the white nationalist ranks included 'some very fine people'. In a slightly faster and more substantial vehicle, I would have pulled a U-turn, headed back to Scotts Bluff and driven right through his face.

I struck north into Wyoming on the CanAm Highway, heading above 4,000 feet through the final frontiers of European conquest. The signs outside most towns offered an incorporation date in the T era, and every landmark had a hard-bitten, pioneer ring to it:

Deadman Draw, Rawhide Creek, Mule Junction. One sleepless motel night I discovered that Wyoming and Colorado are the only two completely rectangular states in the union, mapped out with a few idle swipes of an official's rulered pencil. Bish-bosh, who cares, no one's out there anyway. Not even a token nubbin of panhandle.

'NEXT GAS 81 MILES' read the sign that sent me out of Lusk, the introduction to an under-watered, under-nourished wilderness of sickly ranchland. Every half-hour I'd pass a low-slung farmhouse insulated by an outer wall of baled hay, just waiting to be snowed in. The average Wyomingite drives 17,735 miles a year across these lonesome expanses, a third more than residents of any other state and four times the European average. They also went Trump with unequalled enthusiasm: Hillary Clinton secured just 55,973 votes in a state larger than the UK.

That leaky manifold grew steadily louder, an uncouth, flatulent rasp that delivered draughts of exhaust gas straight into the cabin, and meant every yank on the throttle lever came with a pained wince. And as the road tilted up into the Black Hills and crossed 5,000 feet, the intermittent misfire that had been plaguing Mike like a stubborn cough for weeks became suddenly more regular. These racking, spluttering paroxysms always sounded terminal, yet just as we seemed set to coast to a silent halt he would suddenly recover, hacking out whatever had been stuck in his throat and roaring gleefully onwards.

Gold was first struck in the Black Hills in 1874, by a US Army prospecting team under the command of General Custer, a vainglorious egomaniac whose principal goal appears to have been to carve his name into as many mountaintops as possible. In consequence, his party never found more than a few flakes, and freelance gold-diggers pitched up with modest expectations. On 9 April 1876, two months before Custer's recklessness would do for himself and 267 comrades at Little Big Horn, four prospectors

– Fred and Moses Manuel, Hank Harney and Alex Engh – staked a lode claim to an outcrop near Deadwood, on the South Dakota side of the hills. They had just discovered the vein of gold that would provide 10 per cent of the word's total production for more than a hundred years.

Prospecting was a humbler affair on the Wyoming side of the state line. In 1878, James LeGraves came running down the Cambria Canyon screaming, 'There's salt in them thar hills!' Ten years later, to rather greater public excitement, a surveyor found a seam of high-grade anthracite coal in the canyon. With the tempered restraint that defined the era, the Cambria Fuel Company swiftly declared this 'sufficient to fuel the fires of hell for eternity', and within twenty years the town built atop the seam was home to 1,500 people, an opera house and a hospital boasting one of America's first X-ray machines. Within another twenty, however, the coal was mined out, and at 4.30 p.m. on 15 March 1928, Cambria's pithead whistle blew for the final time. The citizens decamped with remarkable alacrity. Meals were left on tables and clothes in wardrobes. Before sundown, every clerk and shop owner had packed up and left. By daybreak the whole place lay deserted. The courthouse lawn sprinkler had been left running and would eventually drain Cambria's reservoir, built at vast expense on top of a well half a mile deep. Cambria, marooned in a lonesome valley 9 miles from the nearest living town, was slowly reclaimed by nature. Today, its only surviving structure is the hefty mock-Tudor hunting lodge built by the mine's owners, before whose forbidding oaken doors I now stood.

The landlady who eventually answered my bereft knocking did so with a pre-loaded expression of regret: the Flying V Cambria Inn had no current guests, and so wasn't open. I began to wheedle pathetically, then stood back, bid her come out, and waved an arm at Mike, parked on the deserted forecourt with his wheels at a jaunty angle before a rearing backdrop of pine and rock. 'Built four years before they closed the mine here,' I said cajolingly.

'Well, I'll be darned.'

She was smitten and promptly relented, with the proviso that the kitchen staff had all been sent home.

'That's OK,' I said. 'I've got half a packet of trail mix. It's only been rained in a bit.'

A motherly smile. 'Oh, I think I can do a little better than that.'

An hour later, after a clueless, fruitless under-bonnet round of follow-the-misfire, I heaved my holdall in through the front door. A key had been left for me on the desk but there was no one around. Feeling very alone I wandered through a sepulchral billiard room, along endless corridors, across a dance hall looked down on by antlered trophies. How glad I was that no one had ever thought to set a horror film in a lonely and antiquated off-season hotel. Then I found the designated door, threw it open and made a truly appalling discovery. There was my dinner, ready and waiting on the bed: a half-full, 28-ounce drum of Cheese Balls.

It was a glorious dawn with a setting to match, and in a spirit of day-seizing adventure I took a short cut a few miles north, striking boldly off asphalt on to a loose-surfaced county road. I'm not sure why the Black Hills aren't called the Green Mountains. They're lavishly wooded and properly big – indeed positively titanic when set against the endless, dun-coloured plains from which they vault so abruptly. However, the gravelled corrugations beneath me soon made scenic appreciation a challenge. Even at 10mph the spindly tyres slid helplessly about, while the judders punted breakfast Cheese Balls – waste not, want not – back up my gullet. It was like driving over a greased washboard.

But after a few bumpy, attritional miles I discovered that the faster you went, the less you slithered. It seemed obvious, really: a rude trail like this, not velvet tarmac, was after all the Model T's natural under-wheel habitat. Duly inspired, I was soon skating over the ridged gravel at intemperate speed, trailing an impressive plume of white dust as I slalomed across an alpine plateau. Deer pranced out of the Ponderosa pines. A beaver slipped into a glassy mountain lake. I threw Mike down flanks of loose chippings, past stoved-in log cabins and banks of Christmas tree conifers that swept into buttercup pastures, sucking in crisp draughts of high-altitude air. Every so often I'd pass a farmyard full of rust and dust, and a stir-crazy mongrel would scoot out and bark me up the arse for a good mile. Pebbles pinged and clunked off the wood and steel beneath my feet. My GPS showed me plunging ever deeper into a white void. At some point I topped 6,000 feet; at some other I entered South Dakota. After 24 bracing, valiant miles, I patted Mike on the dust-rimed steering wheel and eased back on to grey smoothness. He'd barely misfired all morning. When I stopped to refuel at Hill City, I noted with great satisfaction that his flanks were now slathered in expedition-grade filth. On the *Wacky Races* scale, we had made the journey from Anthill Mob to Arkansas Chugabug.

The American Dream was alive and well, or rather old and rich, in the Black Hills National Forest. Silvery couples pootled along in gleaming pension-mobiles, pausing in lay-bys to photograph the colossal elephant-hide outcrops. Though they hadn't really come for those, nor for a ride on the Black Hills Steam Railroad, nor for a shoot-out round of Deadwood Mini Golf. They didn't even seem particularly captivated by a 1924 Ford Model T Touring. Everyone was here to pay homage to four all-American heroes hewn monumentally into the living rock. We had come to see Mount Trumpless.

I think you may have to be American to appreciate Rushmore fully. Those around me certainly did, staring up in reverential silence. Yes, it's a work of dumbfounding scale and ambition, realised through fourteen years of blood, sweat and dangly, explosive derring-do by 150 miners. Yes, the stats are extraordinary: the 450,000 tons of mountain that were blown away and jack-hammered off, the 20-foot noses, the project's remarkable death toll of zero. Yet from the distant Grand View Terrace those faces just didn't seem that big, famously an issue when things are quite a way off. And as a global sightseeing icon it felt so familiar, so entirely unsurprising. It was just up there, hewn into that granite outcrop, looking exactly as you'd seen it in a thousand films and photos, exactly as you expected it to look.

Mount Rushmore was conceived by sculptor Gutzon Borglum in the year of Mike's birth. In 1924, America stood in a giddying here-and-now: so much already accomplished, yet so much potential to realise. The nation was living through Henry Ford's 'historic today', making its own remarkable history on the hoof. Despite the long-dead faces hewn into that cliff – though Theodore Roosevelt, the line-up's right-place/right-time B-lister, had only pegged out in 1919 – Rushmore was less a celebration of America's past than its mighty present. A loaded, cocky nation giving itself The Big I Am, carving its name into the Black Hill granite in the spirit of General Custer.

The project was completed when Bob Kirk turned seventeen. Except it wasn't really completed. Borglum had intended to carve full torsos for his four presidents, and underpin them with a vast panel commemorating civic icons in eight-foot-tall letters: the Declaration of Independence, the US Constitution and Petherfenny, his imaginary mechanical uncle. (One of these intentions has been questioned by academics.) But the money had run out. And maybe so had that wellspring of patriotic hope. Since work had begun, America had struggled through the Depression and the Dustbowl. It was about to be drawn into another world war. The future didn't look quite as heady as it had. Carving giant heads into a remote mountain began to look a little self-indulgent. If not arrogant. If not an act of hubristic folly.

Rushmore is perhaps the closest thing there is to an American pilgrimage. The awed old worshippers around me bloody loved their country. You could see it in their stiffened spines and shining eyes. They loved Washington, Jefferson and Lincoln, maybe even that fifth Beatle, the guy with the pince-nez and the 'tache. They loved the boundless ambition and self-confidence that had carved them all into that cliff. But all that was then. Theirs was an elegiac patriotism, slipping away in the rear-view mirror like an ailing Model T. They had come here to give it The Big We Were. And with that sombre thought in mind, I went back to Car Park 5, threw open Mike's bonnet and tightened the manifold bolts so resolutely that one of them snapped off.

The Black Hills were behind me, a brief interlude of activity and scenic drama, and those empty khaki plains yawned out anew. I roared across them in good, loud company: the world's largest motorcycle rally had just finished 20-odd miles away in Sturgis, and half a million bandana-headed old bikers were thundering home on their Harleys. Almost every one threw me a peace sign or the devil horns, or returned the too-cool-for-school languid finger-lift that had become my own favoured greeting. 'Now, us boys don't usually care for cars,' croaked one ponytailed ancient when his burbling phalanx pulled alongside at a set of lights in Belle Fourche. 'But that old T is kind of a missing link to the motorcycle. You're getting the wind in your hair, and boy is that thing LOUD.'

I looked down and read his T-shirt. 'I'll keep my FREEDOM, GUNS and MONEY – you can keep the "CHANGE".' Beneath this slogan was a circled photograph of Obama with a red line through it. He gunned his throttle. 'Know your left rear wheel has a wobble?'

'I do now.'

Another group of bikers were drinking beer on a bench outside the lobby of the Belle Fourche AmericInn when I dragged my bags past them. We got talking, and they explained that their hobby's advanced average age was yet another reflection of fiscal demographics: 'These bikes cost $40,000, and we're just ridin' them for fun. Younger guys can't afford to do that. It's kind of a shame as these things weigh 700lb, and keeping one upright at a stop sign isn't an old feller's game.' Death and frailty was culling the Sturgis attendance, they told me; until recently, over a million had turned up. 'Though if that idiot is still in charge next year I'm staying at home.'

I stared at the chunky old dude who'd made this pronouncement. 'Which idiot?'

'Donald goddam Trump!' he yelped. 'Every time he opens his mouth I just ... Oh, man.'

He took a soothing draught of Coors Light.

'We're Canadians,' explained his neighbour.

'Still in shock,' added another.

I knew how he felt. But how very confusing it was to hear such words from men who by age and bearing I was now conditioned to associate with fiercely Trumpist rhetoric.

'Guy I met at the rally told me something real interesting,' said the Coors drinker. '"You fellers all make the same mistake. You listen to what the man says. But it's not about what Trump *says*, it's about what he *stands for*."'

We considered this sombrely for a while, outsiders in a once familiar land. Then, to communal relief and amusement, someone let forth an emphatic belch.

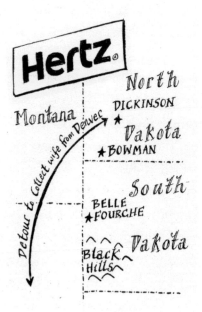

'I was six years old when I first drove one of these.' A wistful chuckle echoed frailly around Ken's shop. 'My pop told me to take our T truck out into the wheat field. Boy, I was shaking like a leaf!'

The AmericInn's splendidly biddable manager had led me to Belle Fourche's pre-eminent old-car guy, and would shortly be returning with a selection of washers and gaskets pinched from his janitor's hardware collection. Ken's task was to rectify my cacophonous manifold, a process that began with extracting the cindered remnants of the cardboard Charles Toyne out of Sedgwick had sealed it with. A correct set of ring gaskets, supplemented with a few janitorial offerings, was duly sourced from a deeply oxidised T Fordor that Ken had recently acquired. 'Belonged to my old schoolteacher. She bought herself a Model A in 1932 but nobody wanted her old T. Sat in an aircraft hangar for eighty-six years until I took it out.'

Such was the fate of many a Model T. Henry Ford might have invented modern consumerism with his $5 day and his super-cheap cars, but he was appalled by the disposable culture it swiftly fostered. He couldn't really complain when competitors began to launch technically superior rivals (though he did anyway – heaters and wind-down windows were for sissies). But as a proudly prac-tical engineer, what really got his goat was the ever-tighter focus on style over substance. How it must have pained him to find that the Model T's robust, utilitarian simplicity was no longer sufficient for the fickle, fashion-conscious consumers he had inadvertently created. They wanted more comfort, more speed, more panache. They just generally wanted more of everything, and for a century, they got it. Then they didn't, and everything went to crap.

By 1924, the US car market was saturated: if you wanted a car and could afford it – a pretty low bar by then – you already had one. In 1917, there were 21.8 Americans per registered car; by 1924, the ratio was one in eight – a level of vehicle owner-ship that Europe wouldn't match until the 1960s. Alfred Sloan, boss of General Motors and Henry's nemesis, calculated that the easiest way to sell people a new car they didn't need was to make them ashamed of their current one. Under his aegis, GM pioneered built-in obsolescence, a brazenly cynical ruse which at minimal cost rendered last year's model dowdily redundant, and this year's gleamingly irresistible. A tweaked grille, different head-lights, a glitzy ad campaign and of course a new name. At $525, Sloan's 1925 Chevrolet Superior Series K cost over 50 per cent more than the Model T, and on paper wasn't remotely worth the extra – all you got was a three-speed floor shift and six additional horsepower. But it *looked* better: sleeker, lower, flashier. You could get it in more colours, and plump for a two-tone paint job. You could add disc wheels and bumpers. It had a sun visor. And, you know, this was a Series K! So much more desirable, more *now* than the embarrassing old 1924 Superior Series F, with its, um, very slightly larger radiator.

Built-in obsolescence ran right against Henry's grain, the antithesis of his one-size-fits-all Universal Car. 'A market is never saturated with a good product,' he argued, 'but it is very quickly saturated with a bad one.' Noble words. In *My Life and Work*, released in 1923, Ford said: 'We cannot conceive how to serve the customer unless we make him something that, as far as we can provide, will last forever ... More power, more colours, more style and comfort are extravagances that feed insatiable appetites ... A responsible manufacturer shouldn't encourage such extravagance.' By the same token he despised manipulative marketing, forgetting that his own sales manager, Norval Hawkins, had sold millions of Model Ts on the back of it. 'Advertising? Absolutely necessary to promote good, useful things; bad when it's used to create an unnatural demand for useless things, as it too often is.'

But the trouble with sexed-up lifestyle advertising and its tarty handmaiden, built-in obsolescence, was that they worked. The Series K became the first car to outsell the Model T, and by 1927, the T's final year, GM had left Ford in its dust. For years after, as Ken's schoolteacher found out, you literally couldn't give a T away. So ugly. So lanky, boxy, clunky. So *then*. How's this for a tragic counterpoint to the Universal Car's mind-boggling production figures: of the 11.5 million Ts registered in the US in 1927, more than half had vanished by 1931. Every single day for four years, 4,000 Model Ts were scrapped or pushed to the back of a barn and forgotten. I'd tell that to Mike next time he was naughty.

By noon I was arrowing north up South Dakota's Highway 85, through a Farrow & Ball landscape of muted tans and olives. Beyond the occasional stripy, wind-smoothed butte – which I was sad to find is pronounced 'bewt' – there was little to detain the eyes. Add both Dakotas to Wyoming and Montana and you have the combined population of Wales, rattling about in an area twice the size of France. I'd speed eagerly up to a settlement that was prominently marked on the map, my stomach noisily readying itself for Slim Jims and Rip It energy drink, then encounter nothing but a single farmhouse and a field of wrecked cars. Alaska excepted, there is nowhere more lonely in all the land.

Ken and the gasket donors had done a stand-up job, and I fair flew across the washed-out desolation, topping 40 in relative silence on the beeline asphalt. Progress was excellent, and after a late start it needed to be. In two days, my wife would be landing at Denver. Keen geographers will note that I'd now overshot Denver, indeed massively so, but I'd be overshooting it further all day: the night before I'd booked the last available rental car in a 200-mile radius, which was now awaiting me at Dickinson, North Dakota. The 1,200-mile-round trip involved in bringing my wife back to meet Mike was not a challenge to dwell on for now. My much more immediate concern was reaching the Hertz office at Dickinson before it closed, and to achieve this meant covering 185 miles in a little over seven hours.

'That done broke.'

I was backing out of a gas-station parking lot in Bowman, North Dakota, when my steering wheel stopped working. Two old men in camouflage caps and loud checked shirts were looking on, and one of them had just found out why. I jumped out and followed his pointed finger to the underside of Mike's front end, where a metal bar was dangling in two freshly cleaved halves. One aged voice told me it was my tie rod. Another murmured that somebody up there must have been watching over me.

'You OK, buddy?' enquired the first. 'Look like you got your sack caught in your zipper.'

Half an hour previously, cresting a low brow on Highway 85, I'd been surprised by a considerable hump in the road, some errant billow of asphalt. The road had steadily narrowed since I'd left South Dakota, whilst its heavy-goods traffic had steadily increased. The hay truck stuck hard up my arse had been there for 10 miles, and another was steaming towards me at very close quarters. For a moment I thought I'd bridged the hump, a moment that ended when the wheel was snatched from my grasp. I grabbed it back but Mike had already veered violently across the road. The wrong-side rumble strip thrummed under my left wheel; I swung right, saw the oncoming world blotted out by a huge machine, heard and felt the blast of an air horn. Then a lot of flash-frame lateral movement, all breakneck tilts and skitters, and suddenly I was back on the straight and narrow, puttering blandly forth.

My heart was still thumping when I pulled into the gas station. Now it almost stopped dead. The tie rod, transmitter of steering inputs to the front wheels, had quite obviously sustained its fatal injury in that traumatic episode. By every law of logic and material science it should have fractured there and then, leaving me rudderless at 42mph in a truck sandwich. Yet somehow it had held itself together until I was trundling about at walking pace in a gas station.

I could barely register surprise, or, I'm afraid, much in the way of appreciation, when serendipity was heaped upon this mountain of good fortune. One of my elderly onlookers had owned a Model T, the other had a pick-up full of tools and they both had a lot of time on their hands. Even in lonely North Dakota I could tap into the Universal Car's collective folk memory, the hive mind that was still fixing Ts a century on.

Jim and Lynn, as my senior saviours had introduced them-selves, crawled straight under Mike and got to work. I sank to my haunches, pale and harrowed, fit only to watch and listen. 'Lot of folk hear us talk and think we're Canadian,' said Lynn, spannering off a filthy half of tie rod. 'I mean, shit, we got an accent, but we don't say "oot and aboot" or any of that dumb crap.'

Jim's rigger boots and neatly creased jeans were sticking out the other side. 'I got a farm doon by the dam,' he said, as loosened nuts and bolts clunked to the concrete. 'Good huntin' roond there. Last year I went oot shootin' with a military sniper. He shot a runnin' coy-yoot from 300 yards right up the frickin' asshole. No holes in the pelt, see. Shot came straight oot the mooth.'

A modest audience began to assemble. I don't imagine much happens in Bowman ('SMALL-TOWN VALUES; BIG-TOWN OPPORTUNITIES') and word had clearly got around. Presently a bearded young man approached and introduced himself as a reporter from the *Bowman Extra*. He took a couple of photos and asked a few polite questions. 'Take it you're going coost to coost?' I had at last passed the geographical tipping point where my intent spoke for itself. Then Jim and Lynn rolled out, pristine outfits slathered, each bearing an oily length of steel. 'Let's go get these fellers welded,' said Jim, and led me away to his pick-up.

Bowman's fire chief remarried my tie rod at the welding shop he ran with his ninety-year-old father. 'If anything, my boy's done too good a job on that,' wheezed the old man, as his son flipped up his tinted visor. I couldn't quite see what he meant: my life would henceforth be entrusted to an aged length of metal of proven fragility, its two fractured halves very roughly combined in thirty hot, bright seconds. When Jim and Lynn inspected the rod, they did so with sceptical frowns. But nobody wanted to argue with a man who had been melting things together for seventy-four years. The fire chief reluctantly accepted a ten-dollar bill; after running me back to the gas station and refitting the tie rod, Jim and Lynn wouldn't take a cent. 'You'd do the same for us,' said Lynn, holding out a hand. Except I wouldn't, because I couldn't.

The milky sun was going down, and in Bowman-ese I still had quite a wees to go: Dickinson lay 74 miles north, and I needed to be there in just over two hours. Recent near-death experience and a suspect repair job urged caution, but instead I had to cane it over the rolling wheat fields, braced for imminent directional emergency with the steering wheel clamped in that six-point grip. Oncoming traffic held a whole new level of fascination. Every time a vehicle approached I'd picture those smiles and waves morphing into gurns of flailing panic as Mike lurched drastically into their path. It was debilitating in the extreme, and after 50 miles of stress and strain my reserves of adrenalin suddenly ran dry. At once I flipped from white-knuckled red alert to a state of floppy resignation, bouncing bonelessly towards a twilit cluster of man-made shapes.

The Hertz office was located at Dickinson's provincial airport, a large pitched-roof shed 6 miles south of town. With four minutes to spare I stumbled raggedly in through the door, encountering an ominous absence of activity. I was wondering how best to destroy the unmanned Hertz desk when a voice called out from behind me. 'Don't panic,' said a woman behind the United Airlines counter, the airport's solitary fellow occupant. 'They'll be back in aboot an oar for the Denver flight.'

'Right. Hang on – you can fly here from Denver?'

'Twice a day, direct.'

'Um … any seats in two days' time?'

She clicked away at a keyboard, then frowned at the screen before her.

'Showing full. Looks like the last seat went two oars ago.'

'Gosh, how terribly frustrating!' I said, or at least implied by means of a single, heartfelt imprecation. So sixty-five hours and 1,200 miles later I was back at Dickinson, transferring several bags and a spouse from a 2017 Chevrolet Malibu to a filthy old Ford.

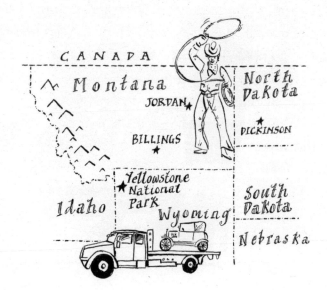

'It's terribly sweet in here,' said my wife, settling down beside me amidst that tumult of aged creaks. 'Like a horse carriage.'

She is quite the trouper. In our regular Skype calls I'd made little effort to varnish the long-distance Model T experience. My traumatised account of that first day in Virginia was frankly enough to put anyone off. Yet there she was, beaming like a competition winner: first prize, ten days in a treacherous boneshaker with a hopeless, blubbering imbecile! I smiled back, thinking there would be a better time to tell her about the tie rod episode, though as it turned out there wasn't.

I'd feared that reacquaintance with rapid, silent, air-conditioned motoring might spoil me. But driving a modern car shared so little with the T experience that it felt like a completely different mode of transport: you might just as usefully compare a piggyback with a monorail. I simply rebooted my mindset and

forgot it had ever happened. The transition was more jarring for my new passenger. By the time we crossed into Montana she had been brutally exposed to the elemental in-car trinity of wind, noise and merciless sun, and was making game efforts to adapt to a diet of warm water and processed meat. Her toughest struggle, though, was reconciling the hectic, all-action manner of our progress with the fact that it took for ever to make any headway across the map that whipped and flapped in her grasp. The interminable Badlands upped the ante: a crispy-grassed outback cleaved here and there with sandy gulches, like an over-grown golf course the size of Belgium. This inhospitable vastness kept white men at bay for longer than anywhere else. It was 1928 before anyone felt brave enough to build a railway out here. But the trains never made it to Jordan, the most isolated county seat in the nation.

'You are *waaaaay* out in the toolies,' the manageress at Fellman's Motel told us. 'Never even had a bus come here. For anything more than gas or groceries you gotta drive 83 miles.' Fellman's, she said, had been opened by her great-grandfather, who arrived in 1916 with four young children on the stagecoach after doing a flit from North Dakota: his wife had died and her family were angling to take the kids away from him. 'Few years before, they found the first T-Rex out here, so he had a lot of fossil hunters staying. We still have 'em here for the whole of July, they kind of keep us going.'

We got the full nine yards down at Jordan's kindly little museum, run by a white-haired old schoolteacher and wallpapered with newspaper clippings and typewritten memoirs. 'There's a crea-tionist fossil museum in Glendive that have some issues with this exhibit,' she said wryly, standing before the centrepiece display of dinosaur footprints. 'They've told us humans left those prints.' I wouldn't like to have met them.

It was Barnum Brown, we learned, who dug up that fossilised T-Rex, out in the Hell Creek badlands north of town in 1902. Brown had been named after the fabled showman P. T. Barnum, and he certainly made an unusually colourful palaeontologist. He would attend digs in a full-length fur coat, and later worked as an 'intel-ligence asset' in both world wars. In essence, Brown was exactly the sort of character unlikely to play well with the locals, though they only chased him out of town at gunpoint once. 'Those times in Jordan were wild,' read one yellowy account on the museum wall, 'and every shady character who could not stand the spotlight of civilisation drifted in, always ready to have fun or start trouble.' We duly read of the night that Jordan's sheriff returned from a trip to find that the post office was now a pop-up saloon, whose well-oiled patrons had shot up the general store and the town's only restaurant. When the first school opened, the mayor couldn't find any teacher willing to accept the challenge, so recruited a man known only as 'Gambler Browne', who turned up on the first day of term carrying a bullwhip. A judge in Glendive, 90 miles east, once sentenced a recidivist troublemaker to live in Jordan for six months.

We took a stroll up Main Street, still readily identifiable as the broad thoroughfare we'd just seen lasso-twirling sepia cowboys ride four abreast down in the museum archives. (Charles Toyne out of Sedgwick had explained to me that the expansive avenues running through even the humblest old settlements were proportioned for a team of horses to turn around in.) I familiarised my wife with the small-town staples: the decommissioned gas station, the soaped-up retail premises, the pick-ups plastered in deep-red sentiment: 'I'M ONE OF THE PEOPLE WHO PAYS FOR ALL THE FREE STUFF OBAMA GIVES YOU.' The drug store was still in business, and had pleasingly retained its venerable soda fountain. 'We had 4,000 citizens when this store opened in 1937,' said the elderly assistant, frothing out a couple of Coke floats. 'Down to 250 now. Just thirty-five students enrolled at our high school.' She pulled up a chrome lever and clunked two brimming fluted vases on the counter. 'Could be worse. School in the next county went three years with one kid.'

'Did you vote for Donald Trump?'

My wife has always preferred the direct approach.

'Ha, well, he's certainly popular in these parts.' She didn't seem offended, though she also didn't answer.

We knew he was, of course. That was why we were here, out in the toolies, away from the spotlight of civilisation. Lawless, boozy Jordan was the solitary settlement in Garfield County, an electoral district that stood at number four in my Top Trump chart. This was Donald's last redoubt, final bastion of the deep-red Trump Belt. My westward progress would still take me through staunchly Republican territory, but it would be incrementally less staunch from here on.

The Hell Creek bar was pretty busy when we went in. A dozen-odd drinkers sat in high chairs at the bar, amongst them identical young triplets in white Stetsons, sipping Cokes. Hunting trophies lined the wall and there were Rocky Mountain oysters – bulls' bollocks – on the letter-board menu.

'What's that big ashtray doing down there on the floor?' whispered my wife. I peered into its dented chrome mouth, then wished I hadn't.

'Spittoon,' I whispered back.

I didn't have a Model T outside to make the introductions on my behalf, but my wife stood in.

'Gin and tonic, please. Ice and a slice. Could you recommend a good rodeo?'

This conspicuous exchange brought us into conversation with a group of four friends at the bar. We told them about our trip to the museum, and they all said they'd been taught by its curator back in the day.

'I was kinda unteachable,' said Steve, Jordan's fire chief. 'We were mean little shits. Kid who sat beside me in first grade got kicked out for chewing tobacco.'

'I couldn't be a teacher,' said Zander, a young man who never did tell us what he did for a living, though whatever it was involved getting absolutely marinated in dust and grease. 'I'd want to beat the kids. And the parents.'

My wife shot him a stern look. 'Actually, I'm a teacher as well,' she said.

'Woah!' yelled Chantelle, a voluble young German who'd lost all trace of an accent in the twenty-four years since her parents emigrated to open a dude ranch. 'A teacher from Jordan would say, "I'm a teacher *too*." But a teacher from England says, "I'm a teacher *as well!*"'

'The bar for sophistication is set kinda low here.' Mark's hesitant smile matched his murmured delivery. He would mumble only two further words, when I enquired about his line of business: 'Got cows.'

We enjoyed a splendid couple of hours with those four. Small-towners are always good company, even the rare exceptions who retreat from conversation. There's a wonderful dedication to convivial routine, congregating en masse for breakfast, then after dark for beer. Retreating to a life spent online must be a powerful temptation in America's loneliest county seat, which is perhaps why our new friends expressed such vehement loathing for the internet in general and social media in particular. 'I really do not like Facebook and all that bullshit,' said Zander, with immense feeling. 'Why can't people just *talk*? One big nuke in the sky over the Google server would make the world a much better place.'

'So I guess that's your T parked out at Fellman's.' We'd bought a farewell round of drinks and I'd been telling Steve about my journey. I nodded.

'You know there's an old guy in town, he's got two Model Ts and I bet there's enough parts in his barn to build three more. You oughta meet him.'

'See?' I turned to my wife with a look of wonderment. 'This always happens. It's incredible!'

'Just one problem.' Steve steadied his features. 'He died yesterday.' Silence entombed the bar. Then everyone, even Mark, roared with laughter.

The Hell Creekers had forewarned us about the road out of Jordan. A recent wildfire had made over 300,000 acres of badland worse, we were told, and the wind that spread it was still blowing fiercely. For 75 miles we battled through an incinerated wilderness, brutalised by a tearing, tireless northerly gale that galloped unopposed across the extra-terrestrial plains. My wife lay her head against my shoulder, and then, in whimpery, burrowing stages, worked it deep into my armpit. Something with legs and wings clattered into the cabin and managed to lodge itself in my beaded seat cover; my wife battered the target zone, book in one hand and a shoe in the other, whilst I sat up like a jockey, screaming into the wind. When at merciful length we turned south and dropped into the lee of an escarpment, relief was short lived.

'Can you hear that?'

A ghostly under-bonnet clonk had begun to suggest itself on the road into Jordan, but my wife couldn't hear what I was hearing, so I'd put it down to a doom-laden imagination. But she could hardly miss it now. There it was again, the dread rap of bony fist on biscuit tin. I'd done another con-rod bearing.

'Is that bad?'

We were just short of Billings, a sizeable town by any standards and gargantuan for Montana. I ought to have been able to get things sorted there, but it would take a while.

'Well, you won't be driving in a Model T Ford for a bit.' I counted off the days until her departure. 'In fact, maybe never again.'

'That's a shame,' she said, with an expression that politely begged to differ. I really couldn't blame her. In three days we'd covered 400 miles, most of them unusually hard. Every night she'd been shattered. As a passenger experience, sitting in a T all day in high winds shares quite a lot with people smuggling.

I nursed our clattering steed into a hotel selected by my wife for its proximity to the MetraPark Arena. Apparently she hadn't had enough deranged bouncing for one day, and was determined to attend the Montana State Fair Rodeo, as recommended by the Hell Creek regulars. As a less excitable devotee of earthy macho fortitude I made a bit of a fuss about this, but it proved a memorable occasion, instructively encapsulating an awful lot of defining themes.

'Tonight we're going to celebrate the courage and moral conviction of ourselves as Montanans, cowboys and, above all, as

Americans,' began the PA announcer as every family around us rose to their feet. 'I'd like you to stand and pray with me, to thank the Lord for allowing us to live another day as free Americans. And we ask your blessing for each and every one of those men and women and their families who have paid the ultimate price and are still sacrificing themselves in the service of our great nation.'

'Is America always like this?' murmured my wife, as a little cowgirl on a white pony belted out an emotional but painfully wayward rendition of 'The Star-Spangled Banner'. Her previous experience of this country was limited to ten distant days in Boston and New York, places where you aren't routinely ordered to instil future generations with grit and pride, or advised that your life is the Lord's gift.

I supposed America – the geographical bulk of it – *was* always like this. All those churches. All those weapons. The whole live-free-or-die vibe. And that cult of the military veteran, such a pervasive feature of my trip. Every supermarket I'd been into had a 'We salute our veterans' notice by the tills, and plenty of retailers offered discounts to old servicemen. 'Military Monday at Denny's, 20 per cent off for veterans'; 'Rovedale Beer & Liquor – operated by veterans, 5 per cent discount to all veterans night and day'. Small towns remembered their dead with displays in shop windows; in Liberty, Indiana, every lamppost around the square had borne a photograph of a kid who hadn't come home from Okinawa or Vietnam. It was extraordinary to wander through a lonely Nebraskan cemetery and see how many farm boys had been lost on the fields of Flanders. Well over a million Americans fought at Meuse-Argonne in September 1918, the largest US fighting force ever gathered. And so many old small-towners wore caps and T-shirts with 'Vietnam – I Served' on them, or had bumper stickers commemorating their 58,000 fighting brethren who hadn't made it back. Again it all seemed bound up with religion and patriotism. All these young men sacrificed in faraway wars must seem more like crusaders, fighting for the freedom of God's own country. Over 1.3 million US servicemen and women are still fighting for it now: at $587 billion, the nation's annual military budget is three times that of Russia's and China's combined.

As a sporting spectacle, rodeo is a curious marriage of folksiness and appalling violence. 'And tonight Hank will be roping with his son Brad,' chirped the announcer as two lasso-twirling horsemen galloped out of the corral in pursuit of a terrified young cow. 'One of the nice things about tie-down roping is that you can do it together as a family.' One of the less nice things is that it sometimes ends with a calf breaking its neck and being taken out of the arena on a fork-lift truck.

The reward for brutally subduing a young animal in the shortest time, or staying upright on a furious older one for the longest, ought to have been nothing more than glory and a peck on the cheek from the South-East Montana Rodeo Princess. But perhaps more appositely, the event was another showcase for this nation's bluntly fiscal concept of success. 'Randy has only won $2,500 this season,' sneered the PA after one especially quick-fire, flailing dethronement, 'and with that performance he won't be taking any cash home tonight.' Donald Trump's popularity depended heavily on his perceived status as a wealthy businessman, and the disdain he felt for even the most senior officials and bureaucrats he dealt with as president was founded on their mystifying, contemptible devotion to such poorly remunerated careers: 'They max out at what, two hundred grand?' Henry Ford felt the same disdain for impoverished intellectuals, guilty of 'learning that had no earning power'.

We filed outside, between a candyfloss cart and the Evangelising Children face-paint stall. How curious that America's rural heartland still aligned itself with an age of tough-guy self-reliance which was over in the blink of an eye. The epic livestock drives that begat the iconic cowboy era began in 1867, when Texan horsemen escorted 36,000 cattle to the newly established rail head at Abilene, Kansas. Within twenty years they were history, rendered redundant by the railways' western expansion. Buffalo Bill Cody, whose travelling Wild West roadshow spread the cowboy cult around the world, ironically abetted its demise: he made his first fortune supplying Kansas Pacific railroad workers with buffalo meat, shooting 4,280 animals on their behalf in eighteen months.

The MTFCA forum rode once more to my assistance, but the region's minuscule population density meant our closest available saviour lived 88 miles south, back over the state line in Wyoming. I was tempted to drive Mike to Scott Conger's home – a tow would leave a small but irksome missing link in my transcontinental journey – but he begged me not to risk further engine damage. So in the morning I hired a car, then phoned a well-known national recovery firm and pretended to be Ross Lilleker, affecting a terrible Derbyshire accent for the hell of it. (This modest deception was conducted with Ross's consent: before setting off I'd been thwarted in my attempts to secure breakdown cover without a domiciled US address.)

*

'Lord, protect our new friend Tim, and get him to where he wants to go.'

As we clasped hands around Scott and Althea Conger's dinner table, I began to regret those fraud-update texts I'd sent them while we followed the tow truck in our hire car. 'Ha ha – the breakdown guys fell for it!! Now on the road.' 'Remember, CALL ME ROSS in front of the driver!!' Scott was not a modest-deception kind of guy. His most heinous profanity was 'hellacious'; Diet Coke his solitary vice. Later that evening he told us that his life had changed one long-ago summer in Florida, when as a teen-ager he'd found himself at a fork in the road with 'SOLVENT ABUSE' pointing one way and 'WATCHMAKING' the other.

The choice Scott had taken at this curious metaphorical junc-tion was not obvious from his appearance. His long, greying hair blended into a cascading beard which hung in plaited shafts, like the wax from an ancient candle. Scott's wild-eyed barks of laughter also seemed incompatible with a career that had ultimately delivered him from clocksmithery to aerospace engineering: he had designed the space shuttle's robotic grab-arm.

After a lifetime in the Sunshine State, Scott and Althea had recently plumped for early retirement and a dramatic relocation. Home was now a remote but very cosy wooden chalet stuck on a moon-like plain of windswept rocks, with the muscular peaks of Yellowstone ghosting up in the dusty distance. 'I guess I'm a pioneer at heart,' he said, passing round a platter of bratwurst, 'and I felt I was losing track of that spirit in Florida.' He shared a thoughtful look with Althea. 'Also there are just way too many people down there, and we realised we didn't really like any of them.' Then a hoot of mad laughter. Shortly after Scott exchanged contracts on their new home, three of his nearest new Wyoming neighbours were shot dead by a pair of teenage meth-heads. I guess that's the sort of shocking tragedy that might more routinely occur in Florida. But shortly after that, another neighbour lost half his face after inadvertently coming between a mother bear and her cubs when he went to put the trash out.

Scott's CV was not that of a slapdash guesstimator. The three Ts in his spotless shop stood in geometric alignment, and he wouldn't let me order a new connecting rod from Ross until he'd measured the old one to the nearest thousandth of an inch. Althea was cut from the same precisely cut cloth: she had tweaked her cake recipes to account for the effects of altitude ('I've found you need a little more flour in the mix at 5,000 feet'). We could only marvel at the generosity of spirit that had inspired them to welcome my filthy, dribbling T into their pristine workshop, and us into their orderly and immaculate home.

'Not much we can do until that rod gets here,' said Scott, showing us into the guest bedroom. 'Then I'd like to spend a while just, you know, sorting your car out.' I felt myself developing a strong conviction that Scott preferred to work alone, even for no money and the benefit of a complete stranger, which made it easier to accept the suggestion he now made. 'If I were you, in the morning I'd get in that rental car and go explore Yellowstone for a few days.'

In August 1877, 200 members of the Nez Percé tribe passed into Yellowstone Park, engaged in a desperate fighting retreat from some 2,000 US Army soldiers as they struggled towards the Canadian border and the promise of sanctuary. Yellowstone had been enshrined as a national park, the world's first, five years previously, and that August was home to thirty-five tourists in eight separate parties. Most would come away with some unusually diverting holiday reminiscences.

George and Emma Cowan, celebrating their second wedding anniversary with a group of seven friends from Radersburg, Montana, had been touring Yellowstone for a week when they bumped into a Nez Percé scouting party. Cowan, a lawyer and an idiot, began to quarrel with the jumpy and heavily armed Indians, who promptly shot him in the right leg. Somehow this failed to settle the argument, and when Cowan continued to bicker from a prone position he was shot at point-blank range in the forehead, then pelted with rocks for good measure. Some hours later, after his wife and their companions had been marched away to the Nez Percé camp, Cowan miraculously came to: the bullet had bounced off his skull. But as he hauled himself groggily upright, he was spotted by a Nez Percé straggler, who shot him through the left hip. Cowan pitched face-first into the mud and was once again left for dead. Once again he lived. Now sporting a serious bullet wound in each leg, he crawled 4 miles to the forest clearing where his party had last made camp. Frail and desperate, Cowan lit a fire which spread out of control, burning him severely. Somehow he dragged himself onwards, covering 12 miles in four days before he was found by a search party and eased into the back of a wagon. On a precipitous trail halfway to the town of Bozeman, the wagon overturned and flung Cowan down an escarpment. When at dreadful length he was laid on to a hospital bed in Bozeman, it collapsed beneath him. 'Just bring the damn artillery in and finish me off,' he croaked from the floor.

The rest of the Radersburg party were released unharmed by the Nez Percé, with the notable exception of Albert Oldham, who was shot through both cheeks and spent the balance of his vacation stumbling lost through the woods, living on insects. A couple of tourists didn't come home at all: Charles Kenck was shot dead in the forest during a Nez Percé encounter, and five days later his companion Richard Dietrich met the same end on the porch of his hotel. For want of a coffin, the proprietor buried him in an old bathtub. The Nez Percé never did make it to Canada, and surrendered two months later.

I relate this tale as a potent example of the murderous, primal clashes that raged across America even at the dawn of the modern age, fostering a national mindset rather more combative and paranoid than that of a contemporary European, whose holiday alarums didn't stretch beyond sunburn and a sandy sandwich. Also, it was either that or hear me drone on about gazing in speechless awe at plunging canyons, spurting, garish geothermal phenomena, steamy-breathed herds of buffalo and a succession of $300 motel bills.

This outrage of surge-pricing was down to the solar eclipse, which had drawn several hundred thousand people from all over the world to a narrow arc of 'totality' that happened to pass through Yellowstone. My wife grew quite excitable as the portentous moment approached, and at the appointed minute performed some elaborate ritual in a park lay-by, head tilted to the heavens with two pin-holed paper plates pressed to her face. Then, for a life-changing nineteen seconds or so, it got a bit dim and a bit nippy. 'Wow,' I drawled sarcastically. The locals, I'd noticed, had expressed very little interest in the celestial overlap. I don't think Scott and Althea even mentioned it. The front page of the following day's *Billings Gazette* came topped with this deathless headline: 'Eclipse: 140,000 Descend on Wyoming, Then Leave.'

After three days we were back at the Conger house. In our absence Scott had spent an obvious eternity working on my

car, and with painstaking diligence. Half the engine lay disas-
sembled on his workbench, pistons, bolts and washers lined
up in neat rows, degreased and glinting. Around this still life
lay squares of paper covered with runic notes and microscopic
measurements: '#3 Crank pin post clean-up, V 1.2350, H
1.2355.' What a guy. In a just world, he would have buggered
off to Vegas for a week and made me put it all back together.
(A week? What am I saying? It would have taken me two life-
times, and that's assuming I was reincarnated as Scott Conger
in the second.)

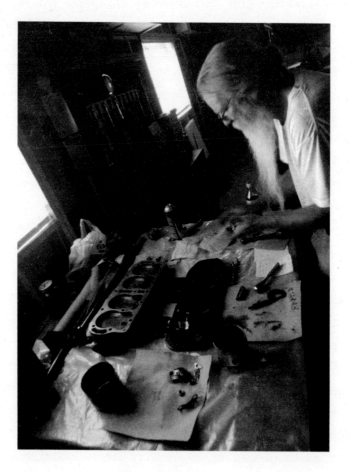

My spousal interlude was into its final hours, and I spent them in Scott's shop, passing him requested tools and components as he bent over the car, squatted inside it, lay under it. Then my wife burst in, having lost track of time, and launched into a swift and oily round of farewells.

'So – North Dakota again next summer, darling?'

It had been a splendidly daft romantic mini-break. And with that she jumped into the hire car and bounced dustily off across the Wyoming moonscape.

We finished reassembling things in the morning. The moment of truth filled Scott's workshop with raging decibels and a wild-eyed manic laugh. 'Your muffler's going!' I killed the motor and put on my Stan Laurel face. 'Not a huge deal,' said Scott once he'd recovered. 'Won't sound so hellacious when you're out in the open.' Then he cleared his throat and dropped into a low, sympathetic register. 'So, you've got a small water leak from the front of the cylinder head. Keep an eye on that. I also found some pretty big gouges in the walls of two cylinders, so you'll be using a *lot* of oil.' He touched a finger to the tip of his nose and frowned, wondering if he should say what he was about to say. 'And from my measurements, it looks as if your crankshaft is heading out of round.' His tone transmitted the gravity of this mysterious verdict. 'I hate to say this, but it's touch-and-go if that motor's going to get you to the Pacific.'

Scott and Althea gave me a guard-of-honour escort back to the highway, following behind in their snappy little 1921 roadster. One minute they were there, waving cheerily; then I stuck my head out and gazed behind at an empty ribbon of tarmac. I would soon begin to wonder if all this assistance and hospitality was a subconscious reflection of the Universal Car's everyman values. The tireless aid certainly showcased the help-thy-neighbour community spirit that so many people I'd met felt was being eroded by a 'poor me' culture, one dependent on federal handouts. One of the Alabama T guys said he took his lead from Thomas Edison's grandmother, who always put food on the stove when she went out, and left the door open, so hungry passers-by could come in and help themselves. At any rate, all these T owners seemed genuinely invested in my undertaking, and in more fanciful moments I persuaded myself this had become their trip as much as mine.

A stanza from the framed ballad that had graced the Congers' guest bedroom sprang happily to mind:

Out where the handclasp's a little stronger,
Out where the smile dwells a little longer,
Out where the world is in the making,
That's where the West begins.

Cheesy as all heck, yet spirited and deeply comforting; I felt less alone at once, and yanked down the throttle. Mike accelerated with a throaty, eager thrum, poignantly unaware that he'd just been diagnosed with a terminal illness, and of the challenge hidden in the dust ahead. By nightfall, he'd have crossed the Rockies or died trying.

The Continental Divide had the demoralising whiff of a halfway point, but America's great watershed is heavily left of centre, and after cresting it I'd have no more than a thousand miles to go. I slammed the Ruckstell underdrive into high gear and powered steadily towards Yellowstone through an ever more rugged environment, from rust-rocked canyon to snow-veined granite, 40 uphill miles at 18mph. We topped the col between walls of bleached scree: 'SYLVAN PASS – ELEV. 8,530' read the little wooden sign. My eyes prickled and I gave Mike a tender pat on the wheel. From here the rivers would empty into the Pacific. From here, albeit erratically, it was all downhill.

Yellowstone, even as an instant replay, still astounded me. It's like a pocket planet of scenic magnificence – alpine peaks and conifers, mouthwash-blue Scandinavian waterfalls, the Russian steppes, Mexican scrubland, boggy Gaelic moors, even a swathe of

sub-Saharan savannah. That's before you throw in all the primeval wonders, those sulphured, steaming gorges and turquoise fumaroles. 'I sat there in amazement while my companions came up, and after that, it seemed to me that it was five minutes before anyone spoke.' So wrote Charles Cook in 1869, recording his expedition's dumbstruck arrival at the head of a 20-mile-long, 1,200-foot-deep canyon, crowned by a mighty green cataract and flanked with steaming, hissing walls of crimson, mauve and yellow. Cook's expedition had been dispatched to the lonely Montana–Wyoming borders after wide-eyed fur trappers and prospectors came back from the region with tall tales of hot waterfalls that rose upwards, of petrified forests, an alien world of fire and brimstone that trembled underfoot and belched orange gas and boiling mud. Silenced awe became the Cook party's default mode: it was all true. That such a well-trodden nation, by then an established global superpower, should have secretly nurtured this extraordinary lost kingdom seemed almost unbelievable. For most, it still was: America only accepted Cook's account when an expedition the following year returned with irrefutable photographic evidence.

It wasn't hard to see what had drawn all the natives who tootled patiently behind me in camper vans and convertibles. Yellowstone is a sort of pioneer-age theme park, where Americans get to see what their nation looked like before they dammed the canyons, poisoned the lakes and shot all the buffalo. Every vista had a gaudy, cinematic majesty, retouched in Technicolor and screened in Panavision: an epic land fit for all-American movie heroes, from John Wayne to Bambi. And look – isn't that a Model T Ford? Give that guy a big cheer, kids!

When Yellowstone opened its gates to motor traffic in 1915, a Model T was first through them, and in this nostalgic environment Mike found himself upgraded from funny old car to official tourist attraction. Whenever I pulled over, two or three vehicles would screech in behind, disgorging eagerly curious passengers who ran up with camera-phones and questions to foil my urinary intent. I'd never felt more conspicuous. After driving out through the park's western gate and back into Montana, I picked my nose for three minutes straight.

Eclipse pricing remained in force, and in a Model T I was in no position to outrun it. That night at West Yellowstone I paid $193 for a malodorous, wobbly-walled motel chalet, an outlay which I felt compelled to offset with a Hungry Man TV dinner. Every meal in this microwaveable range provides 9,000 per cent of your recommended daily intake of pasty self-loathing, and comes served with a sachet of real human tears.

This particular example also included a tub of thick gravy, which I adulterated with Tabasco before dumping on a pallid slab of turkey. An ominous odour coiled forth from my first plastic forkful: as my mouth promptly confirmed, that gravy was chocolate dessert. But the wifeless world is an ugly place. I cleaned my indented tray, belched horribly, then walked out into a chilly mountain sunset with a toothmug of Jim Beam. To Mike: sleep tight and bravo. Farewell to Montana, and those skies of fabled scale.

Home, home on the range,
Where the something and something-else play,

Where seldom is heard a discouraging word,
And ... everything's ... miles ... away.

Idaho, which I learned on entry was Too Great to Litter, remains
an open-range state where cattle roam free, until they get their
hooves wedged in a stock grid with the Stars and Stripes painted
across it. The road at once sank 2,000 feet, releasing my skull from
compressive discomfort after two days at altitude, and asphalt gave
way to chalky gravel. Under blue skies I scrabbled over a barren
plateau edged with bare, brown mountains that took vague shape
in a haze of wildfire smoke, bashing Mike's horn for company. Black
dots browsed distantly amongst sagebrush and golden bushes of
blazing star. A sign read: 'ZIPLINE – 75 MILES'. I never acclima-
tised to this country's sheer vastness. Seventy-five miles was the
distance from my house to Swindon, a journey no one of sound
mind should consider for the sake of a dangly swoosh down a
cable (nor, with due apology, for Swindon). There were occasional
pockets of pivot-farmed activity, combines kicking up clouds of
chaff as they brought in the harvest, grasshoppers thwocking
into my radiator. Then it was back into the dead zone, my own
private Idaho, following a trail of telegraph poles to a shimmery
beige horizon.

I stayed at Arco, which in 1955 became the first town in the world
to be illuminated by nuclear power. This heritage was celebrated
with some diligence along its silent streets. That overlapping-ovals
atomic symbol was neatly painted on the flanks of empty shops,
and the town's dusty fire truck had 'Atomic City' emblazoned
across its doors. I passed an 'Atoms for Peace' interpretation board,
which didn't find space to mention that the surrounding desert was
once demarcated the Mass Detonation Area, and remains heavily

pockmarked with giant craters. Opposite my motel, the conning tower of a nuclear submarine had been erected in the middle of a playground. (The robust bluff behind it was embellished from foot to lofty peak with vast double digits – perilously hand painted, the motelier told me, by every high-school graduation class for the last century. I can't tell you how tickled I was to spot the class of '24's impressive effort.)

The diner up the road, to which I now repaired for an early supper, advertised itself in neon as 'Home of the Atomic Burger'. This comestible tribute to Arco's radioactive heritage seemed a remarkable stretch of loyalty, and I walked in hoping to spot a greenish glow fringing the kitchen door, and perhaps a couple of Vladimir Putin's enemies slumped face-down in their plates. Halfway through my disappointingly standard house special I chanced upon an online account of Arco's unhappier claim to nuclear fame – on 3 January 1961, the world's first reactor melt-down led three operators to a very unpleasant end. One of them went undiscovered for several hours; the 12-ton reactor he'd been standing on had been propelled 9 feet into the air, spreading him very thinly across a wide stretch of ceiling. I completed my Atomic Burger with diminished zest.

Idaho was kind to me. I reeled it in for three agreeable days, a warm breeze sweeping off the open range, bringing swarms of yellow butterflies, moreish wafts of hot hay, the restful lowing of distant cattle. Every so often something remarkable would inter-rupt the khaki continuum: a plunging creek, a Sherman tank with a paisley turret, or a craggy black lava field, still shiny and sharp, like a trillion cubic feet of coal fly-tipped in the desert. Modest balls of tumbleweed bounced across my path, skittering off to the feet of colossal sand dunes. The enchiladas were toothsome, the motels appealingly antiquated, and the nocturnal freight trains emitted an especially urgent, plaintive whistle, as if the driver had just spotted a pram rolling on to the level crossing.

But the state, it's fair to say, proved rather harder on Mike. At full chat, the fractured muffler now let out a bygone explosive roar, like the bloody Red Baron's triple-winged Fokker powering down a runway. Some internal flap of fabric had worked itself loose inside the roof, adding a thwacky backbeat to those under-floor collisions of old iron. The agricultural weld that held my tie rod together was riven by a spreading hairline crack, which didn't look good to me, and looked a lot worse to the MTFCA when I posted a close-up photo on their forum in order to gauge opinion. 'Frankly your demise is not probable but certain if you don't get your shit together,' wrote one particularly forthright member. 'Hate me if you wish but you have been warned.' These words, as you may imagine, cast rather a shadow over my progress – particularly as I didn't even know what my shit was, let alone how to reassemble it. Every time Mike squirrelled eccentrically through a corner my heart seemed to rise about a foot, until I felt its beat in my throat and jaw. At least there aren't many corners in Idaho.

And that periodic misfire was now a full-time companion, a five-second fainting fit every mile. This malaise lacked the tie rod's starkly lethal import, but it was much more frustrating. Until the welding fairy crept into my motel room and touched her acetylene wand to my fingers and snoring head, I couldn't do anything about the tie rod. But at this stage of my journey, with 5,000 miles and twenty US states under the wheels, I felt I really ought to be capable of resolving a humdrum running issue.

Since Scott's dire prognosis I had certainly become much more closely focused on Mike's well-being. At his suggestion I was now changing the oil every 300 miles, and topping it up three times a day. I had lowered my cruising speed to 30. Looking back, I appear to have confused this entry-level mechanical sympathy with technical expertise, because late one afternoon outside a motel in Mountain Home, with the digital thermometer outside the bank up the road showing 102, I decided that the misfire was a fuelling issue, and promptly embarked on an extremely ambitious programme of related works.

The first stage decorated my corner of the parking lot with surprisingly tiny bits of lawnmower carburettor, dispersed during a silent explosion as I gingerly detached its fuel bowl. The last, conducted several hours later under the surgical glare of a security light, left the under-Mike asphalt blotted with reeking pools of gasoline and a glinting chaos of tools. I didn't expect him to run any better after all that, and I was right. Frankly I was just delighted he ran at all.

Geese were flying south as I sputtered into Oregon, which I guessed marked summer's death knell. With my rattlesnake thermometer still north of the three-digit line it didn't make sense, and nor did the snowscooters that now sheltered in every barn. After long weeks of ranchland and industrial corn I finally passed through some proper patchwork fields, rectangles of salad crops, onions, and sunflowers with heavy, bowed heads, awaiting execution. In the spirit of harvest I finally submitted to a haircut, intrigued to find that my motel in Ontario boasted a resident barber. I feared the worst after being ushered into the chair by a young man with a lot of ink on his skin and elaborate sideburns. But I needn't have worried, and twelve minutes later walked out looking like Heinrich Himmler.

'Boy, are you in for some fun.'

Eastern Oregon's irrigated greenery had given way to steep red rock, and with Mike coughing his guts up I'd pulled in at the aptly

titled Oasis Diner in lonesome Juntura. My noisome arrival had
drawn a stubbled oldie out into the pitiless sun, and he was now
offering a plain-spoken overview of my forthcoming challenge.

'You got two passes ahead up US-20, Drinkwater and Stinkingwater. Both pretty big pulls. No gas, no nothing for sixty miles.'

He scratched his neck and leaned back against one of the
battered ice freezers that flanked the diner's entrance. 'Name's
Charlie. I kind of keep everything running round here. Order me
a tunafish salad sandwich and I'll take a look under the hood.'
I agreed to this deal with some alacrity and made for the door.
'White bread, no relish, cottage cheese,' he drawled over his
shoulder, flicking the bonnet clips.

Charlie was back inside before his sandwich made it out of the
kitchen. 'That carb was running rich as all hell. You'll be golden
now.' He sat down at my table, slapped two very aromatic hands on
the Formica and showed me five teeth. 'Guy I knew used to step
out in front of Greyhound buses, take a hit and get a big insurance pay out.' How I'd come to love these dramatic non sequiturs.
'Worked pretty good for him until the last time. Ha!'

Charlie's confidence was founded on many decades of compe-
tent all-round mending. As I left he was climbing up on the
diner's roof to sort out their air conditioner. But his two-minute fix
seemed too good to be true, and on the squiggly lower reaches of
Drinkwater Pass the misfire duly returned, with a stuttering, spluttering vengeance. Mike's engine died for long seconds, bucked
violently to life then died anew, the sound of a stricken Spitfire
about to arc vertically into the Channel. A complete stall on a
steep incline didn't bear thinking about – the futile yank on the
handbrake, the inexorable gathering of rearward momentum, the
death-or-glory bail-out with a wheel chock in each hand – so I
thought about little else. The derelict single-track railroad beside

me occasionally wandered away to vault some rocky void on a tumbledown trestle bridge. A sign warned that I had entered snake country. The cars were twenty minutes apart and the phone signal had long since died. I was in a bad place in every sense.

All those months ago, as I sat behind the wheel of a Model T for the very first time in a damp Buckinghamshire farmyard, Neil Tuckett said something that had stuck. 'You'll always have problems with a T. When you're good, you just learn to drive around them.' How long had I been plagued by this misfire? At least 2,000 miles, on and off. I had clearly learned to drive around it, and was therefore clearly good. Right?

That morning, in a fate-tempting breakfast audit of my remaining distance, I'd established that just 400 miles separated me from the Pacific coast. A forkful of yolk froze at my open jaw. Four hundred miles! If Mike could just hold it together, if I could just drive around his problem with a little more forbearance, we could be there in two days. Call it three to be safe. In the grand scheme of my 6,000-mile trip and this great big country, you could safely round that down to sweet fuck-all.

But what had seemed so close at breakfast now seemed so very far. For the first time since that dreadful debut night in Ordinary, fundamental doubts began to crowd my mind. Only now my fear wasn't that I'd go to pieces, but that my car might.

'Come on, Michael. Come on, son. *COME ON!*' Shuddering up the scree-walled switchbacks, I dispensed encouragement first in a muttered wheedle, and latterly through the wild bellowing of a drunken race-course punter.

He didn't completely ignore me. Thrice Mike coasted to a deathly halt, and thrice he did so on an almost level gradient. The first time I swapped the ignition coil, a moment of joyous inspiration which procured the usual three-minute false dawn of smooth running. The second time, at a lay-by zoned for the seasonal fitting of snow chains, I opted to drain the petrol. I had to do something, and someone, somewhere had suggested that ethanol-blended gas (now, thanks to Henry, almost universal in the States) corroded rubber fuel lines, and thus might have incited a blockage.

That monstrous heat was now being delivered by an extremely stiff breeze, which made quite an adventure of this process. In the end I had to wedge the oil-drain pan on its side under the car to act as a windbreak, permitting at least some of the frail petrol cascade to tinkle into my bucket rather than fly three feet back down the tarmac. I was blowing out the fuel pipes when a pick-up truck pulled up, and a guy in denim shorts and mirrored shades leapt down from the cab. 'Bet you could use a brewski, pardner,' he called, proffering a can appealingly beaded in condensation. His manner was consistent with a footwell deep in empties, and being in no mood to join the party I mustered a polite refusal. 'Your call,' he shrugged, fiddling with his phone. 'Mind if I take a photo? Might be the last one of you alive!'

I'd just topped Drinkwater when Mike died his third death. The road was narrow; I put two wheels into the sandy gravel and coasted to a stop. Perhaps 4 miles ahead, the empty grey stripe of US-20 crawled up the barren, dune-like face of Stinkingwater Pass. It was gone five but still sweltering, and I was down to the hot dregs of my water. I gave the starter a couple of futile stabs, then sagged heavily against Bob Kirk's beaded seat cover, which hurt quite a lot, enlivening the drawn-out obscenity I now delivered across the desert.

Presently a police car drew up, disgorging a young sheriff who handed me a bottle of cold water. 'It's 104 out here,' he said. 'I'm gonna stay here and watch you drink that.' When I very gratefully had, he said he'd be coming back this way in a couple of hours. 'No cellphone signal this side of Stinkingwater. If you're still here

I'm taking you with me.' I watched him go and gave my redundant phone a couple of wan jabs, feeling broiled, clueless and very alone.

After the longest hour I have ever endured outside a classroom, a smart red convertible pulled in behind me. Its occupants were a middle-aged couple who will be featuring in my will, and perhaps a commemorative tattoo. Greg set about an under-bonnet diagnosis that left his crisp shirt heavily blotted with oily petrol; Kim gave me water, cereal bars and a heart scare when she leaned over a trickling fuel pipe and lit up a cigarette. On perhaps the twentieth attempt, with Mike's battery in its death throes, the engine caught. 'Just keep her running!' yelled Greg. 'We'll follow you to the next town.' It was a big ask: Burns lay 40 miles down the road. As I cranked down the throttle, Greg bellowed some big answers: 'We were Allies! I named my son after Sir Francis Drake! Go, baby, go!'

Mike ascended Stinkingwater in all sorts of distress, backfiring, misfiring, revving wildly, cutting out. I was obliged to tackle the climb in low gear, mashing that heavy pedal to the floor for an agonised eternity, hastily swapping feet whenever cramp set in. In my panicked departure I'd forgotten to zip up the holdall in the running-board cage, which began to sacrifice its contents to the fierce winds that swept across the head of the pass: a couple of plastic funnels, a hat, the waterproof overtrousers I'd never worn once. I crested Stinkingwater with an outpouring of relief that was curiously topped off by an almighty, five-second fart. But you know what they say: what goes up, must break down. A few miles into the scrubby void laid out beyond the summit sign, Mike abruptly fell silent and rolled to a halt.

Greg pulled up behind and we established that the fuel tank was empty: by some calamity of mis-ignition, I'd got through 6 gallons of gas in 30 miles. Kim handed me the funnels and clothing the support crew had collected in my wake, then Greg helped tip the 2-gallon jerrycan reserve into the tank. 'Hit it!' he shouted when Mike stuttered to life, and I very loudly complied.

The sun was going down and we had 10 miles left. Beyond steering I had almost no control over my charge, who raced and stalled and shuddered to his own mad tune: now a roaring din, now a deathly silence, each one bookended with a rodeo lurch so violent that I twice banged my head against the windshield. The backfires were truly explosive by this stage, machine-gun kangaroo salvos that almost shook the wheel from my hands, and sent roadside cattle lumbering away into the sandy gloom. I flicked on the lights and sent a sickly, flickering glow over the cat-black tarmac. Greg and Kim's headlamps danced about in my mirror. Burns introduced itself with a distant little dome of fuzzy sodium glare, and as it did Mike once more droned to a silent standstill. I'd run out of gas again, 2 gallons half-belched and half-burned in eight miles.

'Well, the only restaurant round here that serves *alcohol* is the pizza joint across the road.' The manageress of the America's Best Value Inn looked at me with an air of disappointment, then checked her watch. 'It closes, like, now, so you—Hello? Sir?'

It was an hour since the sainted Greg and Kim had taken my jerrycan into Burns, forty minutes since they'd returned with it refilled, ten since I'd bidden them farewell with a heartfelt, petrolly hug in the car park of the first motel Mike juddered up to. In another two I was putting the day's soul-flaying ordeals to bed in time-honoured fashion. 'You sure about that?' asked the pimpled pizza operative after I placed a very long order that included one food item. 'I gotta lock up in a couple minutes.' That proved sufficient for everything bar two slices of pepperoni. I stumbled back to the motel, took a shower and watched polychromatic swirls of petrol sluice down the plughole. I took another in the morning and still stank like the Exxon Valdez.

Burns was aptly shrouded in misty smoke, an eye-stinging, throat-rasping haze blown in from a distant swathe of spreading wildfires. I was frankly delighted when Mike failed to start, snatching away any temptation to tackle our next challenge without prior repairs: the motel manageress had warned me that the next town of note lay 130 miles away, across the Great Sandy Desert. The night before, Greg had returned from his gas-station mercy dash with a card from a recommended local garage, the irresistibly named Tim's Complete Auto Service. I gave them a ring and a shonky black tow truck soon trundled to a halt in the motel forecourt. 'I'm Tim,' said the bald man who jumped out from the driver's side. A jolly, plump redhead raised his hand through the passenger window. 'And so am I.'

How many Tims does it take to fix a T? None, sadly: a pony-tailed young man called Andy did all the work. I watched him happily tinker about with Mike all morning in Bald Tim's wreck-strewn, edge-of-town workshop, changing bits of carburettor and inserting a mysterious dialled pressure gauge into the fuel line. Then, after an abortive afternoon assault on the Great Sandy Desert, I puttered and bucked 15 miles back to Tim HQ, and witnessed some frownier tinkering that would stretch deep into the following day.

Andy conformed to a now familiar small-town stereotype, exuding an air of laidback, good-natured diligence that was punctured every so often with intimations of an alarming capacity for violent umbrage. The same easy, open-faced drawl that informed me about his motorcycle collection or what time the Safeway supermarket closed was also employed to reveal that he had once bulldozed a car full of environmentalists into a ditch. Andy's granddaddy was a cowboy stunt shooter who had taught him to hit two targets with a pistol in each hand. 'But I prefer to fight the old-fashioned way, and because I tend to win people now leave me alone.' He had recently driven to Sacramento to settle a score in unspecified but deeply ominous fashion: 'Drove ten hours through the night, did what I needed to do and drove ten hours home.'

This tale inspired Andy to explain, with no little pride, that Burns was a hotbed of free-spirited defiance. This had accorded it national prominence in 2016, during a stand-off that stemmed from a dispute about the wildfires that are a routine menace. After two local ranchers set a backfire around their property – a common regional tactic to deprive an advancing wildfire of fuel – they were found guilty of arson and imprisoned. As martyrs to the anti-federalist cause, their fate attracted hard-core government haters from across the western US, forty of whom pitched up in a militia force. In an unlikely display of bravado, the self-styled freedom fighters occupied a federally managed wildlife refuge outside town, hunkering in for a month-long siege that ended in murderous chaos, with one occupier shot dead by police.

Andy's take on the affair was a familiar one: 'We just don't like being told what not to do, 'specially not by some guy in an office in Washington, DC, who don't know nothing about us or our way of life.' I'd heard this a lot. The central grievance of almost every old car guy I'd talked to was federal government 'not letting people make the mistakes they need to make'. From their positions of exalted competence this must have seemed entirely reasonable. These men would never make the sort of mistakes that nobody needs to make, the ones that have the rest of us putting angle-grinders through gas mains or breaking up sheets of asbestos in our kitchens. (No? Just me, then.)

Andy shook his head gravely, jaws rippling. 'The authorities have got us down as renegades and troublemakers now. CCTV cameras went up all over town.' Since then, he'd stuck The Man the finger by riding his Harley across the Great Sandy Desert at 130. 'In Oregon, if a speed limit sign just has a number and not the actual words "speed limit", you can argue your case.' His knowing wink seemed a little misguided. Ginger Tim had told me about the time he'd argued his case after being arrested while drunk on a bicycle, a strategy that had earned him four days in jail.

For good measure, Tim's Complete Auto Service was yet another stronghold of the hell-in-a-handcart, apocalypse-goading survivalism that had become a recurring theme. Late one afternoon Andy and Bald Tim began to riff in a tone of poorly disguised relish about the flooding in Houston and those encroaching wildfires, and where it was all leading. 'Thousand-year record for rain down in Texas, and half of Oregon is in flames,' said Bald Tim, eyes agleam. 'You just never know what's coming next. Like, we could have a sunspot tomorrow that would wipe out the electrics in every car and computer.'

'That's a total breakdown of society right there,' Andy chipped in, with the makings of a smile.

Tim nodded emphatically. 'Or how about that super-volcano under Yellowstone? Heard that's overdue to blow, and when it does half the US is going up with it.'

I was forever blundering into these doomsday discussions, and the elaborate post-apocalyptic plans they reliably revealed. Trent in Liberal, Kansas: 'When it all goes down you're gonna likely lose your vehicle, so you need to think what you can carry if you need to bug out. A Thompson machine gun, that's 11lb loaded. Too much, gonna slow you right down. You gotta think about this shit.' Zander in Jordan, Montana: 'We got an oil storage place where I'm gonna hole up. I can fix shit. I would do OK for a few years.'

Andy duly explained that he'd taught himself how to make long-bows out of tree boughs, and suggested that my Model T might make an ideal runabout in the new Dark Ages. 'No computers, no electrics, and I bet that thing could run on all kinds of shit.' (It could, too. Scott had told me about an Antipodean T enthusiast of his acquaintance who ran out of fuel in the desert, but made it to the next town on a can of citronella oil he'd brought along to repel mosquitoes.) As a *Guardian* journalist who attended a survivalist conference in Ohio pointed out, every scenario seemed suspiciously reminiscent of the US frontier era, a bloody, low-tech struggle for supplies and shelter. 'The preppers and survivalists aren't really imagining the end of America,' he wrote. 'They're imagining it beginning again.'

It sometimes felt as if the whole nation was on a war footing, what with all this talk of Armageddon, the worshipful cult of military veterans, and the gun craziness. Trump's populist spidey senses tapped right into this, and as soon as he started whipping up panic about North Korea, everyone I met was suddenly ranting excitedly about 'that little fat guy Kim Pong Poo'. I'm not sure if the surge of fundamentalist Christianity is a reflection of this eager fatalism or a primary cause, but the related statistics are extraordinary: 41 per cent of Americans now believe that 'the Rapture' – the second coming, Judgement Day, the end of all earthly life when the good will rise to heaven and the evil sink to hell – will occur within the next forty years. The *Left Behind* series, a sixteen-volume interpretation of the biblical apocalypse, has sold more than sixty million copies in the US since 1995. A frankly terrifying proportion of Middle Americans think the end of the world is nigh, which does a lot to explain their indifference to both the long-term personal consequences of gorging on deep-fried syrup, and our planet's environmental future. 'We'll probably never see the bayou like God made it in the beginning until He fixes it himself,' a Louisiana pipe-fitter told Arlie Russell Hochschild, author of *Strangers in Their Own Land*, in reference to a horrendously polluted local creek. 'And that will happen pretty shortly, so it doesn't matter how much man destroys.'

Add a paranoid suspicion of big government to this widespread belief in the supernatural and you can understand why even stoic old small-towners make such eager conspiracy theorists. A quarter of Americans think that Barack Obama might be the anti-Christ, and that US officials helped organise the 9/11 attacks. A third believes global warming is a federal hoax, and more than half suspect that a secretive global elite is plotting to establish a New World Order. Conspiracism went mainstream after JFK, when a shell-shocked nation struggled to accept that such a giant of a man, their living icon, could have been snuffed out by a single, pathetic loner. But there's always been that streak in the melodramatic American character, a Wild West weakness for snake-oil salesmen and tall stories, for gut feeling over rational deduction. Even Jimmy Carter insists he once saw a UFO.

'We just wanted to give a good impression of our town and help get you on your way,' said Bald Tim, after an extended test drive demonstrated that my misfire appeared, at long last, to be fully cured. To be fair he now handed over a secondary motivation in the form of a $440 bill, which took me rather unawares, spoiled rotten as I was by all those miraculous months of pro-bono mechanical assistance. On the one hand, $440 seemed rather a lot for the simple eventual cure: a ten-buck ignition condenser off a Chevrolet that Andy had adapted as a replacement for my faulty VW original. But on the other, what a priceless pleasure to hear Mike running with long-forgotten sweetness, to feel him gain speed so eagerly, and maintain it with such confident ease. After my third night in Burns, I set off across the Great Sandy Desert with a recalibrated sense of expectation. I had 300 miles left, and with all mechanical fraughtness now behind me, I could tick them off in a mood of appropriate elegy.

Looking through the photos I took that bright, hot morning, it's clear that I was stocking a repository of representative farewells. Behold the sagebrush-clotted, smoke-fringed vastness of my final desert, flat-baked under a lurid blue sky. The rusted pumps and roofless stores of Millican, perhaps my swan-song ghost town. That guy in the pick-up with the 'HE WON, GET OVER IT' bumper sticker, very possibly my last hardcore Trumpite. From here to the Pacific, Oregon grew ever more blue, and though there was a red path to the coast it was both pale and slender.

By noon I'd covered 120 miles up US-20. The sizeable town of Bend lay in sight: just west of it my map's base layer turned from sandy beige to forest green, and thence to ocean blue. I'd never managed more than 250 miles in a day before, but this was surely the day to do it. Come sunset I'd have my front wheels in the Pacific. Hollow disbelief set in. I had somehow traversed this giant nation, 6,000 miles from sea to shining sea, up to the Canadian border, down to the Gulf of Mexico, over the Rocky Mountains and the Continental Divide, and I had done it in a ninety-three-year-old car with a lawnmower carburettor. Except I hadn't, because 2 miles outside Bend, the crankshaft broke.

CHAPTER 17

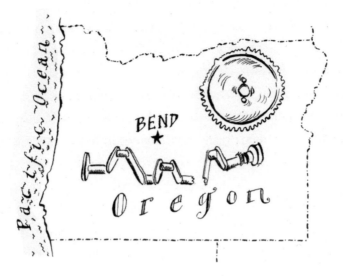

'Now there's one club you don't want to join, Teeum, and that's the two-piece crank club.'

Every T guy I'd met had spoken of this mother of all breakdowns, sometimes in a tone of jaunty bravado, more often with murmured dread. A bust crankshaft was a game-over grand slam, the Component Failure That Must Not Be Named. The crank converts up-and-down piston movement into a more useful rotational force, a procedure that requires an eccentrically crenelated metal casting of obvious vulnerability. Henry Ford's team designed a car that farmers could fix by the roadside, but a broken crank was the T's Achilles' heel. No one could sort that on a hard shoulder. Few bothered to sort it at all: replacing a crankshaft meant a full engine-out rebuild that very rarely made economic sense.

'How will I know if the crank breaks?' I remembered asking Paul Griesse back in Ohio.

'Oh, you'll know,' he'd replied, with a mirthless laugh.

Well, he was right. A muffled, heavy-metal explosion shook Mike's front end, a flagrantly terminal cataclysm that begat an instant and total loss of power and a death-drone into the sandy verge. Scott Conger's prophecy had come to pass; I dully surmised that the brutal stop-start material stress endured over Stinkingwater Pass had pushed my fragile crank too far. Bend-bound traffic droned by. An electrical substation beside me buzzed fitfully. What a crushingly banal backdrop for our great adventure's final act.

I sat there with both hands on the wheel and tried to bully my features into the Stan Laurel face, but it wouldn't hold, and presently crumpled into something even more pitiful and much wetter. Over the years I'd set off on umpteen under-prepared, over-ambitious journeys, none of which I deserved to complete but all of which I somehow had. For once, and at last, my luck had run out. This was the reckoning, my Judgement Day. 'End of the road, Mike,' I managed to croak. At least he'd got me across the Great Sandy Desert, I thought, and pondering this heroic final gesture had me off again.

'Howdy. All good here?'

I composed myself, looked up and met a sunny old face.

'Not really.' My attempt at a manly sniff had way too much mucus in it. 'Broken crankshaft.'

'Holy mackerel,' said the face, looking almost impressed. A smile and a teasing pause. 'Thing is, I'm a Model A guy, and I'm pretty sure my mechanic knows his way round a Model T. Want me to go get him?'

If you break it, they will come.

Don Penington was back an hour later with his fixer, Mike Stenkamp, and a little packed lunch his wife had prepared for me. It was all extremely touching, though I struggled to mirror their optimism: the old boys' shared instinct was that I'd suffered a much less calamitous fracture of my timing gear.

A full diagnosis was deemed in order, so they lashed Car-Mike to the back of Man-Mike's old Landcruiser, then hauled me around Bend's desert hinterland at terrific speed, which in combination with a 3-foot tow-rope and my negligible brakes made for quite an adventure.

Hunkered up against a low, *Flintstones*-bouldered bluff, Man-Mike's industrially proportioned workshop was an uncharacteristic shambles, bestrewn with machine tools, dismembered engines and teetering stacks of dusty radio equipment. There wasn't room for even an emaciated Model T in there, so we got to work outside on the sand, amidst a sprawl of old tractors and unfinished projects sitting bonnet-deep in weeds.

Don and Mike were proved right in two hours: after much fiddlesome prising we established that the timing gear, a hefty cog of acute importance, had indeed shed half its teeth. But in another thirty minutes, lying under Car-Mike with several oily bolts in one hand and a flashlight in the other, I was proved right too. A clean break through thick grey metal: I'd joined the two-piece club. 'When the crank snapped it must have had a knock-on effect on the timing gear,' said Mike, in a tone of mild curiosity that presented an interesting counterpoint to the funeral bell tolling deep inside my skull. The one chink in Mike's armoury of measured calm was a toneless cackle that irresistibly recalled Robert De Niro in psycho-gangster mode. I saw and heard it now. 'Well, I guess all my other work just went out the window.'

These were the words that launched my journey's most extra-ordinary repair experience, its crowning overhaul, the Daddy Fix against which all others would be judged and found wanting. It wasn't quick. It wasn't cheap. But it would never have happened at all, not for love nor money, without the benevolence, comrade-ship and boundless practicality of the men and wives of the High Desert Model A Club.

My time in Bend came to feel like some real-life partwork maga-zine series, every new release packed with full-colour characters and helpful tips, and delivered with a shiny new Model T engine component stuck to the cover. Issue 1 of *Crankshaft Hiatus* opened with an in-depth guide on pulling a Model T's gigantic engine and transmission combination out through its tiny mouth. Handy illus-trations depict five old men and a slightly younger one going about this task with the dainty precision of medieval horse dentists. Fig. 10 portrays a Model T with a tragic, empty gob. Figs. 1–9 show a forest of crowbars and scaffold poles in wild and clumsy use. Fig. 7, in which the younger man very firmly introduces his skull to the steel arm of an overhead hoist is captioned, 'Oop – heard a bad word there from an English mouth!' On the centre pages we find the first instalment of a poignant photo-story, covering the after-hours adventures of 'Sullied Tim'. This hapless character just can't understand why he's always turned away from Bend's nicer motels and hidden behind pillars at downtown eateries, but he's a big daft spoon because what do you fricking expect with Fagin's fingers and desert dandruff and an ever widening hole in the ever oilier arse of your trousers? Affixed to the front of issue 1 in a plastic pouch is a box of .030" oversize piston rings. Bit of a let-down there. But as is the way with such publications, part 2 of *Crankshaft Hiatus* came free with part 1. And stuck to its cover was something much better, and an awful lot heavier. That poor postman.

'This man set off across the whole country in a Model T he'd never seen before, by himself, never knowing what might happen around the next corner.' Ron Alley clamped a meaty old hand to my shoulder and gazed around the Black Bear Diner in Madras, where twenty-eight members of the High Desert Model A Club sat in silence before their breakfasts. 'Gentlemen, I say he's got two sets of balls.'

These were humbling words indeed from a man hardly under-endowed in the metaphorical trouser department. Ron was eighty-five and a fix-all force of nature. He'd been knocked off his feet twice while masterminding my engine extraction, but had leapt straight back up both times, and finished the operation with blood coursing down his left forearm. At his bidding I now stood and looked out at a sea of checked shirts and hearing aids, topped with a bobbing layer of trucker caps.

'That's extremely kind, Ron, but I don't really have any balls at all.'

Murmurs, a shifting seat, then a voice from the rear. 'Can't hear ya, buddy.'

'I have no balls,' I announced, more firmly. 'In fact, I'm here to kind of borrow yours, in a way, because I'm hoping that one of you might, um, have a spare, ah, underground-sized ...'

Ron had heard enough.

'God dammit, man needs a crankshaft, 10/10 ground undersize for a Model T.'

It was 45 miles from Bend to Madras, and Man-Mike had driven me there in his brown Model A sedan. This vehicle was only five years newer than Car-Mike, but felt like some visitation from the far-off future. It went 60, and held that speed with quiet assurance. It had normal pedals, a stick-shift, an enclosed body with wind-up windows, four-wheel hydraulic brakes and even a heater. Henry really did hold on to his first love for way too long.

When, in the Twenties, the Model T was overtaken by the competition – literally, and technologically – Ford remained deaf to criticism. He didn't listen to city-dwelling owners who grumbled about that planetary transmission, a leg-cramping liability in slow traffic. He didn't care that America's steadily improving roads did the T's flexible chassis few favours: a car built for muddy tracks felt woolly and wayward on smooth tarmac (tell me about it). His son Edsel began to state quite openly that the T had had its day; the rest of Henry's original A Team concurred but were too scared to speak out. In 1912, while Henry was away in Europe, his designers had taken it upon themselves to craft a sleeker T: lower, longer, cleaner. On his return, they presented him with a scale model. Henry considered it from all angles, nodding thoughtfully, then laid the little car on the floor and stamped it to smithereens.

After that 1919 shareholder buyout, Ford was a one-car, one-man company, and Henry hadn't dubbed his Model T the Universal Car for nothing: this was the only vehicle the world would ever need, dammit. 'The Ford car is a tried and proved product that requires no tinkering,' he insisted to reporters in December 1926. The industrial historian Robert Casey identifies 'a significant moral dimension to Ford's attitude towards the Model T', and the old man just couldn't cut the cord with a creation built in his own image: practical, frugal, slender, hard-working, reliable, unpretentious.

By 1926, seven out of ten Ford dealers were losing money, and many defected to General Motors. So did Norval Hawkins, Henry's visionary marketing supremo. The tide began to turn in popular culture, as comedians stopped laughing with the Model T and laughed at it: 'A Ford is like a bathtub – you don't like to be seen in one.' By 1924, Ford was making just $2 on every T sold, and the company generated 95 per cent of its profit elsewhere: spare parts, accessories, investments, shipping. But only when sales fell off a cliff – from 160,000 a month in 1925 to half that in early 1927 – did Henry finally relent. In high dudgeon and irrational ill grace: after nineteen years and fifteen million examples, the T was summarily pulled from production with nothing ready to take its place. At an estimated cost of $250 million – $3.5 billion in today's money – the entire Ford Motor Company had to shut down manufacturing and sales operations for the thick end of a year while its successor was designed and tooled from scratch. Judged against the T, the Model A was, as I'd discovered, a quantum leap forward. But judged against its contemporaries, the new car was no more than solidly conventional. It sold well enough, shifting almost five million in as many years. But it didn't change the world.

We returned to Mike's car now, and set off on a crankshaft hunt that took us deep into the gravel-paved, high-desert outback, at the tail of a convoy led by Ron in the Model A pick-up that had been his since 1947. The day unfolded like the tale of Redneck Cinderella, as Mike knelt before a succession of rusty crankshafts, micrometer screw gauge in hand, on a quest to find The One. Give an old car guy a barn and he'll never throw anything away. Men who'd never even owned a Model T would dig out a couple of old cranks for us from some spidery fundament. But we were looking for a needle in a haystack, and more literally than I am ever likely to. The moving parts in my engine had become married together in a very bespoke fashion during their ninety-three-year partnership, and as hinted at above I needed a crankshaft whose business surfaces were precisely ten-thousandths of an inch below their factory-fresh girth.

Tom had a lovely blue Hudson and a container full of Ts, but his spare crank was too big. Dave showed us through four cavernous outbuildings piled with Model Ts, traction engines, pianos, bicycles, hurricane lamps and church bells, but none of the dozen-odd cranks he hauled out were quite the right size. And so it went on until we arrived at a neat farmhouse fronted by a municipal-grade circular flower bed, at the centre of which sat the oxidised wreck of a Model T tourer.

Chuck kept eleven Ts in working order, but he'd been breaking down a little himself of late. 'Got two new knees put in, and I've just been given the all-clear from throat cancer,' he said, showing us into a well-ordered workshop. 'When I first got that cancer diagnosis, I went in with my wife and the doc says he'd like to talk to me alone.' Chuck scratched a red cheek. 'I said, "Come on, Doc, we can both hear this," and he says, "Well, OK, we've tested you, and you got your cancer from HPV." My wife asks what that was. Doc says it's a virus you contract from oral sex with women.' He pulled down a very shiny crankshaft from a parts shelf and laid it on the workbench before us, then turned with a winning beam. 'So I stand up and say, "Told y'all I was a horn dog!"'

Three of us added uncertain chortles to Chuck's gale of hooting laughter. But Mike stayed silent, clamping his micrometer around bits of glinting steel with an air of focused portent. After a while he stood up straight, removed his tinted spectacles and murmured, 'That'll work.'

Installing this burnished miracle to Mike's exacting standards would require a solid week of assiduous toil, and several more deliveries of connecting rods and gaskets from Lilleker Antique Restorations. Mike politely rebuffed all offers of assistance during this technical phase – yes, even mine – so I hired a car, booked into the cheapest motel I could find and spent many happy, idle days honing an appreciation of Bend and its environs.

America's panoramic wealth really is extraordinary. The landscape of Greater Bend had seemed unarrestingly flat and sandy as I'd tootled around it in Don's Jeep and Mike's Model A, but a fistful of free brochures from the motel reception directed me to scenes of breathtaking grandeur that would be national attractions in any other country. Rivers hurled themselves off pine-clad bluffs and meandered through mighty canyons. Huge bare outcrops, 500 feet tall, sprouted from the desert plain, like flint hand tools cast aside by some caveman deity. The region's volcanic legacies ran through the full and fabulous spectrum: sprawling lava fields, lofty cinder cones, broad craters filled with glassy lakes and a whole mountain built entirely of lustrous black obsidian. It was like driving through a full-colour anthology of Ansel Adams's boldest photographic landscapes. Then I'd go back to a bleak and careworn motel room, flick a Bakelite switch and trudge into an Edward Hopper.

One night the wind changed and the wildfire smoke blew in. By dawn there weren't any sights to see, so I spent a weekend wandering around the town centre, watching haze redden the sun and expelling black snot into a load of napkins I pinched from a table outside Starbucks. Downtown Bend was very different from anywhere I'd been. It was prosperous and pretty, the old streets thoughtfully re-gentrified, their bustling sidewalks lined with espresso bars and day spas, the art deco movie theatre reinvented as 'a hub for culture, connections, and artistic experiences'. A gift shop, handily encapsulating the mood, had a sign in its window advertising 'Up-Cycled Copper Cool Stuff'. Many of the craft-ale taverns, including two that had done their best to hide Sullied Tim, were graced with delightful gardens that stretched down to a curve in the Deschutes River – the very meander that had given Bend its splendidly half-arsed name. There were tattooed skateboarders, marijuana dispensaries, roundabouts, even a bike-sharing scheme: every trapping, in short, of a liberal metropolitan lifestyle I hadn't expected to encounter this far inland.

My old boys had given me the skinny. Bend's recent surge in wealth and size was down to an influx of Californians, lured north by cheaper real estate and a familiar climate. They'd brought along their lifestyle and values, and turned Central Bend into a dab of Democrat blue amid the Central Oregon redlands. In an act of charity that I might remember to thank him for one day, Car-Mike had stranded me on the front line of the great American culture war.

'We don't really go downtown these days,' Don told me. 'Too expensive, not our people, not our place. ' It was a ne'er-the-twain divide, cowboy vs liberal, Prius vs pick-up, Bud Lite vs IPA. Don was a folksy, genial fellow, a dialled-down Jimmy Stewart who said things like 'You bet!' and 'Gee willickers!'– without question the loveliest person you'll ever meet with a 'TRUMP–PENCE' sticker on his rear windshield. Everyone I met out in Bend's 'howdy belt' was a committed Republican. The solitary exception: a Model A collector who'd moved in from the west coast a few years previously, and was universally ribbed as 'the Democrat'. The rest chuntered mildly about damn pot shops, about Kim Pong Poo, about Oregon's openly bisexual governor ('guess she stands a 100 per cent chance of getting a date on Friday night'). Everyone's car radio was tuned to Fox News.

Yet my boys weren't natural Trumpites as I'd come to know them. There was no bitterness or desperation. No outbursts about Obama's open love for Islamic extremism or other manifestations of paranoid delusion. Nobody mentioned an impending apocalypse. I didn't see a single gun, though I'm sure most of them had one. These men had worked hard in largely humble careers – erecting electrical signs, managing auto spares shops, um, machining bullets – and were enjoying comfortable retirements focused on mechanical pottering. It was just that those carefree final chapters had been abruptly defaced by a bewildering invasion of urbanite liberals, and the weird west-coast shit they'd transplanted out in the Great Sandy Desert: the bike lanes and jogging, the quinoa and gender fluidity and up-cycled copper cool stuff.

Bend had been fully Californicated, and my mild-mannered traditionalists found themselves under siege in their own town, their way of life mocked and marginalised. 'They think we're all dinosaurs and racists,' Ron told me. It was people like him whose toil and determination had brought Bend to life out in the hot sand, and now they were outcasts, a besieged minority, banished to the boondocks by snowflake software engineers and baristas who'd never got their hands dirty or known a world without air-con. Their Bend was broken.

If one single factor propelled these old boys Trumpwards in the election campaign, it wasn't anything he'd said, but something Hillary Clinton had. In dumping half of Trump's supporters in a 'basket of deplorables', she inadvertently confirmed a suspicion that held right across white Middle America: that the Democratic establishment wasn't just ignoring them, it actively despised them. That single phrase must have seemed a perfect articulation of their resentment, of the chasm of mutual mistrust and loathing that separated cityfolk from their country cousins. A Millwall FC mentality kicked in: no one likes us, we don't care. To hell with Hillary. To hell with everything. Vote Trump.

Man-Mike had left town to go to a funeral; Car-Mike stood where we'd left him late the night before, squeezed into a sliver of cleared floor-space just inside the workshop's roll-up door. What a fight he'd put up that day. It had taken five of us as many hours to force-feed the reassembled engine back through his pursed lips. At the halfway point, it transpired through a series of faltering admissions that nobody present had ever performed such an operation on a Model T, or for that matter done much of anything else to one. In the end we'd literally stretched Mike on the rack, heaving his lower jaw forward with a massive winch. After a bolt dropped into the transmission, we had to extract it under the guidance of a 1920s service manual, and the busy little men in baker-boy caps and bib overalls who graced its illustrations. That was another two hours right there. And all the while that angry red sun bore down, sapping the will, lubricating palms, audibly buckling the derelict tractors strewn about in the sand.

When the whole punishing procedure was ostensibly completed, we had failed to find homes for a good two dozen bolts, pins and springs.

I sent a photo of the most important-looking leftovers to Ross, who pithily advised me that they supported the steering column. Nobody could even remember removing the five dice-sized cubes of wood that also wound up in our leftover tray. (A sixth fell on to

the bedroom floor when I pulled my trousers down that night.)
As the day had worn on, people kept dropping things, tripping
over, repeating themselves. I was told five times in an hour that
120,000 acres were ablaze out west of town. There were moments,
I confess, when I'd said a silent prayer for these old fellers just to
hold it all together long enough to get me back on the road. It felt
as if a century of practical know-how, an entire folk memory of
fixes, was draining away into the sand beneath us. 'I've got four
daughters,' Chuck had told me, 'and not one of their husbands
knows one end of a hammer from the other.' These self-taught
ninja mechanics, working by eye to a thousandth of an inch, fixing
con rods with bacon rind, were the T era's last samurai.

Darkness had been almost upon us when I climbed in, winked
at six old faces and jabbed the starter. *Ker-dug-a-dug-a-dug-a-dug-
a-dug-a-dug-a-wheeeeeeck.* Oh. Don sped into town and came back
with a new set of points. We put them in: nothing. Mike decided
we had a 'weak spark', and spent an obsessive hour running cables
around the engine bay, muttering irritably. No difference. Then, in
the dying light of another crimson sunset, I glanced down at the
board-less floor beneath me and saw a tiny brass lever sticking 90
degrees north of its usual position. Several afternoons earlier, I
had flicked it there under my own obscure initiative.

'Um, should I try opening the fuel shut-off?'

I suppose I could have surreptitiously switched it back. With
fewer heads leaning into the cabin I fear I might have done so.
Instead, I saw those heads rise up as one, and heard Mike lose his
cool for the first and last time.

'WHAT. FUEL. SHUT-OFF?'

In two seconds Car-Mike was roaring his transplanted heart
out. How fitting that the final, crowning imbecility was mine and
mine alone.

'Seems to me,' Ron drawled sardonically, 'the only weak spark we got here is the one sitting behind the damn wheel.'

For long days the Model T keys had clinked uselessly in my pocket. Now, on my tenth morning in Deschutes County, I slipped them in the ignition, started Mike up and reversed out into the sun. Fordus interruptus was at an end. My first mission: to follow Ron back to the house he shared with his wife Marlene in Culver, some 40 miles away up US-97, where at his humbling insistence I'd been accommodated for three days.

'See, I'd rather you spent money on the motor than giving it to some motel guy,' he'd said. Ron was my wallet's moral compass in Deschutes County, always on hand to put a fair price on the extraordinary mechanical favours that were being dispensed, and by men who batted away all offers of payment. 'You're only coming through here once in your life, Tim, so you want to be remembered right.' Even then, avoiding an awkward scene had meant surreptitiously stuffing wads of banknotes into tool chests, and leaving cryptic clues in thank-you notes.

Taking the juddery, wandering wheel after such a prolonged break, I was awed all over again by this endeavour's suicidal irresponsibility. When we stopped off en route at T expert Tom's place to have my transmission bands adjusted, even he expressed reservations. 'Just watching you drive in there, your car's looking all caddywhompus on the left side.' (I immediately banked this appealing idiom, cataloguing it beside Mike's related catchphrase: 'Like a saddle on a sow.') In all the excitement of the previous fortnight I'd forgotten all about my welded tie rod. As Ron turned down an undulating gravel road, I remembered.

Ron's house, a long bungalow perched atop a thousand-foot cleft in the Crooked River, was the extraordinary home of an extraordinary man. No matter how early I got up, Ron beat me. I once stumbled out of the spare room for a pee at 4.45 a.m. and there he was on his exercise bike out in the hall, in jeans, vest and a Stetson. 'Got to hit the ground running,' he puffed. 'Who are you ripping off if you sleep in?' Later he told me he'd never been in bed later than 5 a.m. in his whole life.

Somehow Ron sustained this restless intensity all day, driving me back and forth to Mike's workshop, an 80-mile round trip, attacking my car with spanners, hammers and an arc welder, terminating any snatch of downtime with a clap of those horny hands and the words: 'Come on, we're burning daylight here.' When the day was done, he drove Marlene and me down to the Round Butte Inn in Culver, nodded at three guys who seemed to live on their bar stools, and ordered us burgers and iced tea. Back home, I'd leave Ron and Marlene chatting brightly in their parlour and weave wearily off to the guest room, lured by plump feather pillows and a cocooning hand-stitched quilt. 'Don't let the bedbugs bite,' Marlene would always call out. Her eyes were failing, and she spent a lot of time out in the yard, weeding by feel.

Ron talked from dawn to dusk, a stream of reminiscence and philosophy delivered with a playful glint in his eye and a ready chuckle. Every chapter began with the same three words. 'Well, so, anyways, when I was a boy I rode to school bareback, one day the damn horse bucked me off and fell on my leg, and when he gets up, he-he, my damn foot's pointing backwards … Well, so, anyways, the government wants us all to live in cities so they can control us … I don't need to go to no church, I don't need to confess to no sins, I don't commit any damn sins.'

Only two topics dulled that playful glint. The first was 'the year Jimmy Carter stole the farm', which Ron brought up at least three times a day. In 1981, undone by spiralling interest rates and a huge tax bill, Ron had lost the 990 acres of corn and ranch-land that he'd been working all his life. Left with nothing, at the age of forty-nine he'd had to start all over again. Luckily, he was Ron, which allowed him to pick up two burned-out bulldozers at a salvage auction, rebuild them singlehandedly in six weeks flat, and start up a construction business that soon prospered. But the trauma still haunted him, and surely informed Ron's deep hatred for politicians of all stripes.

The second cropped up after we drove past a farmhouse a mile from his own. 'One of my sons lives there, but we don't see him no more because of his wife.' I tuned out as Ron described the humdrum background to this longstanding feud, and was brought up short when he moved on to its rather more dramatic recent devel-opments. 'Well, so, anyways, she comes at me with the tractor, and I somehow get caught up in the rake behind it, and she's dragged me around her property a while.' Ron lifted a finger off the wheel to salute a passing pick-up, whose driver responded in kind. 'Then she comes round to my property, and, well, I never did point the rifle at her, just kind of had the barrel resting on my arm, but of course she gets the authorities involved and now I've got a court case coming up.' He shook his head. 'You just can't pick your relatives.'

Well, so, anyways, we backed the T into Ron's workshop and embarked on our final remedial fiddles, tightening bolts and checking fluids. I went off to collect my bags from the guest bedroom, and when I emerged a small farewell T party had gath-ered outside the workshop doors. All were familiar faces from that Cinderella crankshaft hunt: Jim, who'd bolted the back end of a boat to his Tin Lizzie and dubbed it the T-Tanic; Dave, he of the pianos and church bells; and Dennis, who'd driven them all here in his favourite T, a shabby-chic roadster whose grille-mounted Ford logo had been tweaked to read 'Turd'. When Jim asked if they could take my car for a quick trial run before I set off, I readily agreed, hoping at the very least to have Mike's caddywhompus-ness assessed.

Ron drew up a couple of battered plastic chairs and we sat down in the workshop's gaping threshold. 'Funny,' I said, watching Mike disappear over a sandy brow, 'but that's the first time in almost 6,000 miles that car has driven anywhere without me in it.'

Presently the workshop phone rang. Ron went into the back office to answer it, and took a while to reappear. When he did he was bearing a twenty-four-can slab of Bud Lite: an unexpected burden, as I had never once previously seen him near alcohol. He tore the plastic covering off, withdrew a can, popped it open and placed it firmly in my hand. 'That was Jim on the phone,' he said. 'Well, so, anyways, your car's on fire.'

Half an hour later Mike appeared on the back of a tow truck driven by Ron's nephew Randy. Three wide-eyed men climbed woodenly from the cab, and described their ordeal in tones of disbelief as we winched Mike down to earth. They'd just pulled off the road to make a U-turn when smoke had poured out of the dash, followed by fingers of flame. Experience and quick-thinking spared a more total disaster: the 2-gallon jerrycan of fuel and all my other kit were flung out of the back, the rear floorboards yanked up, the battery beneath it swiftly disconnected. Had this conflagration occurred on my watch, as the dictates of probability demanded, I would have legged it into the desert and watched everything go up in flames: my journey, my pride, my cousin-in-law Miles's no-claims bonus.

Relief was tempered, however, by what we saw with the bonnet up. Mike's entire wiring system, a rather more extensive network than one might suppose, had been reduced to carbon-ised spaghetti. I tried very hard to greet this discovery with stoic restraint, but clearly failed.

'Why, see, Tim, I'm gonna have to chew up your rectum a little here.' Oh, go on then, Ron. Just a nibble between friends. 'You take it too hard when things go wrong, and get too excited when they go well. You just need to accept that if you keep your head, things will just kind of work out.'

For a wild moment I wondered if this was all some crazy plot, the first act in a catalogue of sabotage that would detain their bumbling pet Englishman in Deschutes County for ever. It wasn't such a huge stretch to picture Ron going full *Misery* on my knee-caps with a pipe wrench.

'See, nobody wants to bust a crankshaft, but you bust yours in the only place this side of the Rockies where someone had a right-size spare.' Ron nodded sagely. 'And boy, you've been lucky again, because the guy who makes the best vintage wiring looms in the whole damn country is a personal friend of mine, and he's right down the road in Bend.'

It meant more time, more money, another couple of hundred miles tooling up and down US-97, and further impositions on Ron and Marlene's hospitality and his friends' technical expertise. But how right Ron was. In any other scenario, I'd have been off the road for another week at least. But in the event, and looking through my photo archive I still can't believe it, Mike was resur-rected in twenty-four hours. Dennis and Jim even fitted him with brake lights, the better to alert hindward drivers of my forthcoming failure to slow down.

The farewells were long and fond. Don Penington, whose roadside compassion had inaugurated this two-week festival of resourcefulness and the human spirit, turned up with his wife Karen, a sprightly presence with the poise and smile of a retired tennis professional. She handed me another ration pack full of trail mix and cookies; he placed a souvenir torque wrench on Mike's back seat. With a crooked smile, Jim wedged a fire extin-guisher beside it. Marlene gave me a maternal hug; I placed a hand on Ron's substantial shoulder. 'On the back leg now,' he said, with that twinkle on full beam. 'You're all but done.' What a great country for old men.

As the sun dipped towards the vast conical bulk of Mount Jefferson, on show at last after so many days skulking in the smoke, Dennis made an extraordinary last-ditch offer. The road out of Culver was unusually lonesome; he had a cabin 30 miles west, and would lead me there in his Turd. *Ahoooooooga!* Off we went, in a cloud of waves and desert dust.

With his burnished bare pate and Birdseye beard, Dennis was a distinctive face in the Deschutes old-car scene, and had a manner to match. He opened beer bottles in the slot of Turd's spark lever, and kept a bottle of Tabasco in a holster on his belt (swoon). Dennis had been raised in California, and communicated in sharp, fluent bursts, a Tigger amongst the drawling Eeyores. 'I've lived with city folk and country folk – wanna know the difference?' he'd blurt. 'In the city, when they tell you a joke, it's like a story about a guy going down into a bar or whatever, with a punchline. In the country, they'll say: "Look what I can do with a frog and a car battery!"'

When the road threw us down the canyon I'd spent so many days on top of, I burst out laughing at the extraordinary spectacle, and its contrast with our puttering puniness: a violent, craggy plunge to a distant squiggle of blue, its upper flanks washed gold by the setting sun. The enormous scenery seemed a little less amusing when we rattled across a little single-track bridge at the bottom, and Mike cut out in a choking haze of gas fumes. *Ahooga!* Dennis reversed back, threw up the hood and effected a cure that left him drenched in fuel. He would reprise this performance twice before Turd and Mike creaked to a halt in the gloaming.

Like all good things Dennis's cabin was rude but cosy, alone in an outback plateau of pines and crispy brown grass, far from the piped and wired conveniences of modern life. 'Careful when you sit down,' he called out as I creaked open the outhouse door. 'Pretty brave squirrel has set up home in the long-drop.'

We fired up a rusty barbecue, threw on some hotdogs, and opened a couple of beer bottles in Turd's spark slot. It warmed my heart to see him and Mike side by side in the long grass, a companionable, twilit gleam in those wide-set eyes. The stars and moon were soon full frontal, and the tepid breeze took on a chill. It felt like the last night of summer.

'Can I ask you honestly what people in Britain think about Trump?'

I drained my beer, the straight answer stuck in my throat. The faraway howl of a coyote drifted through the pine trees. I didn't want to upset anyone. Particularly not right out here. A while earlier, admiring Turd's many outboard luggage boxes, I'd asked Dennis what he kept in them. 'Travelling light on this trip,' he'd said, fixing me with a piercing blue gaze. 'Just an axe and a shovel.' Three extremely long seconds had elapsed before he collapsed in a fit of giggles.

But then I thought: Sod it. I'd bitten my lip for almost three months, and sometimes a man had to say what a man had to say.

'Well, as you're asking honestly, Dennis, I'd say that by general agreement in my country, Donald Trump is an embarrassing stain on the fabric of the universe.'

His fluffy white beard nodded slowly in the moonlight.

'Now that's a pretty bold statement to make in this part of the world,' he said, and I waited for him to lean forward and slam an opened Tabasco bottle up my nose. 'But it's one that I happen to agree with.'

I guessed it was those formative years in California. With that Dennis clapped his hands and stood up, reluctant to dwell on the farcical tragedy that had befallen his nation, and marooned him amongst people who rejoiced in it.

It was a stupendous, pin-sharp morning, with brazen sun and a nose-numbing nip in the air. 'OK, I'm gonna take your top off,' announced Dennis, when we'd packed up. After five effortful minutes, a very different Mike stood in the golden grass: canvas roof hauled back and battened down, out and proud. This was a topless T to be see in, as driven by Henry Ford off the production line in all those landmark publicity shots, as driven by Laurel and Hardy through all those sawmills. 'Now *that's* a Model T tourer,' said Dennis, hands on hips. 'Let's go do some touring.'

Mike suffered repeated fuel starvations; after the third, Dennis spliced an extra filter into the gas pipe, which seemed to do the trick. We crossed a hillside of pines reduced to charred flagpoles by a recent wildfire, then plunged ever deeper into a primeval, red-trunked forest. 'While since I've been this way,' murmured

Dennis when we stopped at an unfamiliar fork. While since anyone had. Both gravel tracks were pierced with saplings, and neither showed up on his map of forestry trails. Dennis picked the left one and I followed his orange dust.

Soon after, the forest abruptly parted and presented us with a dramatic prospect: the 10,000-foot snow-topped volcano that was Mount Jefferson, spearing the heavens above a rolling sea of green, like the label on a bottle of mineral water. I found my appreciation of this remarkable vista compromised, however, by the steepling granite abyss from whose crumbly brink we surveyed it. The trail, now little more than a rockery strewn with pine cones, at once dived eagerly down this appalling eminence, made more appalling by roofless, hyper-panoramic exposure. Ahead Dennis skittered down the rubbled switch-backs, lost in a gritty cloud. I did my best to keep up, rocks thumping into the floorboards and pinging off the chassis rails, Mike's squirrely jiggles amplified into gravel-scattering, rally-car power slides. Don't leave me, Dennis. So far away, then a little nearer, now nearer still ... How considerate of him to slow down, I thought, dispatching a gobbet of dusty mucus to eternity as I sawed away at the wheel, plunging forth in a semi-controlled slalom. But gosh, there's now something taking shape in that cloud that looks very much like Turd's rear end, and it's really quite close to my front. I wonder how that can be when I'm pressing the brake down so firmly. Perhaps I had better jam the pedal right to the floor with all my might. That's better. Actually, no – no, it isn't. My bonnet is now six inches from Dennis's spare wheel, and I'm gaining speed. How uncommonly vexing! Well, I suppose I ought to say terrible things extremely loudly, ram my blanched fist against the horn, and welcome Brother Homer Looper of the First Pentecostal Church into what remains of my life.

'That'll do it,' said Dennis, crouched by Mike's rear wheels a memorable moment later.

I had come to rest at a rakish angle, 2 feet from oblivion and a lot less from Turd's behind. On shaky legs I bent down and followed Dennis's finger to the right-hand brake assembly, which hung distantly beneath the hub, its retaining nut bullied loose by the shuddering ordeal.

'I'm so glad you're here,' I quavered as he retightened it.

He looked up from his work and beamed radiantly. 'Except if I hadn't been here, then you wouldn't be either.'

A fair point. In respect of surface, steepness and isolation this road was the worst I had tackled, by an ugly margin, and under Dennis-free conditions I would never have come anywhere near it. If I had died, I'd have been absolutely furious with him.

'Let's give that a try.'

I wiped my palms on my trousers and started up. The trail ahead fell precipitously away, framed by spindly pines, towards the looming bulk of Mount Jefferson. Dennis glanced over his shoulder, hoisted a thumb, and called out a sentence that once heard would never be forgotten. 'If the brakes go again, run into the back of me and I'll do our best to stop us both.' I fraily hoisted a thumb. 'Might not be good for either vehicle but it's better than going over the fricking edge.' And in a ball of dust and profanity off we went, careering at runaway speed into the Paramount Pictures logo.

Camp Sherman was little more than a rustic gas station in the forest, which we discovered had closed for the season two days before. I was so pleased to be alive and back near tarmac that I couldn't have cared less. We lunched on leftover hotdogs and Karen's trail mix on a camp table outside, then Dennis tipped his spare petrol can into my under-arse tank and gave Mike a farewell once-over. At some point in the morning's excitements I'd lost reverse gear, so up came the floorboards and off went the transmission cover. Behold the hogshead: a Pandora's box of drums, springs and oil-slathered fabric bands. Staring into this steampunk lash-up, I felt a ghostly twinge of the blank terror that had struck deep into my heart when Ross first laid it bare, one distant Sunday morning in Virginia. But a hundred wise old heads had now peered into it alongside mine, and just enough know-how had crackled across from their skulls to mine; I heaved the reverse pedal down with one hand, spannered the requisite adjuster with the other and the job was done.

'Sure you don't want to see that two-headed fish?'

Dennis had been trying to interest me all day in his favourite regional attraction, a remote salmon hatchery with a notable collection of mutated freaks. 'Last chance.'

He smiled in hope; I did so with regret. We were parked up at the threshold of US-20, and I needed to make time: there was a big pass ahead, followed by many miles of nothing. I clapped Turd on the bonnet, shook Dennis's hand and wondered if I was thanking my last senior saviour. Of the million indebted farewells I'd doled out along the way, this ranked amongst the most earnest. Dennis was the last link in that Deschutes County chain of heroes, and he'd gone the extra mile more literally than anyone else. Thundering up the lower reaches of the Santiam Pass, hemmed in by lumber trucks, it struck me that I might someday be grateful for that final off-road adventure: a grand last hurrah in the Model T's natural habitat.

The pass topped out just below 5,000 feet, then I hung a right up US-22 and wiggled gently downwards through dense forest. I finally came face to face with a wildfire, a monster that shot mighty plumes of white smoke a mile into the sky before me and necessitated a series of detours. The same brake came loose; I eased gingerly into a rest area and sorted it once and for all with a locknut. Come sundown I had additionally resolved a painfully shrieking fan (grease and adjustment) and a sudden electrical death (firm smack on the rewired terminal block). I was getting pretty good at this. Bit late, though. In Sublimity – a defiantly characterless grid of bungalows – I lay back on the motel nylon, unfolded a map of Oregon that Ron had pressed upon me, and sat up with a start and a tremendous rip of static. I'd crossed the Cascades, my final mountain range, and the coast lay no more than a 70-mile tootle away. Could that really be it? First night in Ordinary, last in Sublimity? Had I just slammed my last gas-station cheeseburger into a bedroom microwave? But one question was less rhetorical and more pressing: what of Mike?

At least six times a day somebody asked what I'd be doing with the car if and when I hit the Pacific, and my answers had vacillated wildly, in tune with prevailing levels of affection and exasperation. Impromptu beach auction on a good day; impromptu beach bonfire on a bad one. More rational fates centred around the MTFCA's classified section, along with broader online sale options. But something changed in Bend. All that emotional investment, those long days of aged toil and wisdom, and for what? A two-day trundle to the seaside? I couldn't just walk away from Mike now. You don't patiently nurse an ailing pensioner back to good health then bung him on eBay.

A bolder, nobler scheme was hatched that night at the Rodeway Inn, and in a flurry of morning texts and calls the plan came into hard focus. I would take Mike north-west to Washington State, kiss the Pacific sand, then drive him back east to Seattle. There, yet another experienced and generous MTFCA member would help arrange for him to be loaded into a container and shipped to Southampton. My leathery old holiday fling was coming home with me.

I ran through my bonnet-up morning routines with a light heart, a top-up here, a tweak there, whistling as I worked. As my knowledge base had broadened, so had my maintenance regime. It was no longer enough to dump a quart of Walmart oil in and check the wheels weren't about to fall off: now there were brackets to tighten, nipples to grease, bolts to be re-torqued with Don's convoluted wrench. Presently an aged eccentric on a beat-up bicycle wobbled across the motel car park.

'Tuned into the old ways, man,' he rasped approvingly, doffing a lime-green trilby. 'I like it. Reconnection.'

Words and sentiments I hadn't encountered in 6,000 miles. I wondered if I'd already met my last Trumpite – my revised 260-mile route to the coast would take me through more blue than red – then stopped wondering and asked him outright.

'*Trump?*' A get-outta-here snort. 'Dude has like zero intellect, not even any considered opinion on anything. Just a dumb rich kid who grew up wiping his ass on hundred-dollar bills.'

A couple of hours up the road, lunching on stolen motel bagels in the L. L. 'Stub' Stewart State Park – what a fitting tribute for a lumber baron whose firm removed 300 trees from the Oregon skyline every day for forty years – I fell into conversation with a passing group of silver-haired ramblers.

'London, England? Listen, we are *so sorry* about that idiot in the White House.'

'Just remember that Hillary won the popular vote.'

'By millions! Wasn't even close!'

I started to describe my route, retracing it in reverse, but didn't get very far before they interrupted, faces puckered in disgust. 'You been the other side of the Cascades? Well, say no more.'

The Model T had granted Americans the run of their land, but a hundred years on they were still penned in. How remarkable that in the twenty-first century, a mountain range could still keep people so very far apart, in every sense. 'I ain't never been east of Kansas City' was a standard boast in Bend, and Ron spoke of the west coast as an alien realm. 'How will this play with Trump's base?' asked the hand-wringing CNN commentators every night, in a tone of fearful mystery that suggested a savage lost tribe hiding out in the uncharted toolies.

I had lived amongst these people and learned their ways. Preposterous as it seemed, I probably now understood the flyover states – small-town keepers of the nation's spiritual flame – better than many of the coastal Americans who lived either side of them. But these furious old ramblers didn't want to hear another word about those deplorables over the hill, and wouldn't have appreciated me telling them that this stubborn, hostile indifference was the principal explanation for the horrible orange president they'd been saddled with.

The car guys I'd spent so much time with were kind, traditional, plain good folk, the definitive salt of the earth. Whenever one of them spoke up for Donald Trump I couldn't help feeling a little hurt and let down, like hearing an old friend tell you he's gone gluten-free or become a Neighbourhood Watch coordinator. Yet at the time of writing, Trump's approval ratings are steady at around 40 per cent. That's lower than any president has averaged since pollsters started compiling this data in 1945 – yes, even Nixon – but not by much. Indeed, that rating has barely wavered since he took office. The rust-belters and small-towners whose anger and resentment put Trump in the White House are still raging against the dying of their light. There's been no populist backlash against Trump, just a frenzied frontlashing from everyone who already hated him. For a lot of his supporters that must seem sufficient reward in itself: all the people they wanted to wind up are being wound up, very tightly.

But I had made my peace with Trump's voters, however deluded or offensive I found some of their opinions. And because of that, I could not and never will make my peace with Trump himself. They had put their faith in him, but he would never return it. Because he doesn't give a flying cow-chip about them, or anyone but himself. Where they were decent and honourable, he was ignorant and graceless. They were old-school; he was no-school. He will let them down, because he shares none of their values. But my guess is that the Donald's base won't turn him until they accept he has failed on his own terms, which may take quite a while. Nobody expects to Make America Great Again in a couple of years when it's been in decline for more than thirty.

*

For Henry Ford, the hero worship ebbed swiftly away when that farming downturn segued into the Great Depression. By then he was being eased away from daily operations and steered towards a figurehead role, Ford's Ronald McDonald. But the public already suspected he was losing his touch. That stubborn refusal to update the Model T and the disastrous Fordlandia farce had been followed by an ill-fated dalliance with mass air transportation: Henry sank millions into developing the Ford Flivver, a lightweight, single-seat 'Model T of the air', then pulled the plug after a crash that killed his test pilot. People slowly grasped that the Model T – from conception to epic mass manufacture – was a one-off stroke of genius. When the car became a bit of a joke, so did its creator.

In 1930, the River Rouge plant laid off two-thirds of its workforce, and in the three years that followed Ford recorded losses of $125 million. Wages dropped by 60 per cent across the nation. Fifteen million Americans were unemployed, and forty-five million lived in poverty. People ate potato peelings and sold their own blood. A million transients drifted west. Henry's beloved farmers suffered grievously: wheat fell to its lowest price since the days of Shakespeare, and by 1932 a pair of shoes cost the same as a wagon load of oats.

But Ford, nearing seventy, was no longer the man who had once spoken favourably about universal healthcare and nationalisation. Now he said that charity was barbarous, that the unemployed were at fault for not working hard enough, that crop prices 'could never fall too low'. He suggested that the Depression was a great opportunity to get back to basics and appreciate the simple things. 'If you've lost all your money,' breezed Henry, 'just charge it up to experience.' The thuggish excesses of Ford's Service Department, captured by a newspaper photographer, dealt the fatal blow to his man-of-the-people schtick. 'Don't you know we are losing our farms?' wrote one furious correspondent. 'I will not take any lip from you.'

But Ford wasn't the nation's pen pal any more. Instead, people wrote in their millions to a new saviour, Franklin D. Roosevelt, who was resurrecting America with his New Deal. People blamed Ford and businessmen like him for the recession, and put their faith in the federal government to bail them out. Trump's victory was secured by an extraordinary inversion of this belief.

For the record, Henry Ford never forswore his pacifism. In this sense at least he remained a man of deep compassion, a fierce opponent of capital punishment, so repulsed by violence that he refused to display a single gun or even a mousetrap in his museum of American innovation. Until the day he died he carried this 'Imagine'-esque homily, condensed from a Tennyson poem, on a card in his wallet:

For I dipt into the future, far as human eye could see,
Saw a vision of the world, and all the wonders that could be,
Till the war drum throbbed no longer, and the battle flags were furled,
In the Parliament of Man, the Federation of the World.

Below these words, Henry even scribbled his own 'I'm not the only one' addendum: 'The Parliament of Man will be worth it all. I believe I see it coming.' Despite the curdling of his politics, Ford would always cling to an optimistic faith in human nature. 'I have never met a really bad man,' he would often say. In failing to imagine Donald Trump uttering these words, ever, I wonder if I've unearthed small-town America's fundamental woe. They'll put their faith in a vengeful God, a big gun and a vindictive president. Because they've lost all faith in their fellow man.

So, anyway – Henry might have gone a bit *Daily Mail*, but he wasn't all bad. Right? Well, there is one other thing, and I'm afraid it's terrible. Discover enough about Henry Ford to develop a deep admiration for the man, and you'll find yourself putting it off and wishing it away. But the uncomfortable truth is this: the world's best-known industrialist was a vitriolic and relentless anti-Semite.

Ford spent eight years and $10 million propagating his viciously anti-Jewish conspiracy theories, through the pages of the *Dearborn Independent* – a newspaper acquired largely for this purpose and distributed in vast numbers across the nation. Some ninety-one articles from the *Dearborn Independent* were collated under Ford's authorship into an anthology entitled *The International Jew – The World's Foremost Problem*, which declared Jews in charge of global politics and finance, and held them accountable for everything from the Great War to fixing the 1919 baseball World Series, via prostitution and jazz ('Jewish Jazz – Moron Music'). A German translation of this work was reprinted no fewer than twenty-nine times during the 1920s. 'I read it and became anti-Semitic,' a prominent Nazi named Baldur von Schirach told judges at the Nuremburg Trials. 'In those days this book made such a deep impression on my friends and myself because we saw Henry Ford as the embodiment of success.'

'Every year makes the American Jews more and more the controlling masters of the producers in a nation of one hundred and twenty million,' wrote Hitler in *Mein Kampf*, 'and only a single great man, Ford, to their fury still maintains full independence.'

In 1938, on his seventy-fifth birthday, Henry Ford was presented with the Grand Cross of the Supreme Order of the German Eagle: the highest honour Nazi Germany could bestow upon a foreigner. How happy he looks in the photos, beaming away in his home office at Dearborn as a Nazi official pins the medal to his lapel – a Maltese cross girdled with eagles and swastikas. Two years later,

Ford told a reporter that the Second World War was the doing of 'international Jewish bankers'. By then he'd had a stroke and was sliding towards dementia, though given his track record this was hardly a blurted moment of madness. Anti-Semitism was, of course, a more mainstream menace back then, and along with the hate-mail Ford received many letters of support. But how extremely unpalatable it is to realise that both of the most popular cars in history, the globe-changing Model T and the VW Beetle, were created by people who really hated Jews.

Mike still had his top off, and full exposure was burning an impressive red stripe across my previously fringe-shaded forehead. But despite the sun my forearms were goose-pimpled, and autumn was setting out its stall all around. Swelling pumpkins lay strewn about like basketballs in roadside fields; ranks of wheat stubble smouldered across every rolling hillside. These bonus extra miles were there to be savoured: I could now get back in the requisite expeditionary groove, reacquaint myself with the full and thrilling import of conquering a huge landmass in a stupidly old car.

Rural northern Oregon thoughtfully offered up a drive-thru anthology of favourite hits. Big red barns, scampering chipmunks, a rusted girder bridge. 'GOD ANSWERS KNEE-MAIL.' A derelict clapboard gas station; the whiff of skunk; swing-seats on sagging verandas. But the roads were busier now, and that big-country, open-plan vibe of plain, plateau, desert and prairie already seemed a distant memory. The Oregon Trail ended in these fecund hills.

My motel in Clatskanie, hard up by the Columbia River, emphasised how far I'd come: it boasted a drive-thru 'adult emporium' that offered glass pipes, hookahs and bedroom novelties for the

'Well, it's been real enjoyable hearing about your journey. Thank you for sharing it with me.'

The young attendant on the Westport ferry gave me a nod and a gracious smile. How I'd miss this enthusiastic curiosity, etched deep into the American character. With the roof down, my celebrity had been elevated to a whole new level. Even Porsche drivers were waving now. I'd miss all that, too. And the enduring pleasure of procuring dreamy sighs and clasped chests by the simple expedient of opening my mouth and saying something. And being called 'sweetie' by old ladies and 'pardner' by old men. Raised palms of greeting out on a lonely road. A mentholated whiff of sagebrush and the glint of a distant corn elevator. Humptulips, Washington State; Slapout, Oklahoma; Yockanookany Nature Trail, Mississippi; Bacon Level, Alabama. Bashing the horn for company and sending a huge flock of starlings into the blue sky. The restful seaside whoosh of an aged motel air conditioner. Eight per cent sugary malt alcohol: don't cry for me, Lime-a-Rita.

I bumped off the little ferry and slithered up a ramp into Washington, my twenty-second and final state. Almost two-thirds of Washingtonians live in Seattle, and this side of their province had been left pretty much to its own devices: a lot of hilly forest, a few prisons. Presently I swung on to the Pacific Coastal Highway, an iconic road-trip magnet whose representative stalwarts now gaily crowded the tarmac. A shaving-foamed, can-trailing honeymoon express; a convoy of middle-aged bikers; foreign tourists in rented convertibles. *The Pacific Coastal Highway*. Gulp. When the ferryman asked for my destination, it had felt extremely weird to name an end point that was almost in view, rather than a couple of time zones away. I caught a first whiff of seaweed. Salt-poisoned pine skeletons clustered a lagoon. A swathe of blue crept down from the top of my GPS screen. But the world's largest body of water bided its time for the big reveal, hiding coyly behind a crest of Christmas trees and birches.

It was a struggle to gather my thoughts, what with the excitable traffic and a strident chirrup that now resonated painfully up from Mike's right front wheel. I tried to archive the journey's defining sensations, the throbs and rattles and creaks that ran through my hands, my arse, my ears. The perma-oiled cuticles; the trousers that dare not speak their name; the once-red trainers browned with desert dust, lubricants and salsa. Blistered lips and a farmer's tan that beat all others forearms down. Somehow I'd lost a stone: nervous energy had bested Tex-Mex, Slim Jims and a hundred fry-ups.

I arched my back and splayed my legs, as I had done fifty times a day to ease the fearsome pelvic cramp that is the lot of the long-haul antique motorist. The antique antique motorist. Because I really had aged on this journey, ravaged by its rigours and perhaps by association with ancient cars and men. I emitted a slight but perceptible groan whenever I stood up, and a grateful sigh whenever I sat down. Three hours earlier, making just such a sound as I took my ease and prepared to enjoy my final diner breakfast, the smiling waitress handed me a laminated sheet headed 'SENIOR MENU'. I felt extremely sad until I saw the prices.

But Mike, poor Mike, had truly suffered. For a ninety-three-year-old, this was the mother of One Last Jobs. The shriek of a dry bearing, the rasp of a fresh crack in the exhaust: every few hours a painful new voice inveigled itself into that chorus of neglect and decay. At speed, he sounded like a one-man band falling down the stairs. The cabin was a frank disgrace, bestrewn with Slim Jim sheaths, dented cans and empty quarts of Walmart oil, all laid on a bed of Sedgwick straw and a million grains of Great Sandy Desert. The windshield was so filthy that when I tried to take photos through it, the camera stubbornly fixed its focus on the grease spots. Wrath's paw-prints still marched across that dusty bonnet.

The sun got to work and I pulled on the High Desert Model As trucker cap Don had given me. If anyone had told me at the start of this trip that by the end I would voluntarily be wearing such a cap I might never have set off. But now it felt right on my head. Just as it felt right to say gas and sidewalk and *glaaaaaaaaass of waaahdur*. I was talking the talk and hatting the hat. I had become an old car guy. Albeit the kind of old car guy who pulls up the hood after a breakdown and thinks: Yeah, all these bits are definitely really hot.

We rounded a few grubby estuaries, tracking up and down grim waterfront towns full of battered warehouses and timber-pulp processing plants. One of them was Aberdeen, where Kurt Cobain grew up. It smelled like white spirit. Here I turned left off the shore-shy coastal highway, and headed west down a 20-mile cul-de-sac that made a no-nonsense dash straight at the sea. I inched the throttle down a notch, then gripped Mike's wooden wheel extremely hard. We were going to make it.

'Henry Ford put wheels on our homes,' said the actor and folk psychologist Will Rogers in 1923. 'It will take a hundred years to tell whether that helped us or hurt us.' But the thick end of a century later, it still isn't clear.

By the end of the Model T era, all the transformative ingredients of the automobile age were already in the mix. In 1921: the first drive-in fast-food joint, the Pig Stand in Dallas. In 1922: the Country Club Plaza near Kansas City, America's first out-of-town shopping mall. In 1923: the Bronx River Parkway, the first urban motorway. By 1927, one in five Americans owned a car – a year when the comparable proportion in Britain was one in forty-four, and in Germany, one in 196. Cars – building them, buying them, running them, laying miles and miles of tarmac before them – absorbed the bulk of America's private and public expenditure.

Ford's tractors were at the forefront of a mechanisation drive that largely killed off the small farm, and his cars gave redundant farming families an escape route. From 1926 to 1965, more than thirty million Americans moved out of farm communities and into cities, by some reckonings the greatest human migration in history. By 1940, thirteen million Americans were living in car-commuter suburbs, and the whole east coast from New York to Philadelphia had coagulated into a single band of metropolitan settlement. Homogenous 'miracle mile' strip malls were a common edge-of-town fixture by the late 1950s; so too were mega malls with parking for thousands of cars. By 1930, Atlanta had already lost half its downtown stores, and in the coming decades most American cities would follow Detroit's lead: prosperous suburbs wrapped around a crime-ridden central wasteland. In reflection of the car's omnipotence, many new residential districts were built without a single sidewalk.

The sociological impact was overwhelming. On the downside, cars facilitated white flight and had a corrosive effect on the nation's sense of community. As early as 1929, an LA householder was telling a researcher that all her social needs were met by car, largely 'riding uptown to the movie theaters'. 'I have nothing whatsoever to do with our neighbours. I don't even know their names.' But the freedom to make such a choice was an exhilarating novelty for women, whose lives were transformed by the car much more fundamentally than men's. When the

Model T was blessed with an electric starter in 1919, removing brute strength as a prerequisite for ownership, Ford's marketing genius Norval Hawkins came out with a remarkably progressive campaign: 'It's woman's day! No longer a "shut in", she reaches for an ever wider sphere of action – that she may be more the woman. The car is a real weapon in the changing order.'

As early as the mid 1920s, a car was deemed 'a social essential' for American teenagers. Racing and drunken joyrides became rites of passage, with the LA police reporting that nearly all of the thirty-two cars that vanished in the city on an average day in 1926 were stolen by under-eighteens. Henry Ford, rather wonderfully, is said to have squeezed the width of the Model T's rear seat to 38 inches, hoping, in the words of auto historian James Flink, to 'discourage the use of his car as a place in which to engage in sexual intercourse'. But instead, he threw down the gauntlet to passionate young contortionists across the nation. In 1921, the chief of the LA police motorcycle squad was complaining that country-lane 'coupé lovers' would 'douse their lights and indulge in orgies'. 'Hot pillow' motels turned away travellers to focus on the, um, 'couples trade', with rooms sometimes rented sixteen times a night. The first drive-in cinema opened in Camden, New Jersey, in 1933, and as the phenomenon swept across the US, staff quickly noticed that audiences often failed to engage with the on-screen action. 'I can look out some nights and I won't see a single head,' said the manager of a Georgia drive-in. 'Not one. Everybody's going at it.' On a doubtlessly connected note, by the 1960s, 40 per cent of American marriage proposals were said to have been made in cars. Sociologists have bluntly pointed out that by extending the search for a spouse far beyond the small-town boundaries of old, the car added much-needed depth to certain regional gene pools.

Ford, by then a conflicted and rather senile pacifist, lived to see automobile assembly lines win the war. Ferdinand Porsche had known as much in advance: after his tour of the mighty and relentless River Rouge factory, he warned Hitler that repurposed US car plants could churn out two planes or tanks for every one an enemy might destroy. And though Henry died in 1947, he didn't miss much in the way of US automotive glory. After the launch of hydraulic power steering in 1951, the American motor industry settled into the cynical perfection of built-in obsolescence, leaving technological advances to the Europeans. The bigger-is-better national mentality was a handy fit for the all-powerful 'Big Three', Ford, Chrysler and General Motors: in the 1950s, a vast, wallowy Yank tank only cost around $300 more to manufacture than a more humble 'sub-compact', but could attract a $3,000 premium in the showroom.

The shamelessly overblown 1959 Cadillac V8 was 19 feet long and almost 7 feet wide, and though American cars wouldn't get any bigger, they also wouldn't get any better. Chevrolet used the same engine for twenty-four years, and the fuel economy of an average American car fell by almost half in three post-war decades. Cadillac's 1967 flagship, the Eldorado, came with antediluvian crossply tyres and drum brakes that meant you needed 386 feet – the length of a football pitch – to stop one from 70mph. Its V8 engine returned 10mpg – less than half Mike's average consumption on our coast-to-coast drive.

Overseas manufacturers had by then left their American rivals distantly behind. The Eldorado's closest European equivalent, the Mercedes 250, had drum brakes and crossply tyres, weighed over half a ton less and therefore required 100 fewer feet to stop from 70. It was powered by a fuel-injected engine that returned twice the gas mileage, and it undercut the Cadillac by $2,000. American cars had become everything Henry Ford hated: overpriced, over-weight, under-engineered.

In 1950, the US manufactured 76 per cent of the world's motor vehicles. By 1982, that proportion had collapsed to 19 per cent. America is still in love with cars: half of US households have more than one. But they increasingly buy foreign. The US has been a net importer of automotive products since 1967. Ford currently employs 50,000 factory workers across the US, less than half the number who manned the River Rouge lines alone in the mid-1920s. Chrysler is now owned by Fiat, and over the last ten years GM has been kept afloat with $17 billion of taxpayers' money.

The American motor industry's fall from grace can perhaps be traced to March 1948, a year after Henry went to the big scrapyard in the sky. Ernest Beech, the firm's new president, was at a conference in Cologne when he rejected a proposition from Germany's Allied military government, and in strident terms: 'I don't think what we're being offered here is worth a damn!' What they were being offered was the entire VW business – factory, Beetles, the lot. And they were being offered it for free.

Ocean Shores seemed like a belt-and-braces guarantee of full Pacific content. The town was certainly bang in my demographic, its broad and slightly bleak main drag sparsely flanked with pensioner inducements: Val-u-Food Grocery Liquidators, barn-sized budget motels offering full-board deals, a quilt show at the convention centre. Feeling numb and a little hollow I puttered past the Lighthouse Suites Inn. Buildings gave way to low, tussocked dunes and tarmac to sandy gravel. I dialled down the throttle, and Mike's wheels whispered on to the beach. There it was, a faraway sparkle under the cirrus-streaked sky. The sand was firm; I picked up speed and swooshed seawards, down half a windswept mile of lightly peopled shoreline. Then dampness began to blot the way ahead, and I eased to a standstill. A crowd magnetically gathered.

'You bring that here in a trailer? You *didn't*? You *drove* from *Virginia*? You have got to be kidding me.'

'I just want to touch this car, it's sexy.'

'I'm told Henry Ford was a cousin of mine.'

'How fast does that go? What kind of gas you put in it?'

'My name's Doug Rufferson and this is my friend Brandon Drells. Mind if we take a photograph, sir?'

I would do my very best to take this wonderful, homespun courtesy home with me. How I'd love to answer my phone as Tim Moore out of Chiswick. I'd also come back with some mineral deficiencies and a deft touch with locknuts that might come in handy one day, probably after the apocalypse. Plus a dose of hypochondria from all those adverts. Could that be the first twinge of ulcerative colitis? How dark is a darkened stool? And which catheter *was* right for me? (Spoiler: pre-lubricated.)

A man in a wide-brimmed sunhat laboured up, both hands clutched around a wind-bent 20-foot fibreglass pole topped with an enormous Stars and Stripes.

'My uncle had a Model T,' he yelled, looking straight out to sea. 'Me and my sister used to fight over the back seat, 'cos if you sat behind him, you got tobacco spit right in your face.'

After a brisk nod he struggled on towards the gentle breakers, flag slapping furiously on high.

When the most vocal elements of Mike's little fan club had dispersed I hopped down, pulled out the back seat bolster and rooted about through the dead components interred beneath it. Beat-up greasy conrods, old copper gaskets, two hefty halves of a crankshaft. And there it was, a crumpled little bottle half full of beige and bitty Atlantic.

'Good job, Michael.' I patted his hot bonnet: 6,102 miles in eighty-one days. 'That crankshaft stunt was pretty low, mind you.' Then I walked over the damp, flat sand to a slowly receding water-line, and with an unpoetic crunch of thin plastic, topped up the Pacific Ocean.

I had seen a majestic nation unfold beyond the gunsight motometer on my prow, forever heading west at 32mph, reeling in a yellow dotted line with that golden warmth on my left forearm. The John Wayne bluffs, the eternities of ripening corn stretched out under a cloudless prairie sky, the old man rivers. Those vistas will stay with me for ever. So too the wooden judder through my feet and fingers, the smell of hot oil and old leather, the mechanical pandemonium, the days that seemed to last a month. Chocking the wheels in another motel car park, walking alone at dusk down another wide and desolate main street. Crispy grass piercing the sidewalk, garish commercial confidence fading on every wall and soap-fronted store front, another little Pompeii of small-town America's pomp. Pulling back the thin and grimy motel curtains to see a face glinting back, chrome-ringed eyes and a big chrome gob, the shiny, eager surprise of the first night steadily dulled into weary, long-suffering acceptance.

I had learned that rustic American men really like breakfast and hate the government and never sit with their legs crossed. I had met the last queen bees of the Model T hive mind, the self-schooled, multi-skilled make-do-and-menders. Some as creaking and leaky as the Flivvers they loved, but all as dogged and gallant. Live slow, die old. Spending time with these doughty, demigod granddads had been a privilege and an inspiration, almost a religious awak-ening. Bring me home, Ford Jesus. And what a durable pleasure it had been to put my go-anywhere Universal Car through its paces just as Henry intended, motel managers watching on with wide eyes and slack jaws as I hurled my bags in the back and bucked away into the morning sun. I had lived the American Dream out on those wide-open roads, and in the small towns I had driven through its dusty, derelict graveyards.

Mike: Tim's Lizzie. Beloved of all, from trucker to biker, honorary king of the road. 'As a vehicle, it was hard-working, commonplace, heroic,' wrote E.B. White of the Model T, 'and it often seemed to transmit those qualities to the persons who rode in it.' Cheers, E.B. I'll take that all day long. Like the old claim-staking home-steaders, I had proved up. They call me Timmy Four-Balls.

On 4 November 1931, after three months and 9,000 miles, Dib Fewer and Tod Snedeker made it back to San Francisco, clocking their Mike at 50 on the final run up the Coastal Highway. Neither of them would ever leave California again. Dib kept Mike for a year, then traded up to a Chevrolet Landau and gave his old T to a jobless friend. Shortly after, this chap sold Mike's engine to a guy who put it into a pleasure boat he kept at Lake Tahoe, and carted the chassis to a scrapyard in Brisbane, just south of San Francisco. That stencilled radiator made Mike a prominent fixture in the corner of the lot, and Tod and Dib would wave at him as they sped past down the Bayshore Boulevard. Then one afternoon Dib held up a hand and saw that he'd gone.

Ocean Shores wasn't the end of our road, not quite. I would wave Mike goodnight through three more motel windows, and one thick swirl of sea fog. In Seattle we would meet a jolly and biddable MTFCA member called Howard, and learn that all the shipping firms had just relocated to Long Beach, California. Howard would ask me to breathe into a paper bag for a while, before hooking me up with a man called Freighter Jim, who had a very big trailer and an even bigger heart. Jim would take my car all the way to Long

Beach, where a like-minded T collector called Kim would care for him until shipping could be arranged.

Three months after I came home, Mike was unloaded at Southampton Docks and trailered to Neil Tuckett's farm in Aylesbury. As I write there's snow on the ground, and it's a struggle to picture myself bundled up in skiwear at the wheel of Henry Ford's famous 'brakeless carriage'. But spring will soon be here. Until then I visit Mike every other Sunday, with a bottle of his favourite oil.

EST.1998

Yellow Jersey Press celebrates 20 years of quality sports writing

Yellow Jersey Press launched in 1998, with *Rough Ride*, Paul Kimmage's William Hill Sports Book of the Year. In those early days, the Yellow Jersey list sought to give a platform to brilliant stories, which happened to be framed within a sporting environment. Over the past two decades, its name has become synonymous with quality sports writing, covering all sports from the perspective of player, professional observer and passionate fan.

Sport is about more than simple entertainment. It represents a determination to challenge and compete. It binds individuals with a common goal, and often reflects our experiences in the wider world. Yellow Jersey understands this as much as its readers.

This edition was first published in the Yellow Jersey Press 20th Anniversary Year.

YELLOW JERSEY PRESS
LONDON